Voluntary Effort and Rural Development

Voluntary Effort and Rural Development

G. SATYANARAYANA

RAWAT PUBLICATIONS
Jaipur • New Delhi • Bangalore • Mumbai • Hyderabad • Guwahati

ISBN 81-316-0086-6

Published by
Prem Rawat for **Rawat Publications**
Satyam Apts, Sector 3, Jawahar Nagar, Jaipur 302 004 (India)
Phone: 0141 265 1748 / 7006 Fax: 0141 265 1748
E-mail: info@rawatbooks.com
Website: www.rawatbooks.com

New Delhi Office
4858/24, Ansari Road, Daryaganj, New Delhi 110 002
Phone: 011 2326 3290

Also at Bangalore, Mumbai, Hyderabad and Guwahati

Typeset by Rawat Computers, Jaipur
Printed at Nice Printing Press, New Delhi

Dedicated to
Mrs. Lucy Francis & Mr. C. Francis
.who have suffered to remove the suffering of others

Contents

Preface

This study of voluntary effort of Weaker Community's Action for Development and Liberation (WCADL) of Mahabubnagar District in the Telangana region of Andhra Pradesh (AP) has a distinct academic importance in the field of development studies. India has been primarily an agricultural country where 75 per cent of the population lives in villages in rural environment, depending on agriculture as their main occupation. Almost half of India's population lives in a hand to mouth living condition even after 60 years of independence in spite of visible advancement in science and technology and the country emerging as one of the few powerful nations of the world. It is interesting to note that the ironical situation of Indian society is that it constitutes a composite population, of both, educated and uneducated, affluent landed gentry and people living in utter poverty. In spite of the growth of industries a lot of rural and urban population are still unemployed. Rapid advancement in science and technology and unshaken rigid tradition bound communities, over populated towns and cities exist side by side the hamlets and village settlements mostly in dilapidated conditions.

To reduce the gap between the rich and the poor, the educated and the uneducated, industrialised cities and rural bound villages a consistent effort has been made through various programmes of five-year plans, community development programmes, Panchayati

Raj, cooperative movement, land ceiling and land reforms and various subsequent rural development programmes for the past five decades. Despite this, the problems of rural people have not been solved, and instead they multiplied. Hence, the Indian development process has been characterised as "vertical development" wherein rich became richer and poor became poorer and all the programmes of development ended in confusion and in chaos rather than in realising the objectives and goals of bridging the gap between the rich and the poor and to construct an egalitarian, equal and just society in accord with the philosophical richness of Indian ethos and culture which lay emphasis on equal human worth, humanism, giving importance to collective approach rather than individual outlook.

However, of late, there is a shift in the development process and more emphasis has been given to weaker communities development through voluntary effort which has been the main focus and gaining importance all over the world, and more so in India for more than a decade. Even the international organisations such as the World Bank, the IMF, etc., are officially emphasising the conditions in their programmes of "development assistance" to various national governments to involve NGOs in the process of development of the underdeveloped and directing the governments and their machinery to play a minimum role in the process of development and to avoid the duplication of work and expenditure, corruption, favouritism, nepotism etc.

This shift and the new paradigm of development, though objectively good, could not actually take its roots at the grassroots level in the development approach. Though the governments, are realising the importance of the shift, while implementing the development projects at the grassroots level, could not be in a position to scrutinise, regulate, control and command the voluntary organisations, i.e., NGOs which inherently lack the necessary spirit and approach of human service and the reformistic, and philanthropic mindset to derive the motivation of service from their constant internal urge, by and large, adapt voluntary effort for external value, professional service and as an occupational pursuit.

As such, in the process thousands of voluntary organisations have been cropping up in India in recent times than in the past, as also in the world. There has been a lot of debate all over the world in the planning and academic spheres with regard to the nature of development in the voluntary and NGO sector and its prospect and retrospect in the context of handling the social problems and issues of development.

In the process, the focus is shifted from development programmes of governments to development programmes of the voluntary sector; from integrated community development approach to individual community; from resource use to resource development; and finally from mere development to sustainable development and from context development to contact and continuous development.

In view of the above theoretical and empirical importance of the role of voluntary effort in the development process of weaker communities such as Scheduled Castes (SCs), Scheduled Tribes (STs) and women, this study has been initiated. The main purpose of this study is to examine and evaluate the effort of a selected voluntary organisation in the development of rural societies specially the weaker communities. The other aims of this study are to explore the various dimensions of the development process such as philosophical convictions, commitment and sincerity of the authors of the voluntary sector, their financial resources and constraints in seeking financial assistance, approaches of development, organisational structure, cooperation of the government, banks, and the general public, at large, sincerity and commitment of the paid workers, beneficiaries and ultimately the problems, and prospects of development through voluntary effort which would go a long way in the process of developing the underdeveloped and socio-economically deprived and suppressed sections.

G. Satyanarnyana

Acknowledgements

It is really difficult to thank every person who has contributed directly or indirectly to this academic work which aims at a scientific appraisal of voluntary effort. But I should acknowledge the help and encouragement of those people in completion of this work to the extent my memory permits to place on record.

First of all, I have to thank the devoted social workers Lucy Francis and C. Francis who readily accepted to cooperate in this study of evaluation. But for their wholehearted cooperation in providing information and encouragement, this work would not have been completed.

I am, also very much indebted to F.D. Vakil who has been a constant source of inspiration and a role model for human and intellectual concern for the development of the underprivileged. He is the person who introduced me to the voluntary organisation (WCADL) under study and its main organisers. I am also very much indebted to A. Subba Rao who has given valuable suggestions in improving the draft, for effective presentation.

I am also very much grateful to my friends who have sincerely worked with me inspite of the innumerable troubles during the period of this study. They underwent a lot of hardship, working from morning to evening in all seasons even in the hot summer, heavy rains and cold winter and moving in the interior villages and Tandas (tribal settlements) of Mahabubnagar district for meeting the respondents individually and collectively for collection of data and subsequent processing of the data and analysis. In this regard and also for the completion of the work, the contribution and cooperation of B.V.M. Sudheer, T. Venkatesh and P. Koteshwar have been of immense value.

I thank Jangaih, the Programme Coordinator and P. Rajender Reddy, Transport Incharge of WCADL who have helped us in the fieldwork by guiding and taking us to every village and introducing us to the beneficiary respondents and explaining to us the living and working conditions of the weaker communities in the past and the present.

I also thank all the other field staff of the WCADL including C. Narayana Goud, K. Devaiah, K. Mallesh, P. Narsimha, Pentaiah (watchman) and all the respondents who spared their valuable time to give us the information sought.

I also thank all my colleagues, scholars and students who have been a source of inspiration in my academic pursuits. I also thank Prem Kumar who used to attend to my needs sincerely while I was writing the report. Further, I thank my students who are sincere, gifted with a lot of academic talent and whose help is also of immense value in completion of this work, particularly Kavita Shinde, N. Mrudula and P. Madhusudhan Goud.

I also thank my research students Madhavi, Shivani Rawat and Niranjan Rao who have been a constant source of inspiration in completion of this work.

I should also extend by sincere thanks to my wife Udaya Sree and my children Arun Babu and Nivedita who have silently contributed to all my academic pursuits and who have been a constant source of encouragement and support.

Lastly, I thank Ram Lingam and Somasekhar who have helped me in computer processing of the data and typing the script.

G. Satyanarayana

Glossary

Abstract	Existing in theory rather than in practice, not concrete.
Academicians	Member of an academy.
Adivasis	A member of the aboriginal tribal people of India.
Affluent	Abundant, tributary stream.
Aggravate	Increase the gravity of (an illness, offence, etc.)
Allied	Having similar origin or character.
Ambiguous	Having more than one possible meaning; doubtful, uncertain.
Atrocities	Wicked or cruel act.
Census	Official count of population.
Clemencies	Mild, merciful.
Conscientised	Obedient to conscience; scrupulous assiduous. Conscientious objector person who refuses to do military service on grounds of conscience.
Dalits	Persons belonging to weaker sections.
Deteriorated	Become worse.
Deteriorating	Becoming worse.
Disbursement	Pay out.
Diviner	Search for underground water or minerals by using a stick which dips when these are present.

Downtrodden	Oppressed; down under in Australia; have a down on colloq, dislike, be prejudiced against.
Dummy	Imitation object, serving to replace real or normal one.
Egalitarian	Advocating equal rights for all.
Elites	Selected group or class; the choice part.
Emancipation	Set free from legal or social or political or moral restraint.
Feasibility	Practicable, possible, plausible.
Grounding	Basic instruction in subject.
Hamlets	Small village.
Harijans	Member of the class of untouchables in India.
Hermit	Person living in solitude.
Ideologies	Schemes of ideas at basis of politics etc., theory or system; characteristic way of thinking.
Illegitimate	Not authorised by law; born of parents not married to each other.
Ingrained	Deeply embedded, inveterate.
Inhibition	Restraint of direct expression of instinct. Emotional resistance to thought or action.
Karma	Buddist's or Hindu's destiny as determined by his actions.
Mahila	An adult female person.
Milch	Kept for milk.
Mirage	Optical illusion produced by atmospheric conditions; illusory thing.
Mortgaging	Conveyance of property as security for debt until money is repaid.
Multifaceted	Having several facets.
Nominal	Like noun; in name or word only; not real or substantial.
Philanthropic	Love of all mankind; practical benevolence.
Pivotal	Pin on which something turns; cardinal or crucial person.

Plight	Condition, state, unfortunate, pledge, engage oneself.
Polemics	Verbal attack, controversy, controversial, involving dispute.
Praxis	Accepted practice or custom.
Random	Without method; without aim or purpose having all parts directly accessible.
Reformist	A policy of reform rather than abolition or revolution.
Sarpanch	The headman of the village.
Self-aggrandisement	The process of enriching oneself or making oneself powerful.
Slack	inactive or sluggish negligent.
Solicited	Repeatedly, earnestly for or seek or invite. For immoral purpose.
Sporadic	Occurring in isolated instances or very small number scattered, occasional.
Stagflation	A state of inflation without a corresponding increase of demand and employment.
Sturdy	Robust, hardy, strongly built.
Subsidiary	Serving to help. Controlled by another.
Tubectomy	Surgical removal of a fallopian tube.
Undermine	Injure, reputations, influence, etc.
Voluntarism	The principle of relying on voluntary action rather than compulsion.
Vulnerable	That may be wounded, open to or not proof against attack or injury or criticism, etc.
Watchdog	Charged with protecting rights, etc., dog kept to guard property, person, etc.

1

Introduction

Voluntary effort in rural development is increasingly gaining importance in India in contemporary times. However, voluntary effort in the emancipation of various sections of the deprived and suppressed population in particular, and society in general has been a worldwide phenomenon since the dawn of human civilisation. The human mind is increasingly realising the various socio-economic and cultural problems of changing times, as human civilisation is growing and expanding. To resolve these problems is beyond the capacity of the very people who suffer from them and in some cases the sufferers may not be even aware of their suffering. Consequently, individuals and organisations have taken up the responsibility of mitigating the sufferings of the people through organised effort with available resources, tools, techniques and methods. Thus, a large number of people and associations have been making their efforts in this direction by adopting different philosophical, reformist and philanthropic approaches for the mitigation of human suffering in their respective societies all over the world, in different times. Despite this, the sufferings continues to exist due to the inherent structural problems and the consequent socio-economic inequalities perpetuated in any given society. Hence, as long as inequalities and suffering exist among individuals, groups, sections, people and societies, individuals, groups, voluntary organisations and governments have to continue to make their efforts to mitigate human suffering and its root cause, 'inequalities' of all forms.

Sisir Basu (1994: 8),[1] in his article "Rural Poor: Failure of Growth Models", highlighted the plight of the rural poor, loopholes of planned development, policies and programmes and the necessity of organising the poor. Stating that the need for organising the poor is debated without any intensive analysis conceptually or operationally, Basu underscores the skepticism and vagueness that surround this concept. He opines that for the success of redistributive laws, policies and programmes, the poor should be organised and made aware of the benefits intended for them. Basu emphasises:

> Organised tenants have to see that the tenancy laws are implemented. Organisations of the landless have to see that surplus lands are identified and distributed to them in accordance with laws within a reasonable period... After more than four decades of planning the rural sector has become an island of mass poverty... growth models adopted by us have failed to eliminate rural, urban dichotomies.

Using the term 'stagflation' which combines stagnation and inflation to represent Indian growth model, Basu identifies the following factors as responsible for this failure:

> ...choice of wrong theory, wrong technology, preference for dependence on international systems rather than our own effort, planner's propensity to assume, instead of building into the model, objects such as removal of unemployment and reduction of the gap between the rich and the poor. These are the most important flash-points of failure, though there are other causes as well (ibid.).

Basu further adds:

> The real problem of the power elite has been found deficient in meeting serious challenges of the rural destitution. They are unable to explain the slowing down of the growth rate of rural economy and despite what is called the 'green revolution' and the continuous increase in the number of people being pushed below the poverty line in villages (ibid.).

Concept of Rural Development

Katar Singh (1999: 288),[2] while highlighting the importance of NGOs in rural development, states that rural development should be considered as a joint effort of the people, corporate, cooperative and private sectors, for which a systems approach has to be adopted for an all-round and balanced development of the economy. In this effort as he points out NGOs have a special role in educating and training rural people and in ensuring their participation in rural development programmes, by working along with them (ibid.: 289).[3]

Thus, it is clear that there is a need for understanding the concept of rural development. In this context, D.N. Singh (1985: 1),[4] in his introduction, observes that rural development which is associated with the downtrodden, neglected vast backward areas have not been given adequate focus as a thrust area of planning.

Singh and Singh (1985: 24)[5] elaborately discuss the concept of rural development. They consider rural development as a scheme of development for rural (non-urban) areas and therefore implies a special focus on irrigation facilities, electricity and the techniques of cultivation and the like, in these areas. In a narrow sense, in rural development, agriculture is not only the heart but almost the whole of rural development (ibid.: 25).[6] Singh and Singh (1985:25)[7] while referring to Harris (1982) who explained the need for rural development, they state that as a policy and process approach, rural development is broader than 'agricultural development' and should take care of the development of the economy of the rural people and should lay particular focus on poverty and inequality in the rural society. It has an implied concern with reduction of inequalities in income, employment, access to public goods and services and with the alleviation of poverty. Further, Singh and Singh (ibid.: 25) referring to World Bank (1975a), emphasise that rural development is a specific strategy to improve the economic and social life of a specific group of people, i.e., the rural poor and involves extending the benefits of development to the poorest among the rural people like small-scale farmers, tenants and the landless.

Madhusudan Pal (2002: 10-11),[8] in his paper "Rural Development and Easy Money" discusses some of the latest important programmes of rural development and their priorities and problems in realising goals. As he observes, planners and the government authorities are aware of the slow pace of the rural development programmes and were taking remedial steps to bring balanced development. In 2002, the Ministry of Rural Development enhanced the budgetary outlay to Rs 12,265 crore from Rs 9,760 crore of the previous year with 25.6 per cent increase coupled with state share and bank credit, this would be about Rs 18,000 crore. As poor connectivity reflects poor socio-economic indices, the Pradhan Mantri Grama Sadak Yojana envisaged an investment of about Rs 60,000 crore for providing connectivity to all unconnected habitations in two stages by the year 2007. Under Pradhan Mantri Gramodaya Yojana drinking water, rural housing, primary health, education and nutrition were to be covered with a priority to provide access to safe drinking water to 1,410,723 out of 1,422,664 rural habitations in the country. Further, as Pal states, various poverty alleviation programmes in the past have contributed to the reduction of rural poverty from 56.44 per cent of the country's population in 1973-74 to 37.27 per cent in 1993-94. The Swarna Jayanti Gram Swarojgar Yojana was launched in April 1999, to widen self-employment programmes, to organise the rural poor into self-help groups and their capacity building, training, infrastructure build-up and technology and marketing support.

Madhusudan Pal (ibid.: 10-11),[9] in his concluding observations, underscores the importance of various rural development programmes and states:

> All these show that rural development programmes have been taken up seriously and with an urgency never before witnessed. It however, remains to be seen how the petty politicians befog and undo these schemes to reap personal benefits out of them and how much of allocated money the bureaucracy-political party-contractor nexus can take away to hinder and halt rural progress.

Katar Singh (1999: 21-22)[10] referring to Todaro (1977) identifies the basic elements that constitute the true meaning of rural development. They are: (i) basic necessities of life such as food, clothes, shelter, basic literacy, primary health care and security of life and property; (ii) self respect: every person and nation seeks some sort of self-respect, dignity or honour. Absence or denial of self-respect indicates lack of development; and (iii) freedom: it refers to political or ideological freedom, economic freedom, and freedom from social servitude. As he points out, so long as a society is marked by the servitude of men to nature, ignorance, other men, institutions and dogmatic beliefs, it cannot achieve the goal of "development". Servitude of any form reflects underdevelopment.

Mehta (1994: 1)[11] points out that development has to provide increasing opportunities to all the people for better living. It has to bring about more equitable income and wealth distribution to promote social justice and efficiency of production, provide a variety of facilities like education, health services, nutrition, housing, etc. Mehta (ibid.: 1),[12] referring to International Labour Organisation (ILO), states that development which involves humans, as distinct from material produce, is a process which brings about improvement in the quality of life of the weaker sections and a greater participation and involvement of the masses in the process of decision-making in the economic, social, political and cultural spheres. Citing Denis Goulet's *Cruel Choice* Mehta adds: "development is not a cluster of benefits given to the people in need; it is rather a process by which a populace acquires a greater mastery over its own destiny (ibid:1)[13]".

In consonance with the "United Nations, Development Administration: Current Approaches and Trends in Public Administration for National Development", according to Mehta (ibid.: 2)[14] states that the primary aim of development is to boost national as well as per capita income and the standard of living of the people and to ensure justice, freedom, equality and security for them. As he points out, the focus of development is now increasingly on (a) equitable distribution of wealth and income, (b) full utilisation of manpower, (c) better utilisation of natural resources, and (d) protection of human environment. In summary, by development he means "change plus growth, i.e., it includes growth, modernisation, increase in social facilities, etc".

Importance of Voluntary Organisations in Rural Development

Vasant Desai (1988: 47)[15] in his *Rural Development: Experiments in Rural Development* (Vol. IV) highlights the problems of the rural community and explains the approach of voluntary organisations in rural development. He states that "the problems of the rural community are not so simple as to be solved easily. Over the years, their problems have been aggravated and there is a feeling among the downtrodden that everybody who approaches them has a selfish and exploitative motive. Therefore, the task of the implementing agency is to regenerate confidence in the people about its selfless and dedicated approach to their problems. To solve their problems, a fair degree of technical and managerial competence is essential in a variety of fields, like agriculture, irrigation, plant protection, storage, marketing, education, animal husbandry, cottage industries, health and sanitation. Further, social service areas like health and education also require innovative approaches, beyond just opening a dispensary or construction of a school building. For this, voluntary agencies should develop "professionalism with the human touch".

Sisir Basu (op. cit.: 8)[16] points out that to counter the leakages in the delivery system and ineffective administration there is a need for an organised pressure group of beneficiaries to counteract the administrative deficiencies and the vested interests. He identifies five ways of organising the poor on the basis of history and the experience. One is rural unionism like Kisan Sabha. However, he is aware of the limitation of peasantry for being radical in a Marxist sense, which resulted in rural poor being kept out of cooperative movements. The second method is organising the poor by mobilisation by political parties for building up a mass political base. The third way of organising the rural poor is by deliberately transforming the political, administrative and social structure into a highly decentralised system of power in the form of democratic institutions of participatory rather than mere representative nature. The fourth is the cooperative method since there is a limitation to trade unionism to be extended to rural areas. The fifth method is widely advanced and practiced by voluntary associations in organising the weaker sections and the urban underprivileged. India has a great tradition of voluntary organisation in the fields of health, education and social service.

Likewise, India has its great tradition of working for the upliftment of people for the mitigation of their suffering through various means and approaches. One of those approaches has been voluntary effort (voluntary action) for the emancipation of the economically poor, socially deprived, psychologically depressed and politically suppressed sections of the society. Such unfortunate people belong mostly to backward classes, SC/ST communities and women of all castes. Various types of voluntary organisations are engaged in this gigantic task of rural development. Some voluntary organisations are working in various parts of the world, and there are some organisations working only in some parts of the globe depending on the resources available, encouragement from various governments, philanthropic organisations and individuals as well as the response of the target people.

As a consequence, there is a phenomenal growth of voluntary organisations all over the world and more so in India. As such it is increasingly felt by the planners, administrators and intellectuals of the world to evaluate, voluntary organisations scientifically, to assess their strengths and weaknesses and to involve and strengthen them in the process of development as a support base for the governmental efforts in order to uplift the people in general, and weaker communities in particular, in an uneven society like India where a lot of planned and unplanned effort is made to create opportunities and facilities to the poor and deprived, if not on par with better-off but at least in the creation of better human living conditions, which is the prime concern of all the nations of the world specially of India. Hence, it is imperative and challenging for the academician to systematically evaluate voluntary organisations, which are working for the poor, deprived and suppressed sections of Indian society.

If we examine the history of the past reform movements of the world and those of India particularly, it is revealed that reformist activity was basically philanthropic in approach and aimed at the alleviation of suffering of the deprived, and that it was not based on any rational method nor was it aimed at establishing any legitimate position in relation to those who were deprived in society.

This kind of approach was mainly initiated under the influence of religion and humanistic ideology. Subsequently, rational and scientific methods of organising people were evolved for upholding the socio-economic and political rights of the deprived and suppressed, including the rights of women. Such a movement was started in India in the beginning by Raja Ram Mohan Roy who relentlessly fought all through his life for the abolition of 'sati' and other social evil practices in Indian society. Later on, a number of individuals and organisations such as "the Brahma Samaj, Prarathana Samaj, Arya Samaj, Ramakrishna Mission and some Muslim religious organisations fought against 'sati', infanticide, bride price, prohibition of widow remarriage, child marriage, purdah, temple prostitutes, illiteracy and the like. Raja Ram Mohan Roy, Dayananda Saraswati, Swami Vivekananda from outside the State of Andhra Pradesh and Gurajada, Veeresalingam Pantulu, Raghupati Venkata Ratnam Naidu, Madapati Hanumantha Rao and others from within the state of A.P. did make their efforts to remove these disabilities" (Ranga Rao, 1998: 5).[17] Ramakrishna Mission's movement became popular through the work of modern Indian philosophers like Swami Vivekananda whose concern for the poor was so great that it reflects in his popular slogan, "Service to Mankind is Service to God". Likewise, Gandhi's concern for outcastes, i.e., Harijans, Adivasis and women, especially for their emancipation as part of freedom movement set a new direction for the future destination of weaker communities. It has been furthered by Ambedkar's life mission to fight for social justice of Dalits in particular and socio-economic political rights of weaker sections of the Indian society, viz., Harijans, Adivasis, Backward Classes, minorities, women, etc., in general by his courageous struggle as part of freedom movement and subsequent provision of constitutional guarantees, made an everlasting impact on the future of weaker communities of Indian society. At the state and regional levels, i.e., in Andhra Pradesh, the contributions of the social reformers mentioned above for the emancipation of the suppressed and Veereshalingam's special reformist efforts to bring women into the mainstream of life and to educate them against orthodox thinking, changed the entire social status of women in Andhra Pradesh. Subsequently, a number of voluntary organisations also started working all over the country for the emancipation of the depressed and suppressed classes with the help of individuals and organisations of national and international importance.

Concept of Voluntary Organisation

It is appropriate to consider at this juncture, what a voluntary organisation is and how it is defined: "Generally, voluntary agencies and non-official organisations are treated as one and the same. This may not be so. All non-official organisations are not necessarily voluntary. Voluntary organisations are spontaneous in their origin whereas non-official agencies may also be government-sponsored" (Lawani, 1999: 17).[18] Interestingly, Lawani (ibid.: 18-20)[19] in his work *NGOs in Development* offered several definitions of this concept as given by various scholars. The prominent among them are as follows. According to Lord Beveridge "A voluntary organisation, properly speaking, is an organisation which, whether its workers are paid or unpaid, is initiated and governed by its own members without external control". David-Sills's definition of a voluntary organisation is that it is "a group of persons organised on the basis of voluntary membership without state control, for the furtherance of some common interests of its members". Further, Lawani (ibid.: 24-25),[20] while referring to Paul Chowdhary, mentioned the following characteristics of a voluntary organisation:

(1) It is the result of the voluntary effort, which though motivated by different factors, is spontaneous in nature.
(2) It is an organisation initiated and governed by its own members on democratic principles without any external control.
(3) It is registered under an appropriate Act to give a corporate status to a group of individuals so that they get a legal personality, and individual liability may give place to group liability.

(4) It has a general body and a regularly constituted managing committee, representing all interested men, women, professionals, public men, etc.
(5) It has definite aims and objectives and a programme in socio-economic fulfilment of these objectives.
(6) It is known and accepted by the community in which it is formed.
(7) It has considerable autonomy, flexible planning and management of its programmes and services.
(8) It has a sense of commitment to human development/welfare.
(9) It meets people's needs and helps to solve their socio-economic problems.
(10) It plans and implements its own programmes through its own voluntary and paid workers.
(11) It raises its funds from the community.
(12) It maintains its accounts and is accountable to people and the government as far as it receives grant.

Even though the above-mentioned factors are the characteristics of a voluntary organisation, the roots of a voluntary organisation are grounded in human virtues like friendly touch, dedication, flexibility, innovation, nearness to the community. That is, voluntary agencies strive for certain human virtues and values. The following discussion throws further light on the characteristics of voluntary organisations. (ibid.: 25)[21].

Rajesh Tandon (20 January, 2004, *The Hindu*)[22] in his "Policy on Voluntary Sector", while referring to Planning Commission's policy document, clearly highlights how the government is giving importance to the role of voluntary sector and that, "as if they were primarily charitable, service delivery, welfare-oriented, relief and rehabilitation type of voluntary organisations which primarily work at the grassroots level to alleviate sufferings of the poor and the marginalised; to respond to failure in government services by filling gaps in social services delivery and in the welfare of the weaker sections".

He further, states that "voluntary organisations are those where people give of their time voluntarily and, therefore, do not receive any compensation. Such people are expected to earn a livelihood elsewhere. This is the old concept of philanthrophy, charity and doing good, where the rich and the well-off occasionally, through some daan, opened charitable clinics or schools or fodder camps or food kitchens, etc". But, according to him, "this definition is far from reality of the voluntary sector in India and elsewhere" (ibid.). The definition "continues to confuse between volunteer and voluntary. Volunteers are individuals who give of their time, skill and capacities freely, in the service of others in the community, without any expectation of return. On the other hand, Voluntary initiatives are self-determined, self-organised, self-governed initiatives with independent mission".

He emphasised that "the government policy suffers from defining very clearly, what type of contributions voluntary sector makes in today's context in India. It should identify precise irritants that are faced by the voluntary sector organisations through Income Tax provisions, outmoded society registration procedures and the draconian Foreign Contribution Regulation Act (...). The policy should clearly state that it would like the voluntary sector to function in an independent, autonomous, innovative and flexible manner, which is its key strength. The legal framework should be an enabling environment and not a regulatory one... The policy should also define the role of the government in encouraging and implementing such an enabling environment".

"It is important that the government does not get involved in either building capacity, coordinating or networking in the voluntary sector. That should be left to the sector's own wishes, capacities and requirement. However, the most important thing that the policy should address is to direct its attention in changing the mindsets and attitudes. No public policy can be effective without promoting better understanding of the current realities, contributions and constrains of the voluntary sector in the minds of political leaders, government officials and the public at large" (ibid.).

Classification of Voluntary Agencies

Singh and Singh (1985: 138-139)[23] classified the voluntary agencies as per their approaches in dealing with various kinds of problems of the people and the areas, as given below:

(1) Charity: Giving food, clothing, medicine, alms in cash and kind, land, buildings, etc.
(2) Welfare: Providing facilities for education, health, drinking water, roads, communication, etc.
(3) Relief: Responding to call of duties during natural calamities like floods, droughts, earthquakes and man-made calamities like refugee influx, ravages of wars, etc.
(4) Rehabilitation: Continuing and follow-up of the work in areas struck by calamities and starting activities durable in nature.
(5) Services: Building up infrastructure in depressed and backward areas, like tractor hiring services, providing or facilitating credit, supply of seeds, fertilisers, informing, technical know-how, etc.
(6) Development of socio-economic environment and all-round human beings: Socio-economic transformation on the area basis, covering all the people in a given area or concentrating only on a particular group normally neglected and in need of help.
(7) Development of human beings: Conscience-raising, awakening, conscientising, organising, recording of priorities to suit social justice, redeeming the past and opening doors to opportunities to the oppressed and exploited.

Mehta (op. cit.: 48-49)[24] states that voluntary organisations are not homogeneous in nature. There are various categories of voluntary organisations, depending on their aims and objectives. They are broadly categorised as "socio-economic, socio-cultural, rural development societies, cultural organisations and service-oriented organisations and societies". As he observes, "generally voluntary agencies and non-official organisations are treated as one and same. This need not be so. All non-official organisations are not necessarily voluntary. Voluntary organisations are spontaneous in their origin whereas non-official agencies may be government-sponsored. A unique feature of voluntary agency is that it stimulates voluntary action among the community served and progressively involves enlightened individuals belonging to the served community in the higher echelons of its decision-making machinery".

Charyulu in his study (1981: 219),[25] while explaining the concept and importance of voluntary organisations, states: "A distinction is drawn by some writers between non-official organisations and voluntary organisations. To them, all non-official organisations are not necessarily voluntary. The test for voluntariness is that the organisation has to try and stimulate voluntary action in the served community. It has to also progressively incorporate enlightened individuals belonging to the community served in the higher echelons of its decision-making machinery. Another distinguishing point made out between these bodies is that voluntary organisations are spontaneous in their origin whereas the non-official agencies may be sponsored by the state."

Mehta (op. cit.: 49),[26] while explaining the various stages of voluntary action, points out that "in a developing country, voluntary action has a three-stage process. First, it is based on social conscience which has been defined by Beveridge in his work *Voluntary Action,* as "the feeling of discomfort on the part of people in comfort about the people in discomfort". Second, voluntary action has emerged from social consciousness generated by organised interest groups of people who are committed to people-centred approach. Third, organisations of various target groups, particularly from among the weaker sections, have emerged. The membership of these groups of associations generally cuts across traditional boundaries of caste and occupational groups. Voluntarism in India is going through a process of evaluation from altruism for its own sake, to conscientious activity dictated by the needs of the situation, i.e., requirement of the area and the people. So, the voluntary agencies choose a particular area for a particular task of development or welfare of the societies".

It is also appropriate to mention here that in spite of successive plans and programmes in India, for the overall development of the society in general and the weaker sections in particular, by successive national and state governments, for almost half a century, poverty and suffering of people have been increasing day by day due to increase in population and a drastic decline in natural resources such as water, forest, etc., thereby creating problems of ecological, environmental and other socio-economic and cultural nature which have become a hurdle for making use of political independence and the future objective destiny of weaker communities in Indian society.

Also, a number of scholars and administrators have observed that in spite of successive planned efforts of more than half a century, the nature of Indian socio-economic development programmes benefited only the "haves and have-nots". This is obviously a vertical development whereby "the rich became richer and poor became poorer". Further, all the development programmes such as Community Development Programme, Cooperative Movement, Land Ceiling, Land Reform's, Panchayati Raj and Green Revolution, etc., instead of improving the condition of marginal and small farmers, tenants and share croppers force them to sell off their land and to become agricultural labourers or urban migrants. This has further increased the misery of the poor who have been already suffering. The mute sufferers are the working classes mostly belonging to the lower strata of the society. The social harmony ingrained in the traditional mode of production through its functional interdependence has been increasingly crumbling due to the invasion of growing science and technology while the consequent latest policies like liberalisation, privatisation, globalisation, etc., would further marginalise the rural masses who are scattered now, may have to go to far off places without address. This will not only affect the deteriorating socio-economic cultural fabric of majority rural working class population but also the whole of Indian society.

It will be a powerful challenge to the voluntary organisations to keep intact at least the existing marginalised earthbound village population, i.e., rural poor to sustain and survive in line with the spirit and dreams of Gandhi's "Gram Swaraj", Vinoba Bhave's Bhoodan Movement and subsequent efforts by our national leaders like Nehru, etc., who laid the foundation through planned economic development by giving equal importance to agriculture by land reforms, decentralisation of political power through Panchayati Raj and Cooperative Movement, which have been forgotten and become already obsolete programmes, though they have set in motion a holistic development of all sections of the Indian society. This is due to lack of political will of the present governing class to implement the development programmes for the objective goals of all-round development. As such, there is not only a serious challenge to the India's established patterned development but also to the Indian society and its cherished socio-economic and political equality. After Nehru, the subsequent national leadership and governments instead of following his footsteps, mishandled the situation of the take-off stage. The Indian working classes missed once again the golden opportunity. This is not due to the lack of patriotic spirit but due to lack of conviction, scientific knowledge and wisdom on the part of the leadership of the country. The subsequent leadership was heavily burdened with the national and international capitalist forces on the one side with vested interest and on the other, with the higher and middle level feudal forces all over the country which were dominating the socio-economic and political solution of independent India and which had taken an upper hand waiting for a chance to reverse Gandhian Gram Swaraj and its socialist model and Nehru's mixed economy and his parliamentary form of democratic socialist vision and foundation. This process, coupled with the weak political democratic process, where most of the people still remained bound to tradition and illiteracy with rampant merciless political and bureaucratic corruption had weakened the self-esteem of the common man. The basic reason is that mostly rulers and bureaucrats came from feudal background due to their socio-economic advantages and they never represented the problems of the poorer sections of Indian population. Hence, even after half a century of native rule, villages are without basic amenities. More than half of the population are illiterate, without work, or assets, suffering from disease, hunger, social and economic deprivation, poverty, and various other related social diseases.

Hence, as a last hope, the philanthropic organisations all over the world are emphasising the role of NGOs in the sustenance of programmes for underprivileged of underdeveloped societies. Further, there were some human rights and civil rights organisers like Lok Nayak Jayaprakash Narayana, who led a movement of "total revolution". At present, in India, Padma Bhushan Anna Hazare's "collective action and micro planning", Dr. N. Jaya Prakash Narayana's movement of "Loksatta" are playing a crucial role in strengthening grassroots democracy through their various programmes and campaigns. Their slogan is "people are masters, leaders and bureaucrats are their servants". This has become the watchdog of civic governments and their programmes.

Hence, voluntary organisations with their special, professional skills and commitment are gaining importance with their efforts for the mitigation of human suffering. There are also a number of voluntary organisations in the field of rural and urban development in general and in the area of uplift of the weaker sections of the society in particular. These organisations are increasing in number day by day, more than in the past and are gaining more importance than the governmental means of bureaucratic development in contemporary times. As a result, the emphasis and recognition of their role by funding national and international organisations like CAPART, the World Bank, International Monetary Fund (IMF), and philanthropic organisations like Bread for the World, etc., acquires importance in this local and global context.

Lawani (op. cit.: 45-46)[27] while tracing the history of voluntary action in India states that "it is the product of social, ethical, economic, political, democratic, cultural and religious values and considerations". Its recorded history is around 150 years old. Today the number of voluntary agencies working in different fields of social services, social welfare and rural development may be more than 25,000. If rural Mahila Mandals, youth clubs and other small voluntary groups are added to this, the total number might exceed three lakh. According to the information available with the Ministry of Rural Development, there were in the seventies around 60,000 Mahila Mandals, 90,000 Youth Clubs working in rural areas. "In addition, there may be many more agencies which are unregulated, not receiving any grant, are in the nature of kinship group, based on mutual aid, self-help, private and public trusts and ventures promoted by business houses."

"Voluntary action in India is of great historical, importance for it lit the spark for political, social and economic freedom."

Pradip N. Khandwalla (1988: 28)[28] referring to Parsons (1956) states that "the potential of voluntary organisations to contribute to socio-economic development of poor, underdeveloped societies may vary markedly. To survive, organisations must meet one social need or another".

Singh and Singh (op. cit.: 141)[29] commenting on the limitations of governmental effort in rural development, focus on the importance of voluntary organisation as follows: "The voluntary organisations have to focus especially on the underprivileged and improve their resource-creating skills and their opportunities of gaining access, to the government-sponsored programmes and assets like land, house sites, etc. Provision of technical and other services in ways that build up people's initiative and enhance their resources are their essential tasks".(...) The authors while quoting Kabra (1985), further observes that "voluntary efforts have to be at best catalytic agents to energise the backward sections dominant articulation and mobilisation potential for development. Voluntary action does not have to move totally along lines parallel to plan programmes; but it must not merge with them or become dependent on them. As a watchdog and corrective, it has to build an alternative fact of power so that politics of planning changes in favour of the poor" (ibid.: 141).[30]

Mounting Critique on Voluntarism

However, there is a lot of criticism, in recent times, on many voluntary organisations, that they are being started without any firm commitment and conviction for the development of the deprived and suppressed people, but only working with a professional motive of self-aggrandisement. The money they receive from governments, philanthropic, national, international organisations and agencies seems to be misused. Target people and donor agencies are also usually cheated because there is no effective control by government and other sponsors over the social work or voluntary work of those individual organisations. As social work organisations are growing in number, this problem has also been increasing further because of the ignorance of the target people for whom those organisations are started. Target people are always in a helpless condition. The culture of poverty makes them believe that receiving benefits from any organisation is not their right and that the benefits are because of the kindness of organisers. They are poor because of their *karma* or religious sentiment. They cannot question the misuse of funds by the voluntary workers. Further, they know that if they question, even the small benefits they are getting may also stopped. Sometimes, organisers and workers of voluntary effort warn them. The importance of civic sense and civic rights of people as can be expected are almost unknown to the people of underdeveloped societies. In India, politicians, bureaucrats and social workers, always go scot-free due to the interconnectedness of power structure. Mostly, they come from rich capitalist and landed gentry. Whatever may be the class background of a person in Indian society, if one belongs to upper castes the whole system at all levels, turns in favour of them.

Nobody will dare to question them. If anybody questions nothing will happen to the person who violates the procedures of a democratic system and on the other hand the person who exposes the truth has himself to risk punishment. The punishment may be in many ways. It corresponds to the nature and level of questioning persons in the positions of management. It may assume any shape from expelling to elimination. The poor always watch helplessly the torture of right minded persons by the brutal and cruel persons, for their pathetic existential conditions of living. It is also no different where politicians and officers are from the lower strata of the society. This is so, because the ratio of people in authority is disproportionate and uneven. Almost all decision-making positions are held by upper caste people. A few of the lower positions are held by people of lower castes. It is very rare in India that the nature of work goes with the nature of persons and skills though it is popularly propagated that recruitment goes according to democratic norms. Most of the ministers, politicians and officials who belong to the lower rungs of the society invariably, willingly and readily mend their ways of life and behaviour in public affairs in favour of the dominant sections of ruling class leadership and their agenda, rather than in favour of the agenda of democracy, humanism, secularism and human rights. At all levels and in all affairs in the Indian society the people of lower strata are placed at the receiving end and not at the giving end. This inequality was rationally opposed by free and post-independence intelligentsia but gradually overpowered and subsequently squinted, mediocre feudal and capitalist groups handled the apparatus of power structure to crush the dignity and human rights of hungry millions of downtrodden population.

However, there are a number of external and internal problems identified by various scholars as objectively as possible. There is a need to pay attention to those problems to make the voluntary effort a more viable, scientific and dependable means of development. It has no other alternative except to correct or rectify the inherent or non-inherent factors of hindrance that effect the development of those unfortunate people who suffer from lack of basic human amenities. Lawani (op. cit.: 199-204)[31] has identified a number of "problems, difficulties and deficiencies of voluntary organisations" such as absence of erstwhile spirit of voluntarism, lack of dedicated leadership, lack of funds, inadequately trained personnel, lack of coordination, centralisation in urban areas, deterioration in quality of services, misuse of funds, lack of public participation, monopolisation of leadership, etc. Further, Lawani states: "A large number of local and regional organisations had expressed that the main problems faced by them while dealing with the communities are non-cooperation of the people and internal community politics" (ibid.: 215).[32]

It is a well known fact that the dominant feature of Indian society is unity in diversity. But this diversity of castes and classes has always been a hindrance for the development of the deserving poor and deprived. It is really difficult for real leadership to emerge for the good of the poor. Leadership in the context of the poor is always manipulated by the rich and dominant castes for their own advantage and as a result, even after 55 years of democratic rule in India, still the upper castes continue to rule. Political murders and other types of elimination tactics prevail very freely and threaten those who want to live freely and to question the illegitimate acts of the ruling castes and classes. Satyanarayana (1980)[33] in his unpublished article "Conflict in Country Side", presented at the All India Sociology Congress held at Meerut, while discussing the conflict in rural villages of Telangana in Andhra Pradesh, concludes that conflicts are increasing day by day in rural Andhra Pradesh and may be all over the country. Of late, it is not due to the manipulative ability of the upper castes and ruling classes but it is due to the weakness of some people who belong to weaker sections who are willingly mortgaging their own community class interest for the meagre and minute benefits and even against their kith and kin to the extent of killing them for the advantage of the ruling classes. This weakness of the weaker section people is perhaps due to their conditions of survival. They align themselves with the upper castes without any substantial benefits to themselves or to their community, but for the false social prestige of aligning themselves with the upper castes. Normally, the leaders of upper castes make use of members of the lower castes by the method of giving loans, patronising a single person or a family of lower castes. For instance instead of giving Rs 100 for ten people or families during the period of elections which is a democratic demand, only one leading person or family is given against all other persons or families due to intolerance of leading person or family towards other weaker section of persons or families.

Better Side of Voluntary Action

Srivastava (1999: 13)[34] while referring to Verghese (1977; 1979) and Pandey (1991) focused on "The Better Side of Voluntary Action". He stated that "the strident criticism of voluntary action groups in India does not, however, undermine the value of voluntary action in the current development phase. It is true that what the critics are condemning is not voluntary action as such, but only certain kinds of voluntary work done by certain people. The general consensus borders round the fact that the growth of NGOs signifies the search for alternative development paradigms with emphasis on popular mobilisation or to supplement the state endeavours in several critical development sectors. The Government also recognises the fact that voluntary organisations perform the function of fillings up the gaps in the statutory welfare services for people in need. Verghese (1977; 1979) hailed voluntary action groups as new missionaries. Many of these have made important contributions to the well-being of a select group of neglected local people and the general public. Another contribution has been in the formation of a counter force or a credible critique mechanism of government policies (Pandey, 1991). Many such groups have demonstrated immense organisational and managerial efficiency in empowering people. Several of them have envisioned innovative ways of organising people according to their cultural aspirations and indigenous goals. By experimenting and acting against the existing systems and development paradigms, some groups have increasingly stressed human development and structural transformation. They represent a new force in the developmental policies of the developing countries. By working as effective pressure groups they publicise the perceptions of peoples front and bring pressure to bear upon authorities to make adequate provisions for poor peoples felt-needs. The biggest advantages of the expanding voluntary sector in the developing countries in their freedom from officialdom and redtape, are spontaneity in responding to peoples needs; flexibility in procedures and economy in operation. These and many other features of good and committed voluntary organisations necessitate their presence in implementing the planned programmes of social, economic, educational and political empowerment of the disadvantaged sections of society.

Andre Beteille (2001: 298-299)[35] in his "Civil Society and the Good Society" states that "the interest in voluntary action, voluntary movements and voluntary associations has been given a new lease of life by the concern for the creation or revival of civil society, particularly in the countries of Asia, Africa and Latin America. It has acquired a global dimension. A democratic society cannot function properly, not to speak at its growing, if everything in it is left to the state or even to statutory bodies. Mere statutory action will be infructuous if it is not underpinned by voluntary action. The significance of voluntary action and voluntary associations in the life of a democratic society has been brought to light by many".

Rakesh Kapoor (1996: 13-14)[36] while writing on "Voluntary Action: Survival, Politics and Transformation" broadly identifies the various areas of voluntary sector such as "registered organisations and unregistered groups, grassroots organisations and urban support groups, networking organisations, development groups and welfare groups, apolitical organisations and politically active formations, non-profit organisations and not-for-profit organisations".(...). Further, Rakesh Kapoor (ibid.: 14)[37] has shortlisted the various activities of voluntary sector which include voluntary actors or voluntary organisations, which are as follows.

(1) provide relief, charity and welfare services, like health;
(2) organise and mobilise people and do advocacy on their behalf;
(3) engage in 'developmental' work – usually economic or ecological activity, sometimes linked to infrastructure building;
(4) provide formal-informal educational services;
(5) carry out scientific and technological work (research and intension);
(6) engage in policy research; and
(7) provide legal services.

As may be seen from the above, most of the activities voluntary organisation do are also done by the state or the market. If the activities are the same as those of the state or the market, what makes it different? The motives with which activities are carried out distinguish the voluntary sector. The motive of the state is governance, the motive of the market is profit, the motive of the voluntary sector is to react to the sins of omission and commission of the state and the market, and thus to strengthen the civil society. In a more positive way, the motive is to stand up for the values of freedom, democracy, justice and self-reliance.

Impact of Voluntary Action and Limitations

Rakesh Kapoor (ibid.: 15),[38] in his discussion on the weaknesses and impact of voluntary organisations, quoting Anil Bhatt (1995), states that "a meeting of voluntary organisation in Gujarat, speaker after speaker mentioned the limitations of the micro-efforts and the frustration emanating from the fact that their ability to fight the forces of corruption, oppression and injustice was very limited. As a result, in the context of the country as a whole, it has not been able to achieve significant 'empowerment' of the people, whether economically, politically or culturally".

Rajesh Tandon (1996: 1)[39] in his work *Changing Context and Challenges for Voluntary Action in India Today* discusses the recent controversy in regard to CAPART 'blacklisting' 500 voluntary organisations for misuse of funds. This has resulted in a debate centreing around the authenticity and accountability of voluntary action.

Rajesh Tandon (ibid.: 7)[40] further stated that "most of the founders and leaders of such voluntary organisations (called 'social entrepreneurs' by some) have now become burdened by the day-to-day personnel and financial administration. The growing size and complexity of operations makes it difficult for such founder leaders to allow for more direct field and programmes related contributions from them"(...) Referring to the voluntary organisations and challenges of professionalism, he (ibid.: 11)[41] states that "there is increasing pressure on voluntary organisations to function in a more 'professional' manner and it has not been clear what professionalism actually implies in operational terms. Most people confuse it with the hiring of professionally trained people like (engineers, doctors, accountants, managers, etc.). It is a very narrow and inadequate interpretation of challenges of professionalism (...). It essentially "implies a more efficient and productive utilisation of resources in pursuit of the mission set by the organisation themselves.(...) Professionalism will also entail ability to produce results in a time bound and well defined manner".

Sharma (1996: 28-39)[42] states that "philanthrophy is not charity, or doling out money to the distressed and the poor (...). It is a universally acknowledged fact that philanthrophy is a creative work which puts a check on the degeneration of the persisting institutional mechanism with a view to reconstruct a better and the desired type of society. Religious revivalism, health and hospitals, literacy and education, civic and public amenities, social services for the distressed people, etc., are the most known activities undertaken by the voluntary action groups all over the world".

Sharma (ibid.: 30),[43] while quoting Dhanagare (1993), states that "the NGOs are variedly known as 'voluntary action', welfare groups, etc., supposedly these groups have emerged to educate conscientise and mobilise the marginalised groups and the oppressed poor. The action groups function at the micro level, and associate themselves with the weaker sections to bring about social transformation".

Sharma (ibid.: 35-36)[44] further states that "voluntarism has generated a lot of interest as an idea and as an approach to tackle India's problems of poverty, unemployment, health, environment, etc. It focuses on a common action programme at the grassroots, the revitalisation of corporate philanthrophy and social responsibility. But it is also viewed as an imperialist strategy".

Sharma (ibid.: 36)[45] also states that "the voluntary organisations have taken up activities and programmes relating to family planning, rural development, literacy, health and hygiene, environment, socio-political awakening, upliftment of women and children, rural and urban poor, etc."

Lakshmaiah (1999: 45)[46] in his *Tribal Development: The Role of Voluntary Organisations* states that "the need of voluntarism was felt inevitable even in the first five-year plan. It was with this reason, the Government of India had made a provision to voluntary organisations to work in tribal areas as the people from voluntary organisations can stimulate the interest in the community with their innovative attitude, with their pragmatic approach, it is easy for them to break the ice and make inroads into their problem situations. They are at ease to inculcate leadership qualities among the tribals by building up awareness and instilling conscientisation measures. The basic philosophy behind voluntary effort is to make the people aware and lead them to the goal of self-reliance. Since the government programmes are time-bound and target oriented, the government functionaries are unable to make adequate rapport with the tribal people in the process of their interaction".

He (ibid.: 46)[47] points out that "a large number of voluntary groups sprang up all over the country working with the grassroots in the development of the tribals outside the ambit of state activities. Many of these organisations showed excellent results. As a result, due recognition was given to voluntary organisations by the government. The effort of these voluntary organisations was perceived as developmental rather than welfare role. At that stage, it was felt that voluntary organisations whichever had high morale, commitment and dedication, which had established their credibility with their clean record of service shown in the tribal areas, were to be drawn into these areas".

According to Lakshmaiah (ibid.: 47),[48] "misuse of funds has become common phenomenon. Just as the local elite exercise their influence on the government agencies for fulfilling their own vested interest; they also influence the government with the help of their connections with politicians of higher ranks for getting financial help from the government. In turn, politicians also work for the voluntary organisations so that they get benefits from them. It is also noticed that enormous amounts of money flowing from foreign countries to the voluntary organisations to utilise it for the development of weaker sections. There is no suitable mechanism evolved to examine whether the money they received is properly utilised or not. It is the government that should take all measures to nip such malpractices in the bud. Any organisation at fault shall be taken to task and the government should see such things do not recur further."

Gopal Krishna Sahu (2000: 20-21)[49] while discussing the "Role of Voluntary Organisations in Rural Development" observed that "during the 1980s the country witnessed tremendous proliferation and growth of voluntary issues. Since then, in the eradication of poverty illiteracy, ill-health and overall backwardness of the villagers, voluntary organisations played a commendable role. They were instrumental in initiating, stimulating and accelerating the process of change in the tradition-bound rural societies. They also created awareness among the people about the developmental programmes". Thus, he concludes that voluntary organisations have a great role to play in the socio-economic transformation of rural people, as they can lend support to the government and other developmental agencies concerned with rural development. He also attributes the success of these organisations depends on the financial assistance provided by the government and other funding agencies.

Lucy (1993: 421),[50] in her "Social Reforms to Voluntarism in India", traced the history of voluntarism. According to her, "voluntary action, synonymous with community action is as old as community or civilisation itself (...). Voluntary action is a part and parcel of Indian Society". Further, while quoting Paul Chawdhary, she explains the difference between voluntary action and non-official organisation: "Vinobhaji equates voluntary action with the concept of 'Janasakthi'. So long as the activity is undertaken by an agency, organisation or institution which is native to the people concerned and which works without interference or dictation from outside, it should be regarded as voluntary action". She further observes that "the test for voluntaries is that the organisation has to try and stimulate voluntary action in the served community. It has to also progressively in corporate enlightened individuals belonging to the community to serve in the higher echelons of its decision-making machinery. Another distinguishing point is that the voluntary organisations are spontaneous in their origin where as the non-official agencies may be sponsored by the state".

Role and Characteristics of NGOs in India

Nityananda (2000: 36-43),[51] in his study *The Emerging Role of NGOs in Rural Development of India*, discussed the challenges of development, evolution of NGOs in India, state-NGO relationship in India, new development paradigm and increasing role of NGOs and challenges and concerns for NGOs. As he points out, the term 'NGO' is quite loose and ambiguous. The role of NGOs is increasingly considered as vehicles for development. Conceptually, the term 'NGO' refers to a wide variety of non-profit organisations including religio-political institutions, welfare wings of religious organisations, business associations, cultural or scientific associations, associations for promotion of sports and arts, etc. (ibid.: 36-37).[52]

Nityananda (ibid.: 37-41),[53] while examining the role of NGOs in India, from a historical perspective states that "voluntary or social service has been an integral part of socio-cultural and religious ethos in India from ancient times. But, in modern times, indigenous forms of voluntary organisations began to appear in the early colonial period during the Renaissance of Bengal with the demands on the colonial state for social or religious reforms on issues like polygamy, child marriage, promotion of women's education, etc. Gradually, this issue-based voluntarism spread to western India during the latter half of the 19th century" (ibid.: 37).[54] But secularist and development oriented voluntary movement became popular during the freedom struggle and the 'ashrams' started by Gandhiji were considered to be the first generation of modern NGOs in India. As he further states: Though there is a long history of voluntarism in India, the term NGOs is comparatively a new term to Indians. Indians still believe that 'voluntarism' is essentially inspired by self-initiative, social commitment and dedication and the western concept of NGOs does not fit in here. In fact many Indians dislike the label NGO and preferred to be called 'voluntary agencies', 'development organisations', 'voluntary associations' etc. It should also be noted here that NGOs in the West are mainly engaged in advocacy and focus on four major issues viz., environment, human rights, consumer rights and gender issues. On the other hand, in India, NGOs are mainly oriented towards welfare modernisation or empowerment. However, Indian voluntary agencies would not like the term 'NGO' and we continue to use the term 'NGO' interchangeably with voluntary agencies or development organisations (ibid.: 37).[55] While highlighting the importance of NGOs he says that "off late the World Bank and UN agencies are pressurising the state to involve NGOs to implement the projects supported by them" (ibid.: 39) (...).[56] But, the ground realities are fiscal deficit of the state accompanied with low productivity of state employees and higher project administration cost, this is forcing the governments to gradual withdrawal and encourage the NGOs to provide services to the poor. Further, the NGO sector also has undergone some changes. Today, the NGO sector is dominated by young professionals motivated by job prospects rather than social commitment. Moreover, the competition within the NGOs has also increased. Thus, NGOs are also willing to get involved with government projects even with more control" (ibid.: 39-40).[57] Drawing attention to the shift in new development paradigm and to the increasing role of NGOs, Nityananda states that the rural poor are to be seen now in various interacting levels, i.e., normative, conceptual, empirical and practical. According to him, first, in the context of knowledge of the poor, earlier it was believed that the poor are ignorant but now the poor are knowledgeable and indigenous technical knowledge is more useful. Second, in the context of resources, poor people lack access to resources and need an injection of outside resources. But this idea has been changed. The poor have resources but they are not properly utilised and need identification and use of local resources. Third, the poor are highly dependent and will remain so. But now the changed idea is that they can also move from dependence to interdependence. Fourth, the poor were thought to be incapable of organising themselves (ibid.: 40-41).[58] But now it is considered that they are capable of forming their interest-reliant organisations. In conclusion, he points out that the practical level of the paradigm should be integrated with the other three levels. "The central thrust is to involve the people to enable them to identify what they want and empower them to obtain it. Participation is the key word in the new paradigm" (ibid.: 41).[59]

Baviskar (2001: 5),[60] while highlighting the importance of "NGOs and Civil Society", in India, refers to Fisher (1997) and states that "the NGO sector in India is characterised by tremendous diversity and heterogeneity. Ignoring this diversity, unfounded generalisations are often put forward and unfair comments and criticisms are offered. NGOs differ from one another in size, in funding, in functions, in the levels at which they operate, and in organisational structures, goals and membership.

There are over 14,000 NGOs registered under the Foreign Contributions Regulation Act. In all, there may be over 30,000 NGOs in India". Aid and help is also sought from individuals, groups, governments and national, international organisations working for the upliftment of the deprived. This has become a worldwide phenomenon in contemporary times. Governments of various countries are also increasingly realising the need for the participatory role of voluntary organisations in the amelioration of conditions of the sufferings of the poor, i.e., weaker sections without depending on governmental 'formal', political, bureaucratic machinery and their effort which lacks commitment, professional skills, humane touch and approach.

Baviskar (ibid.: 1)[61] states that "in the years after independence people exhorted the state to take the initiative with respect to social transformation, now the expectation is that NGOs will perform the same role. Be it in the field of education or health, providing drinking water, organising forest management groups, or thrift societies for working women, NGOs are supposed to take the lead".

Baviskar (ibid.: 4)[62] made an observation in regard to the limitations of NGOs. He points out that "although NGOs claim to believe in openness and transparency, many of them are not open to scrutiny by outsiders. Those who have achieved a degree of success and fame are often hostile to any objective studies by outsiders not approved by them". The reasons are obvious.

Voluntary Effort, NGOs and Sustainable Development

In addition to the socio-economic and political policies and programmes considered above, the overgrowth of knowledge in science and technology all over the world has weakened the people. The uneven and to unaffordable cost of science and technology made rural masses fish out of their water, in the sense that they are thrown out of their traditional mode of living based on indigenous skills and talents, due to lack of subsequent alternative support base for their sustenance. Substantiating the above idea, Francis (1996: 12)[63] referred to Smitu Kothari and stated that "despite the various programmes of development by the

Government of India, the percentage of people below the poverty line has remained constant with, 40 per cent of the population living below the poverty line and another 20 to 30 per cent just above it". As a result, development agencies and people are also losing faith in the sincerity of the formal bureaucratic machinery and in governments.

Baviskar (op. cit.: 8),[64] referring to Gibbs et al. states that "many international agencies, such as the World Bank, which were earlier working exclusively through national governments, now prefer to work through NGOs in implementing some of their projects". In one of its reviews of such programmes, the Bank (Gibbs et al., 1999) has noted several positive aspects of working through NGOs without giving up some of its reservations. It is noted that the NGOs are far less constrained by bureaucratic procedures and administrative inefficiencies. What is more important for the Bank is the relative absence of blatant corruption and leakages in the channelling of funds. This results in a much greater share of benefits reaching the targeted groups than is likely to happen while working through the state machinery".

Nityananda (op. cit.: 41)[65] emphasises the role of NGOs and observes "that their approaches to development tend to be more participatory than the state strategies. They unusually have closer links with the local people and thus have more direct knowledge of local needs and opportunities. This knowledge allows them to better recommend and implement truly sustainable development, which uses and regenerates local resources and enhances local capacity to identify and solve problems. Closer links with the local community also allow the NGOs to play a more important role in empowering the poor as they usually involve the local community actively in the identification and resolution of development problems".

Further, Nityananda (ibid.: 41)[66] referring to Farrington and Babbington (1993) has identified the challenges and concerns for NGO's. He states: "Like state and its agencies, they also face formidable challenges – both external and internal. NGOs do not always perform as effectively as expected in terms of poverty reach, popular participation, sustainability, cost effectiveness, flexibility and innovation. These shortcomings usually originate from NGOs perpetual shortage of funds and other resources. Sometimes they do patch work of social services in which only certain regions are serviced by well equipped NGOs while neglecting most of the areas. In addition they run the risk of duplicating services in the same region due to lack of communication and coordination among NGOs". Besides, according to Nityananda (ibid.: 42),[67] "excessive dependence on large donors for funds may sometimes encroach upon their autonomy and flexibility. They have to be very careful to maintain their identity and autonomy otherwise they lose their credibility. The performance of NGOs may also be hampered by working with donors.(...) They have multiple accountability to their donors and beneficiaries. But it is not so easy to maintain a balance due to absence of measurable parameters".

For understanding the magnitude of the problem of corruption in the sector of NGOs, the latest report entitled "Stealing from the Poor" by Arun Bhatiya (2002),[68] Head of the Tribal Research and Training Institute, is quite useful. Bhatiya who conducted a study on watershed programmes undertaken by NGOs in Maharashtra villages observed that "villages are steeped in corruption in the absence of physical audits. Grants meant for the works have been siphoned off". He further states that "it is easier to steal from the poor precisely because they are poor. They neither see nor understand programme guidelines, false measurement books of work done and false receipts of payments made. The expenditure under the scheme was Rs 24 lakh of which Rs 15 lakh is the estimated misappropriation". Baviskar (op. cit.: 9)[69] also states that "there is the case of an NGO in A.P. in animal husbandry sector that systematically misappropriated funds for several years, while the Delhi office of their foreign donors turned a blind eye to this for fear of attracting adverse publicity". He further says that "state corruption and NGO complicity had a field day in the Council for Advancement of People's Action and Rural Technology (CAPART), the government body set up to fund grassroots NGOs, where funds were disbursed and later evaluations favourably conducted if bribes were paid to the CAPART staff".

Further, Baviskar (ibid.: 12)[70] referring to Ramachandran (1998), observes that "the economy and efficiency claimed on behalf of NGOs is only relatively superior. When the late Prime Minister Rajiv Gandhi revealed that less than 15 per cent of the total money spent by the government on development programmes reached the targeted beneficiaries, there was a wave of shock and surprise. According to some calculations, this proportion may be 20 per cent in the case of NGOs, which also spend substantial amounts on their own salaries and infrastructure. The difference in terms of benefits to the poor may not be so great after all".

Likewise, Baviskar (ibid.: 9-13)[71] identified a number of drawbacks of NGOs. "They are mainly failure of imitation of some successful programmes of some other NGOs, the leadership and authority invested with one charismatic person who started the organisation, no structure of organisation to deal with grievances of employees, personalised management practices impersonal rule-based practices more often force the workers to leave the organisation at the behest of the founders, and the spirit of voluntarism is sometimes used to obscure exploitation and manipulation". He further states that NGOs more often practice double standards: "they plead for openness, transparency and democratic participation but they do not seem to observe the same in their functioning. Crucial decisions are taken at the top without any scope to participate for grassroots workers in the deliberation of decision-making. "The leaders are most reluctant to openly discuss the matters relating to funding". Further, "many NGOs find it hard to resolve the problem of succession and routinisation". There are also other problems faced by NGOs. They often have been entrusted with the task of fulfilling physical and financial targets and to show some tangible results. But it is difficult to measure the output in the sphere of 'social development' and 'cultural transformation'. Competition among NGOs is also a problem which often leads them to indulge in unhealthy practices to attract the attention of the public and the government machinery. In this connection, Baviskar (ibid.: 12-13)[72] emphasises the importance of NGOs by stating that "NGOs have been around for quite sometime and they are likely to remain with us in the foreseeable future". Hence, systematic studies by sociologists of organisations, political sociologists and sociologists of development are essential. The spirit of study should have a holistic framework and approach in which the essence is human development with available resources of money and manpower for optimum use and satisfaction. Katar Singh (op. cit.: 25)[73] also underscores the need for studies of the human being and his/her relation to other human beings in the context of development. According to him, "human beings are both the cause and consequence of development: it is the human factor that is the pivot of the process of development. Though the study of the human being is basic to the study of development, it cannot be of a human being in isolation, but rather of human beings in relation to their fellows, or of humans in society and in their environment" (ibid.: 25).[74]

Voluntary Action: Women and Sustainable Development

It is appropriate to mention here the role and importance of women in the process of development. The United Nations on the advancement of women in the *Blue Books Series* (Vol. VI, p. 57)[75] clearly mentioned that "the central role of women in fighting poverty, creating productive jobs and strengthening the social fabric was proclaimed in the international agreement adopted at the world summit for social development in March 1995 in Cophenhagen". This declaration built around 10 commitments for achieving social development, included an acknowledgment by the world leaders that more women than men live in absolute poverty and that they carry a disproportionate share of the problems of coping with poverty, social disintegration, unemployment, environmental degradation and effects of war. "We acknowledge that social and economic development cannot be secured in a sustainable way without the full participation of women; the leaders stated that "equality and equity between women and men is a priority for the international community and, as such, must be the centre of economic and social development". Even today, this goal remains unachieved. Women are still undeveloped not only in underdeveloped countries but also in developing and developed countries. Of course, the size of their population may vary from country to country. It is still an astonishing fact to note and a challenge for and moral responsibility of the people who have abundantly enjoyed the gifts of nature for generations. If that enjoyment has to be sustainable enjoyment, there needs to be a little sacrifice of time and share of public money from those who have abundantly enjoyed for generations the gifts of nature and the labour of the innocent. If that enjoyment has to be sustainable, there needs to be a change of perspective in favour of those unfortunate brothers and sisters, sons and daughters and mothers and fathers who had never seen light in their life. After all, it is not a charity in a democracy. But it is their political and human right. Their suffering still continues in its various forms in advanced societies even in urban and industrial societies, leave alone the rural and tribal societies. It is due to lack of will of the people who are engaged in management of human affairs to serve fellow human beings, on the one side, and the failure of bureaucratic and administrative machinery which lacks the spirit of service to mankind, on the other. However, historically, some people like Abraham Lincoln, Martin Luther King, Nelson Mandela, Karl Marx, etc., in the western world and Raja Ram Mohan Roy, Jyothi Rao Pulle, Sri Narayan Garu, Ambedkar, Gandhi, Vivekananda, etc., in India laid the foundation for the service of the mankind. Thus, there have been great personalities in the field of social work who dedicated their life to the service of mankind, for example Mother Teresa. Today, the living giants of social work in India are Baba Amte, Anna Hazare, etc. Ironically there are also professional social workers, who use the cause of the sufferer, for their self-aggrandisement.

It should also be stated here that there are some committed organisations which are working for the development and emancipation of the suppressed people. Similarly, there are workers in these organisations who are really sacrificing their time and energy for the cause of the poor. As such, there is an increasing hope on the role of the voluntary organisations that they can really work for the weakest of the weak, rather than for the corrupt, non-committed formal, governmental, bureaucratic machinery. This fact may be the reason for the Indian Government's recent policy of increasing dependence on non-Governmental organisations for the execution of various developmental and other socio-economic developments, political awareness programmes of various communities. Further, Baviskar (op. cit.: 13)[76] referring to Baviskar and Attwood (1995) and Dhanagare (1988) questions: "Why is there widespread voluntary effort in the field of education or health in some regions but not in others? We also need to know about the internal structure and functioning of NGOs. What is the composition of membership, and who are the leaders? What motivates them to undertake such work? Dhanagare (1988) noted the middle class background of activists in most NGOs. We need to know, why is it so? We also need to examine the NGO links with the outside world. What are their achievements and failures? What contributes to the rise and decline of NGOs"? The last question on sustainability of organisations is perfectly answered by Katar Singh (op. cit.: 286).[77] According to Katar Singh, "government funded rural development programmes are vulnerable to changes in policy and budgetary allocations. Involvement of private corporations and their executives, who are not affected by political changes, in rural development projects could help make those projects sustainable. Sustainability depends on both availability of funds as well as commitment of institutions and their employees over the long term. Commitment of government employees to rural development is often short-lived, as compared to that of their counterparts in private sector development organisations. How many Kurians of Anand and Anna Hazares of Ralegon Siddhi can you find in Government organisations"?

Satish Deshpande (2003: 263)[78] while discussing the plight of "Indian Social Science in the Contemporary Era" highlights the importance of non-governmental organisations. He states that "non-governmental organisations (NGOs) have proliferated and are now important sources of funding and demand for research;

they are also fast emerging as preferred employers for young researchers".

Raj Kumar (2002: 64)[79] while explaining the role and importance of NGOs in capacity building of panchayats for rural development states that "a plethora of development programmes run by government could not reach out to the poor due to various reasons. A closer examination of the views expressed by think-tanks in this regard reveals that adoption of alien development paradigm, incompatible with the social-cultural ethos, ossified bureaucratic set-up, corruption and pilferage, are some of the commonly discussed factors inhibiting developmental initiatives. Many factors are responsible for this change in perspective. These include persistent failure of the political and permanent executives in taking policy benefits to the citizens, leading to erosion of their confidence, changing perceptions of the United Nations and other specialised international agencies towards development with a human face and worldwide recognition of NGOs for championing the cause of people's empowerment, environment and sustainable social development".

Raj Kumar (ibid.: 64-65)[80] further states that "the widely acknowledged role of NGOs in such numerous fields as socio-economic change, welfare, mass mobilisation, empowerment and development, has generated an idea that these organisations are capable of creating such enabling conditions. Thus, this needy section of the society can secure influence and leverage through the intervention of NGOs. These organisations, commonly known as the 'third sector' (the government and business are considered as the two other sectors) and their success as reported in the media, these days, regardless of criticism have received appreciation for their strong community ties, social capital, authority and resources at the disposal of their members or participants."

Nayar, while quoting Kothari (1995) and Roy (1995), highlights the importance of NGOs in "Civil Society and Gobalisation". As he points out "International Agencies like the General Agreement on Tariffs and Trade (GATT) and World Trade Organisation (WTO), and the World Bank, are blamming many countries in the Third World for their inability to observe the rules of the game of globalisation and are pressing governments to share the burden of national development with local NGOs" (Nayar, 2001: 213).[81]

Further stating that modern civil society in India is a post-independence phenomenon he says that (ibid.: 216-217)[82] within half a century of existence as a free nation, India has witnessed the birth and development of a multitude of small and large civil society organisations (CSOs) at the local, state and national levels. But, only very few of them have lived up to their objectives. According to him, the gap includes lack of proper leadership, inadequate economic base, and structural and ideological contradictions, even in those that are working efficiently to some extent. There is availability of foreign funds propped up many NGOs in India, but their real contribution to civil society objectives is yet to be examined. A few NGOs, have even attracted the attention of researchers. The findings ironically do not augur well for many of them. Therefore there is a need for the UNO and other international organisations to share funds with the state, as NGOs are better in development activities than the state agencies. Many of these organisations have no accountability to their client's or beneficiaries (ibid.: 216-17).

Srivastava (op. cit.: 1)[83] presented an excellent critique of the change in the "Nature of Voluntary Action in India Today". He refers briefly to the historical aspect, and devotes more attention to the present. From his historical perspective we can see where change lies and why and with what consequences. As he points out in pre-independent India, or even before, voluntary action was characterised by two dominant features:

(1) to help the helpless persons, and
(2) to root out social evils to bring about social reform.

Srivastava (ibid.: 6-7)[84] further states that "some people still think that voluntary workers, like hermits, are indeed living in a world of unreality. The immoral dimension of these organisations is gobbling up the grant money received from national and international sources". While quoting Kundal Commission he further observes that "the findings of the Kundal Commission testify the financial mismanagement and corruption in the Gandhian

NGOs". For instance, CAPART, a government initiated funding agency has black listed the NGOs found to have misappropriated their funds. A big new class called 'social activists' has emerged considering voluntary action as a big business, a lucrative activity and self-serving endeavour. This attitude led to a big spurt in the number of isolated or even invisible NGOs who came into existence with mercenary motives with the patronage of politicians and bureaucrats. The point was also emphasised by Ramachandran (1996), who referred to the corrupt practices of these bodies which function as family establishments with majority of the governing board members and organisational leaders drawn from a single family. The assets of the organisation are treated as family property with implied inheritance rights. Therefore, some scholars have pleaded for greater transparency and accountability of NGOs.

Srivastava (ibid.: 10-11),[85] while classifying the NGOs, states that it is a difficult task, because of the bewildering variety of them that defies any pattern or classification. Broad categorisations have been made on the basis of objectives, ideologies, sources of funding and areas of operation. However, such classification does not capture the reality as most NGOs have a mixed bag of objectives, ideologies, sources of funding and areas of operation. According to Srivastava, the most understandable classification of NGOs is under the following categories:

(a) that are fully supported by state and/or foreign funding sources;
(b) that are partially supported by state and/or foreign funding sources;
(c) that are supported by state agencies alone;
(d) that are supported by state and voluntary contributions; and
(e) that receive no grants-in-aid from any source, national or international (ibid.: 10-11).

Srivastava (ibid.: 11),[86] while explaining the kinds of activities normally NGOs undertake, states that the activities are many with a wide range. The areas are diverse with quite different settings, like in urban areas and tribal areas for rural development they involve people. Some very important activities include service delivery, environmental protection, urban renewal, education, training and conscientisation, people mobilisation, capacity building, organising the poor, promoting social change, uniting people for political empowerment, safeguarding human rights, fighting out injustices to the marginalised sections of society (women, children, Scheduled Castes/Schedule Tribes), providing relief to the diseased, disabled and displaced, and in conducting research and doing consultancy. Normally NGOs work has been set up by outsiders who came to the community to support grassroots networks and many of them have been founded by the local people.

As for the criticism on NGOs, Srivastava (ibid.: 11-12)[87] states that their structural, organisational and operational aspects have been viewed critically. Besides foreign funding with external links, the criticism focuses on other limitations, defects and drawbacks. The problem of fragmentation of NGOs, of brickerings, mutual suspicion and jealousy, down playing of role of colleagues and hurlings of changes can also be the defects. Lack of unity, cooperation or coordination among the NGOs when they are working in the same sector and in the same region also is another problem. These problems affected their collective strength and the development of a vibrant unified NGO movement. Empire building is another problem. Established groups develop the necessary terminology and the funding agencies (Pandey, 1991) are impressed by it. The smaller NGOs (especially those of remote areas) are treated with less appreciation. More dominant and well-connected NGOs manipulate to have approach to government funds whereas the less prominent NGOs are denied funds and facilities (Ramachandran, 1996). Powerful NGOs, however, by and large, fail to tackle the root causes of the problems and to solve the problems of structural change. They succeed in creating own spaces outside the orbit of political parties, outside the framework of power politics and also outside the institutional framework of state (Dhanagare, 1988). It is, however, heartening to note that many NGOs have made important contributions in the areas they are operative, but, they have yet to make a significant dent in the age-old problems of poverty and inequality. Therefore, biggest challenge for NGOs in the developing countries, like India, is to remove the systematic inequalities and injustices. They are unable to accomplish this being the product of the same system which they claim to change.

Andre Beteille (op. cit.: 300-301),[88] while discussing the role of NGOs in bringing about socio-economic change, observes that "the late 1990s has to be called the decade of NGOs which have become a part not only of the Indian social scenario but also of the discourse of practically languages in many parts of the world including India." A growing body of literature is available now in which the of NGOs and their contribution to economic growth and social transformation is widely debated, particularly with reference to the catalytic role of the NGOs, and more so in the Asian, African and Latin American countries where corruption and oppression have become the normal features of weak democratic agencies.

Beteille (ibid.: 301),[89] while referring to Jain (1955) states "that NGOs have advocated the concept of a third sector in society, state and market being the first and second sectors". In this philosophy, NGOs are different from the state because they are non-governmental organisations; they are also separate from the market because they are non-profit organisations. Though this concept of a third sector is attractive, it is difficult to define it in precise terms. From a sociological perspective, it would be unreasonable to argue that NGOs can fill the space in society untouched either by the state or the market. It must be remembered that an NGO may achieve autonomy, especially financial autonomy, but its autonomy in the global sense is questionable.

Further, Beteille (ibid.: 304)[90] points out that "the NGOs in India are too diverse to have one organisational form and too recent to acquire a definite one. Most of them fade and disappear, but as a social phenomenon, the NGO has come to stay. It is difficult to foresee their form in future. However, when an NGO is large and successful, it will be able to overcome the problems of bureaucracy with its rational accounting and adequate incentives for its employees".

Sharma (op. cit.: 35)[91] referring to Karat (1984) says that "in more than five thousand NGOs are receiving funds from foreign countries to finance their activities meant for the landless, tribals, women, slum-dwellers and unorganised labour. Karat raises certain questions relating to the motivation, of these diverse groups, their ideological basis, whether their overall strategy is that of the imperialist penetration, and their implications for the working class movement and the Communist Party of India (Marxist).

Sharma (ibid.: 39)[92] examines the positive and negative aspects of NGOs and identifies two obvious implications of the emergence of the NGOs namely: Streamlining the state bureaucracy with a qualitatively superior performance, and educating the middle class which is at the helm of affairs. But spurious NGOs have been detected. The misappropriation of foreign aid has also been found out. Consequently, NGOs came under suspicion of clan/family domination in functioning.

Ganesh Bhat (1999: 15-16)[93] in his article "Rural Entrepreneurs and NGOs" points out that in the recent past, efforts are made to produce entrepreneurs, with the participation of governmental and non-governmental bodies. The role of NGOs has assumed great significance at the grassroots level. Some NGOs in India have succeeded largely in imparting skills of income generation and micro-entrepreneurship development among the weaker sections of the society – women, tribals and others.

Bhat (ibid.: 17)[94] further refers to the development of entrepreneurship as a national movement not only for industrial development but also for its strength to solve the problems of unemployment and upliftment of economically weaker sections of the society. Their traditional areas of operation, namely, health, sanitation, education, family planning, environment protection, etc., have used this opportunity to entrepreneurise the lesser known target groups. Some government agencies engaged in this activity started collaborating with NGOs mainly due to the sheer magnitude of the operation and their inability to reach the lower strata of the society.

Sudha and Bhargava (2000: 21),[95] while writing on the role of "Panchayats and NGOs in Social Change" states that "the role of voluntary organisation is seen as complementary and supplementary to that of the government, as because they can act as watchdog to see that the development programmes are implemented properly. Without people's voluntary participation, no development programme can be a success. Panchayati Raj Institution (PRIs) have, therefore, to provide opportunities for the NGOs to involve in the task of making democracy and its fruits available to the people. These agencies must foster growth of grassroots leadership operating within the frame work of the state". Public participation can be encouraged by combined efforts of voluntary agencies and the government. Both are the main institutions of rural development and can lead to democratic decentralisation by enabling the citizens to acquire self-confidence, self-reliance and participation (ibid.: 23).[96]

Soorya Moorthy (1997: 63-70),[97] while highlighting the importance of NGOs in the development process of the Indian society, maintains that pre-independence NGOs limited their role to charity, relief and welfare activities. The complexion of NGOs changed in the late seventies. Presently, they are operating in almost all areas of human activity. However, there are also some limitations which are mostly common to the NGOs. There is a lot of criticism against the NGOs in relation to their sincerity and faith in service, corruption and organisation etc. In this context Soorya Moorthy (ibid.: 66)[98] states that "on the close examination one gets the impression that NGOs are founded to harness funds and resources not necessarily for the people always". The birth of an organisation is not always closely linked with the needs of the people or region where they start work. But, they remain as self-employment ventures of the founder and his or her team. Some are only organisations existing only in letterheads (ibid.: 66).[99]

According to Soorya Moorthy (ibid.: 66)[100] NGOs in India began to grow institutionally. Informal activities has changed to a formalised frame. Building staff and funds become the prerequisites of voluntary action. Employing professionals and experts, paying good salaries to staff and implementing projects designed by donor agencies have turned out to be the features of modern NGOs. But, as Soorya Moorthy (ibid.: 68)[101] points out while concluding "the frequent criticism is that the funding of NGOs has been highly local and only a limited fraction of the population is catered in their coverage. Networking and co-ordination of activities have yet to be effective. It is necessary for the NGOs to emulate NGOs abroad to share experience and knowledge".

Y.V. Rao and C. Francis (1993: 651-657)[102] in their "Action Oriented Adult Literacy and Education in WCADL", highlighted the importance of adult literacy in the development process of rural poor. They stated that "in organising the adult education centres, WCADL has not adopted 'Sarpanch-Patel-Patwari' approach". "In such an approach the sponsoring agency simply approach the local administrator or the local leadership and with their help try to establish a centre in that particular village." These centres will not succeed for the reason that elite class will not take interest in educating the working class with the fear that if they become conscious of their right, they may not work freely and for more time and may demand more wages. WCADL method of working with the people was interpersonal by meeting and discussing with the perspective learners of their convenience. WCADL has also adapted 'mass approach' where large numbers of people both illiterate and neo-literate gather on the occasion of Independence and Republic Days, etc. In these meetings men and women, boys and girls are mobilised in which the neo-literates exhibit and express benefit of literacy through speeches, songs, role-plays, dances, etc. Further, WCADL used to motivate the rural poor by giving financial assistance for income generating programmes for those families and individuals who are conscious of literacy education and who are actively involved, cooperating in organising literacy programmes. However, it is concluded that WCADL is in the field of adult education for the last 17 years. It has made its sincere effort to bring about a real and lasting change in the lives of the poor who mostly belonged to Scheduled Castes.

Francis (1993: 205-210)[103] in his "Rural Development, People's Participation and the Role of NGOs", highlighting the importance of people's participation and the role of NGOs in rural development, stated that the participation of rural poor "who are the victims of exploitation in more than one way, victims of illiteracy, ill health, superstition, underfed and undernourished.(...) Their participation is limited to nothing; other than receiving a few doles that too at the mercy of politicians or bureaucrats". He further, stated that "in spite of all the talks about people's participation they are not given a chance for meaningful participation in any aspect of rural development programmes". Francis (ibid.: 206)[104] states that there are a number of advantages for NGOs to make people to participate in the development process unlike the government initiated programmes which suffer from rigid rules and regulations, and lack of flexible approach and commitment of the bureaucrats. Further, NGOs would adopt different approaches to reach the target groups such as interpersonal contact and communication, formulation of 'sanghams' (village associations) division of villages into orderly accessible and manageable clusters and areas and creation of infrastructure facilities for further interaction and solidarity.

Lucy (1995: 224-231),[105] in her article on "Empowerment of Women for Sustainable Development", rightly highlighted the meaning of sustainable development and empowerment of women. While explaining the role of WCADL in empowering women, she states that "empowerment of women and their equal status etc. are more easily said, than put in the practice". It is more difficult in an orthodox and conservative society like India. Realising the male dominance of Indian rural society, WCADL adopted a distinct approach of empowering the women. For this, they first organised the men for a change in their attitude towards women and discussed in the training programme the role and importance of women in improvement of their families and nation. Subsequently, they organised training camps for women in which duties and rights of women were discussed including their right to demand their husband's cooperation in household work, etc. Subsequently, a meeting-cum-training programme was organised separately for men and women and lastly a combined meeting for men and women. Through these training-cum-meeting programmes, they helped the people to develop proper understanding among the men and women and subsequently, empowerment of women and the family and society.

Francis (1994: 42-44),[106] in his article on "Conscientising Through Cultural Activities," explained how the WCADL organisation has brought a socio-economic and cultural transformation in the lives of Harijans and Adivasis. "The animators and the coordinators are selected by their own community. This enhances the appeal and effectiveness of the programme. Some of the general achievements of this group media educational programmes are; immense self-confidence, political awareness and active participation in politics, planned parenthood, knowledge in health and hygiene, children's education, equality of women, courage to speak out in meetings in which even the upper castes are present and enhanced thinking capacity and functional knowledge especially in agriculture. All these made them realise a new meaning in life. Religious prejudice and superstition decreased" (ibid.: 43-44).[107] Further, following are the marked changes among the women: "Consistent attendance in the literacy classes, encouraging the children to attend the literacy classes, motivating the husbands to take active participation in group discussions and meetings, and saving habits. Knowledge in maintaining dairy animals and marketing of dairy products, bargaining for better wages, increasing feeling of equality with men, receptiveness to family planning, knowledge in childcare, good food habits, hygienic way of life, decreased instances of child marriage and early childbearing and better public relations, etc".(...) (ibid.: 44).[108] He further stated that "90 per cent of the small and marginal farmers who had earlier left their lands idle earned their living as daily wage earners and bonded labourers now cultivate their lands and have better living conditions. This resulted in a shortage of labour supply thereby increasing labour's bargaining capacity. The wages of the daily wage earners and bonded labourers were raised by the rich farmers and other employers" (ibid.: 44).[109]

The upper caste people feel that "now the Harijans, both men and women, wear clean and neat dress. Their streets are swept and they send their children to learn. It is nice to see them improving". (...) Harijan men say that "our women are more militant now. They demanded and got better wages. They even question us about our daily earnings and personal expenses like drinking, etc". (...) Our women now encourage and compel us to take active part in the cultural actions and group discussions. They ask us to help in the household chores, something they never did in the past". Further, they said that "we Harijans in the past never had the habit of sitting together and discussing about our welfare and development. Now we are able to stage cultural programmes and stand up and speak in public, a chance we never had in the past" (ibid.: 96).[110]

"We feel elated when we are able to perform cultural programmes and give speeches in front of the upper castes" (...) "These programmes are a great source of inspiration and learning for us. Now we feel less inferior" (...) "There is a steady decline in child labour; we try to send our children to school", (...) "Now we, Harijans have cultivated in ourselves saving habits, we improved our functional knowledge, we learned to sell our products for better prices. The cultural action media helped us realise our worth and improve ourselves" (ibid.: 97).[111]

"As translated into action by WCADL, the cultural action centred group media is found to be an effective media to bring about change for the better among the socially and economically depressed sections by inculcating in them the seeds of self-reliance and self-confidence" (ibid.: 98).[112]

Satyanarayana (1999: 142-154)[113] in his "Voluntary Organisation and Emancipation of Dalit Women" highlighted the unique effort of WCADL in emancipation of Dalit women. He discussed the marked changes which had taken place among Dalit women due to the efforts of WCADL in terms of socio-economic cultural transformation and the assessment of organisational effort in terms of success failure. He concluded that "there is a remarkable and striking change not only in the socio-economic, cultural and political milieu of the Dalits in general, but also among Dalits women in particular. Further, there is a perceptible change in the psyche of the Dalit women and men in relation to their style and perspective of life which reflect dignity, individuality, confidence, expression, effectively as a section and activity not only in the life of the Dalit women, but also in their families, community, and village in comparison with their position in the past" (...). He stated that, "whatever may be the criticism in relation to the voluntary effort for the emancipation of depressed and suppressed sections of the society, commitment and quality of the people really go a long way in building the gap between various sections of the society for establishing a just and human society".

Scope of the Study

Against the backdrop of the above theoretical and empirical reality, this study mainly aims at an objective and scientific understanding of the voluntary effort of a rural development organisation, namely, "Weaker Communities Action for Development and Liberation" (WCADL), which has been working in the backward Mahabubnagar district of Andhra Pradesh for uplifting the weaker sections of the society, i.e., Scheduled Castes (SCs), Scheduled Tribe (ST) communities mainly and other weaker sections of the rural society in general. This organisation has been working since 1976 through various rural development programmes. The assumption is that every organisation has its own merits and demerits, success and failures, unique approach of working with people for the upliftment of the poorer and deprived sections of the rural community. Further, this study aims at examining the nature and types of programmes designed by WCADL for beneficiaries in terms of organisational objectives and goals and their relevance to the target people. Further, it also examines the achievements of the organisation in terms of money spent, effort made and realisation of goals in terms of quality and quantity of money spent and effort made. This study also aims at a scientific evaluation of WCADL as a representative voluntary organisation when there is a lot of importance in contemporary times in the context of increasing criticism against the approach and objective sincerity of voluntary organisations and their leadership in terms of commitment, misuse of funds, method of working, unchecked activities, unaccountability, transparency to the ignorance of the people and lack of control of the government and the sponsors. Finally, it also examines the socio-economic and cultural impact and implications of the voluntary effort on the target people in the view of sponsors, governments, functionaries, beneficiaries and people at large. Finally, it aims at understanding the prospects of this organisation in terms of its continuity and its relevance to meet the needs of the deprived sections.

Some Crucial Aspects of Voluntary Development

Organising the rural poor must be one of the primary prerequisites of any rural development organisation aimed at improving the lot of the poor. As quenching of hunger is the primary need of the poor, they may not be willing to get organised at first on a mere ideological ground. Hence, economic programmes have to be used as entry points to make the poor come in and to be organised on any ideological ground at a later stage. In this process, sometimes the poor who are being conscientised may not be aware that they are being conscientised. This is a gradual process. Even after attaining a certain degree of conscientisation, the conscientised poor may not be able to explain to a researcher or to someone else outside that they reached a certain stage of conscientisation. But, the kind of coscientisation which they receive is a practical one and it is internalised. This means that what they have learned that programmes of awareness has become realisable in their day-to-day activities. The success of any developmental programme (economic or social) depends upon the process of conscientisation (creation of awareness) preceding it, accompanying it and continuing it even after the completion of the programmes. This is what is lacking in several of the developmental programmes of the government and in some of the programmes undertaken by voluntary organisations.

As such, bureaucrats and politicians may take up or pretend to undertake some developmental programmes for the poor, but not for the fuller development of the poor. If the poor are fully developed, the position of the politicians and bureaucrats will become redundant and questionable. That is why they want only apparent development of the poor but not the fuller development. In this context any sort of organisation of the poor becomes a threat to the politicians and bureaucrats. Radicalism, Naxalism, etc., are being opposed and suppressed, not because they stand for the poor, but they are felt as threats to the vested interest. In this context, the aims and objectives (memorandum of association) of a voluntary organisation, which should have some legal entity, by way of registration, may not reflect the actual aims and objects which are clearly spelt out. The bureaucracy who process the registration may not register it and WCADL will be forfeited of the legal status which is very much important for it to function. It may also happen that at times the real objectives may be hidden or may have to be read in between the lines. Besides, the success of any voluntary organisation depends to a large extent on the managerial ability of the leader/leaders/coupled with their, commitment to the cause, sincerity, uprightness, backed up by moral values, rather than on the amount of money spent, utilised and the number of professionals employed, etc., although these become necessary to a certain extent. An organisation need not necessarily commence its activities after framing out or spelling out its philosophy or ideology. It is necessary to have a broader view of developing the poor. Philosophy or ideology can be developed and spelt out after commencing the work or during the process of the work, after a good deal of interaction with the target people. People who often wax eloquent on philosophies in seminars and workshops on development may not be very often the practitioners of any ideology. In other words, their ideology is merely confined to polemics. They do not put into practice what they speak. This is one of the disastrous aspects of voluntarism. Several of the present-day voluntary organisations, it is said, lack the charisma and commitment as it used to be in the past. Voluntarism has become somewhat occupational professionalism in the sense that any person, who is unemployed or otherwise, registers an organisation on the brand of voluntarism and gets indulged in malpractices. This sort of 'voluntarism' tarnishes the image of real voluntarism. Mushrooming of voluntary organisations may be due to the fact that money is available, both foreign and local.

Whatever may be the sources of money, it is to be spent to draw maximum benefit to the maximum number of the poor. Even if money comes from foreign countries, it does not come out of affluence, but as a result of several sacrifices. People of developed nations seem to excel in making more sacrifices than the people of the developing nations to collect money for the underdeveloped and developing nations. This fact is not sufficiently understood by several voluntary organisers. Government is seeking more and more cooperation of the voluntary organisations in the implementations of the government sponsored development programmes for more than one reason. One reason may be the fact that voluntary organisations can better implement their programmes. Another reason may be due to international pressure for example in the case of money, coming from World Bank, International Monetary Fund, etc.

In any case, money for developmental programmes from foreign sources whether it is through the government channel or through the channel of voluntary organisation should be in accordance with the terms and conditions of the receiving end and not merely on the dictates of the donors. In practice, often it may not be possible but in such a case, care should be taken to minimise the imposing conditions as much as possible. Donor-recipient attitude may not be welcomed by all. Donations will become meaningful only when the aid-giving agency, institution or country views the recipient on equal terms rather than as alms-giving and alms-receiving relations. This is possible only when the aid receiver is assertive of his own position and is prepared either to put up with the situation or to make alternative arrangements rather than receiving aid on conditions imposed by the donor.

Method of Funding

Voluntary organisations in developing countries receive funds mostly from developed countries, through a centralised organisation there. This centralised organisation, in turn, receives money collected by grassroots level groups in their respective countries. For example, "Parishes" raise money by way of donations, selling old clothes, or by arranging fetes, etc. Money thus collected is being sent to the central organisations in their country. These centralised organisations accept project proposals from voluntary organisations from the developing countries and approve them depending on the merits and demerits of the project proposal and the terms and conditions which satisfy the donor agencies. Representatives of the donors make visits at times to the project area or they will have their reporting agencies in the developing countries. These reporting agencies very often comply with the ideology and other aspects of the donor. The reporting agencies and individuals are paid for their services. At times it might happen that the reporting agencies or their henchmen of the donor organisations, make reports as directed or expressed by the donor agencies. In this process, neither the fund-raising grassroots level groups nor the functionaries in the highest echelon of the donor agency (e.g., Board of Directors of their Governing Body) are not able to get reports about a voluntary organisation on the actual and factual reality except what the field level functionaries of the donor agency want them to know. Things would be much better if the grassroots level fund-raising groups are able to have direct contact with the grassroots level voluntary organisations as happened in the case of WCADL. But very often it may not be possible for the grassroots level fund-raising groups to have a direct contact as they lack the resources and expertise for this purpose and language barriers. Moreover, the grassroots level fund raising organisations may not know to which voluntary group in the developing countries the fund is going. At times, it so happens that a certain fund-raising grassroots level organisation may not be able to collect enough funds in a prescribed period of time to meet the requirements of a particular project of a voluntary organisation. Hence, the shortage can only be met by the central donor organisation. In any case the upper hand is with the centralised donor agency rather than anyone else. There are cases wherein the fund-raising groups have broken this monopoly of the central aid giving organisations. But the exceptions are very few. But in the case of WCADL the grassroots level fund raising groups succeeded in establishing direct contact with the grassroots level, project level implementation which will be dealt with in the following chapters.

Against the above theoretical and empirical background, an attempt is made here to understand the programmes, strategies, success and failures of the selected organisation, viz., WCADL in Mahabubnagar district of A.P. in terms of its objectives.

Notes

1. Sisir Basu, 1994. "Rural Poor: Failure of Growth Models". *Deccan Chronicle,* October 8, p. 8.
2. Katar Singh, 1999: *Rural Development Principles, Policies and Management*, p. 288.
3. Ibid., p. 289.
4. D.N. Singh, 1985: "Introduction" in *A Prologue to Rural Development Strategies in India*, p. 1.
5. Madhuri Singh and K.N. Singh (1985: 24).
6. Ibid., p. 25.
7. Ibid.
8. Madhusudhan Pal, 2002: "Rural Development and Easy Money", in *Frontier,* April 28–May 4, pp. 10-11.
9. Ibid., pp. 10-11.
10. Katar Singh, op. cit., pp. 21-22.
11. P.C. Mehta, 1994: *Voluntary Organization and Tribal Development*, p. 1.
12. Ibid., p. 1.
13. Ibid.
14. Ibid., p. 2.
15. Vasant Desai, 1988: *Rural Development: Experiments in Rural Development*, Vol. IV, p. 47.
16. Sisir Basu, op. cit., p. 8.
17. K. Ranga Rao, 1998: In an edited book *Women in Developing Society Aiming Towards 21st Century* by J.B. Abibasayulu, p. 5.
18. B.T. Lawani, 1999: *NGOs in Development*, Rawat Pulications, Jaipur, p. 17.
19. Ibid., pp. 18-20.
20. Ibid., pp. 24-25.
21. Ibid., p. 25.

22. Rajesh Tandon, "Policy on Voluntary Sector", 20 January, 2004: *The Hindu*.
23. Madhuri Singh and K.N. Singh, 1985: "Voluntary Agencies: The Role in Rural Development in India". In K.N. Singh and D.N. Singh (eds.), *Rural Development in India*, R.L. Singh Foundation, Varanasi, pp. 138-139.
24. P.C. Mehta, op. cit., pp. 48-49.
25. U.V.N. Charyulu, 1981: *Voluntary Organisations and Rural Development*, edited from Rural Development in India: Some Aspects, NIRD, Hyderabad, p. 219.
26. P.C. Mehta, op. cit., p. 49.
27. B.T. Lawani, op. cit., pp. 45-46.
28. Pradip N. Khandwalla, 1988: *Social Development: A New Role for the Organizational Sciences*", p. 28.
29. M. Singh and K.N. Singh, op. cit., p. 141.
30. Ibid., p. 141.
31. Lawani, op. cit., pp. 199-204.
32. Ibid., p. 215.
33. G. Satyanarayana, 1980: in his unpublished article "Conflict in Country Side".
34. S.P. Srivastava, 1999: "Nature of Voluntary Action in India Today", *Social Action*, Vol. 49, January-March, pp. 1-13.
35. Andre Beteille, 2001: "Civil Society and the Good Society", *Sociological Bulletin*, Vol. 50, No. 2, September, pp. 298-299.
36. Rakesh Kapoor, 1996: "Voluntary Action: Survival, Politics and Transformation", *Social Action*, Vol. 46, January-March, pp. 13-26.
37. Ibid., p. 14.
38. Ibid., p. 15.
39. Rajesh Tandon, 1996: "Changing Context and Challenges for Voluntary Action in India Today", *Social Action*, Vol. 46, January-March, p. 1.
40. Ibid., p. 7.
41. Ibid., p. 11.
42. K.L. Sharma, 1996: "The Indian State and the NGOs: Some Reflections", *Social Action*, Vol. 46, January-March, pp. 28-39.
43. Ibid., p. 30.
44. Ibid., p. 35-36.
45. Ibid., p. 36.
46. T. Lakshmaiah, 1999: "Tribal Development: Role of Voluntary Organizations", *Kurukshetra*, August, p. 45.

47. Ibid., p. 46.
48. Ibid., p. 47.
49. Gopal Krishna Sahu, 2000: "Voluntary Organization for Rural Development", *Kurukshetra*, June, pp. 20-21.
50. T.V. Lucy, 1993: "Social Reforms to Voluntarism in India", *Legal News and Views*, December, p. 421.
51. Nityananda, 2000: "The Social Change: The Emerging Role of NGOs in Rural Development of India", Sept-Dec, 2000, Vol. 30, No. 344. p. 36.
52. Ibid., pp. 36-37.
53. Ibid., pp. 37-41.
54. Ibid., p. 37.
55. Ibid.
56. Ibid., p. 39.
57. Ibid., pp. 39-40.
58. Ibid., pp. 40-41.
59. Ibid., p. 41.
60. B.S. Baviskar, 2001: "NGOs and Civil Society", *Sociological Bulletin*, Vol. 1, March, 2001, p. 5.
61. Ibid., p. 1.
62. Ibid., p. 4.
63. C. Francis, 1996: "Poverty Eradication through Employment Generation in WCADL", in *Indian Poverty Eradication Foundation Bulletin*, July-Sept, 1996, Vol. 1, No. 1, p. 12.
64. B.S. Baviskar, op. cit., p. 8.
65. Nityananda, op. cit., p. 41.
66. Ibid.
67. Ibid., p. 42.
68. Arun Bhatiya, 2002: *The Hindu*, English newspaper November, 24 entitled "Stealing from the Poor".
69. B.S. Baviskar, op. cit., p. 9.
70. Ibid., p. 12.
71. B.S. Baviskar, op. cit., pp. 9-13.
72. Ibid., pp. 12-13.
73. Katar Singh, op. cit., p. 25.
74. Ibid.
75. United Nations Assertion, "The Advancement of Women", in the *Blue Book Series*, Vol. VI, p. 13.
76. Baviskar, op. cit., p. 13.

77. Katar Singh, op. cit., p. 286.
78. Satish Deshpande, 2003: "Indian Social Science in the Contemporary Era", *Sociological Bulletin*, Vol. 52, No. 2, September, p. 263.
79. Raj Kumar, 2002: "Capacity Building of Panchayats for Rural Development: Some Emerging Areas for NGOs", *Man and Development*, March, p. 64.
80. Ibid., pp. 64-65.
81. P.K.B. Nayar, 2001: "Civil Society and Globalisation", *Sociological Bulletin*, Vol. 50, No. 2, September, p. 213.
82. Ibid., pp. 216-217.
83. Srivastava, 1999: "Nature of Voluntary Action in India Today", p. 1.
84. Ibid., pp. 6-7.
85. Ibid., pp. 10-11.
86. Ibid., p. 11.
87. Ibid., pp. 11-12.
88. Andre Beteille, op. cit., pp. 300-301.
89. Ibid., 301.
90. Ibid., 304.
91. Sharma, op. cit., p. 35.
92. Ibid., 39.
93. S. Ganesh Bhat, 1999: "Rural Entrepreneurship and NGOs", *Kurukshetra*, November, p. 15.
94. Ibid., p. 17.
95. Sudha and B.S. Bhargava, 2000: "Panchayats and NGOs in Social Change", *Kurukshetra*, July, pp. 21-23.
96. Ibid., 23.
97. R. Soorya Moorthy, 1997: "NGOs in Development Process of Indian Society", *Journal of the Kerala Sociological Society*, Vol. XXV, No. 1, June, pp. 63-70.
98. Ibid., p. 66.
99. Ibid.
100. Ibid.
101. Ibid., p. 68.
102. Y.V. Rao and C. Francis, 1993: "Action Oriented Adult Literacy and Education in WCADL", *Journal of Rural Development*, NIRD, November, pp. 651-657.
103. C. Francis, 1993: "Rural Development, People's Participation and the Role of NGOs", *Journal of Rural Development*, NIRD, March, pp. 205-210.

104. Ibid., p. 206.
105. T.V. Lucy, 1995: "Empowerment of Women for Sustainable Development", *Social Action*, Vol. 45, April-June, pp. 224-231.
106. C. Francis, 1994: "Conscientising Through Cultural Activities", *Sonolux Information*, September, pp. 42-44.
107. Ibid., pp. 43-44.
108. Ibid., p. 44.
109. Ibid.
110. Ibid., p. 96.
111. Ibid., p. 97.
112. Ibid., p. 98.
113. G. Satyanarayana, 1999: "Voluntary Organization and Emancipation of Dalit Women", pp. 142-154.

2

History and Functioning of WCADL

The main aim of this chapter is to discuss and present the nature of the voluntary organisation selected for study. For his purpose the following aspects are considered: the origin and growth of the organisation, its philosophy, aim and objectives, organisational structure and functions, the method of organising the people, the membership, and the areas of operation and its significance.

The organisation under study, i.e., Weaker Community Action for Development and Liberation (WCADL) is a non-profit making, non-political, non-religious comprehensive voluntary rural development organisation established on 3 June, 1976, with the registration No. 405 under the Andhra Pradesh (Telengana Area) Public Societies Registration Act 1350 Fasli. It is also registered with the Ministry of Home Affairs, Government of India, under the Foreign Contribution Regulation Act and also registered with the Department of Income Tax for exemption of tax.

This weaker community development organisation mainly works in the backward rural areas. It was visualised and established by a devout, philanthropic, service-minded, sensitive, young Malayali catholic Christian couple in the year 1976, with a strong determination to dedicate their lives for the service of the needy and deprived. Hence, they decided not to have children of their own, but later adopted a girl by name, Ansy, from a close relative of their family in her very tender age on her own choice to be with Mrs and Mr Francis. This incident also they considered as the Will of God and accepted her as their own daughter, brought her up in a very disciplinary way, gave her the best of education and got her decently married, which also they considered as part of their social work, service done to God and to the nation. Above all, Mrs and Mr Francis saw to it that Ansy was brought up in a strict disciplinary environment and trained her to be self-reliant and self-dependent. But all the same Mrs and Mr Francis have done this not with expectation of any returns. Incidentally, it may be mentioned here that Ansy was helped for her studies by their friends in Germany.

They started their career at Vishakhapatnam, later worked for some years in the Rayalaseema district of Ananthapur came to Hyderabad in the early seventies and started WCADL, a voluntary organisation at Mahabubnagar for the service of the poor, needy, deprived and suppressed.

Philosophy and the Founders

It was through prolonged discussion and interaction over a decade with the authors of WCADL that I could understand that Mrs Lucy Francis and Mr Francis have derived their inspiration as can be expected, through the inherited culture of their Catholic parental family background which imparted to them rational, modern, liberal education, love, compassion, and a deep sense of service to the needy and deprived. Their decision of not having children itself convinces anyone of the fact that they dedicated their lives for the cause of the deprived and suppressed sections, and to bringing awareness among them for development and liberation.

Philosophy

WCADL believes that the major causes for underdevelopment are illiteracy, lack of awareness among the masses; their backwardness and their inability to organise themselves, to oppose the exploitation they are forced to live in. Therefore, the oppressed masses are to be motivated to analyse and reflect on their situation and to take suitable actions for their own development. The final outcome of such reflection and analysis and actions, is expected to minimise the ever-increasing gap between the rich and the poor, if not the establishment of an egalitarian system of society. This means that the final outcome is expected to culminate in a change of structure to be brought about by the oppressed communities themselves to their own advantage and benefit. Here the role of WCADL is limited to that of a catalyst.

Founding Members

As mentioned above, WCADL was founded by the efforts and initiative of Francis and his wife Lucy. From their early days onwards they were very much concerned about the poverty, illiteracy, ill-health, and other social and economic evils to which the poor and oppressed sections of the society are subjected to. They were also concerned about the violation of human rights that prevailed in the society in various forms and the helplessness of the victims to come out of the miserable situation in which they are trapped. Initially, in their individual capacity they did what they could to minimise such suffering. But their effort met only with a very limited success. Later on, they joined different organisations to work for a change in the existing situation of the suffering victims. Here too they had only very limited role to play in human development and liberation. In the final analysis, both Francis and Lucy decided to leave such organisations and founded an organisation of their own with their own ideology in which they could play a very major role. The outcome was the birth of Weaker Community's Action for Development and Liberation.

The motivation for Francis and Lucy to play a developmental, and liberative role came from a person none other than Paulo Freire himself, who is a social activist and who brought about revolutionary changes in the lives of the poor and oppressed in Brazil. Paulo Freire himself drew his inspiration from Christ who wanted to bring about revolutionary changes in the Jewish community by questioning the hypocrisy, orthodoxy and conservatism of the Jewish leaders, which posed a hindrance for the development of that community at that time. Christ had to pay for it with his own blood. In this context, it is worth mentioning the ideas of Francis and Lucy, in the words of Paulo Freire himself. He says:

> I thought how difficult it was for the masses of the people to start to be and I felt challenged since I was a child. More and more I felt the need to become engaged in the understandings of the situation of the people were. Of course, my Christian formation, background, had something to do with this. I used to say that it was a serious contradiction to continue to say, to proclaim my Christian faith and to look at the situation of exploitation of millions of people without trying to do something. *Reading and Writing Reality: Explorations into Adult Education* by Paulo Freire (Vishwa Yuvak Kendra, 1979, p.14).

It cannot be denied that the founders of WCADL were also influenced indirectly by Marxist ideology. Here, in this context also, it is worthwhile to quote their thoughts in the words of Paulo Freire who said:

> In my case I did not go to the slums of my country because of Marx. I went because of Christ. It is very interesting and I have nothing to deny this truth. But when I arrived there, the reality of my people sent me to Marx and after meeting Marx, I never had the need to stop meeting Christ (ibid.: 23).

In spite of their deep faith in God and firm conviction about the religion they practised, the founding members of WCADL never, at any moment of time, permitted religion to play any role in the day-to-day activities of WCADL. For they believed that service rendered to humanity is service rendered to God. According to them religion is a personal matter of each individual and that no one has any right to interfere with it.

Further, in the due course of my long interviews with them I could grasp that their thinking reflected the elements of rationality, reasoning and scientific spirit. This fact was revealed clearly in their association with rationalists, secular, liberal and democratic minded intellectuals and academicians.

Their way of life shows that they do arduous works, meticulous planning, leading a simple life, without any inhibition and vices and they mingle with the people easily. They also believe that ignorance of the people is a real cause of all ills and evils and they can be removed by simple reasoning of social education. Unity is the strength of the weaker community people. To develop any individual or a group of people, unity is essential. The poor are to be organised to muster the strength of unity, so that they cannot be exploited and suppressed. Unity is the basic requirement for the individual dignity, social equality which recognises the cultural, economic and political needs of individuals and groups. This would be the basic requirement for a level of living, by pooling the resources, designing micro- and macro-level planning for the active participation of the target people. They also believe that guidance, organisation and the unity of the people are essential to overcome ignorance, scarcity and suffering.

They also believe that to organise the poor, no external skill is required but using the people who are well-motivated by their local wisdom can bring a tremendous change rather than a highly qualified professional apart from social workers. This approach really helps the poor and weaker communities with self-confidence and enables them to share their day-to-day problems which need immediate attention.

Aim and Objectives

The main aim of WCADL is to eliminate the barriers in living together by building unity among the poor to use the scarce resources to the optimum level, to tap and extract local resources by giving a scientific and functional education to all, to raise the human dignity and respect to all, irrespective of the background of caste, class, sex, clan, region, religion, etc. Further, as a catalytic agent, WCADL aims at imparting awareness of generating education to the rural poor especially to the members of Dalit communities and Lambada tribals to organise them to work for their own socio-economic development and liberation by promoting and encouraging the spirit of self-reliance and self-dependence and by discouraging undue and undesirable dependence on others.

Their approach of upliftment was not based on any contradiction or conflict, but on peace and harmony and on 'live and let me live' policy which helps them to develop clean and healthy habits. They are also encouraged to work hard to earn to the optimum and to spend less, to save and invest for the future of oneself and one's own family.

As such they trained the illiterate local men and women to maintain accounts, to train others by giving lectures in all forums including local and state and national level programmes and occasions such as International Women's Day, International Literacy Day, etc.

The main aim of the founders of WCADL is to eliminate human suffering by removing the ignorance and illiteracy with minimum aid and help. They want to build a society of strong, healthy individuals with all the required facilities for human dignity with the help of united effort and use of the scarce resources to the optimum level with minimum aid, help and expenditure. Further, they also aim at elimination of all kinds of inequalities caused by caste, class, sex, region, religion, etc., in order to build a just human society.

To this end, WCADL strives to:

1. develop backward villages by promoting agriculture, its allied sectors and village industries, etc;
2. develop rural skills by organising training to encourage farmers and other cooperative efforts;
3. organise functional education and to organise welfare activities to provide common infrastructural facilities in basic health and in marketing;
4. initiate the dynamics of development in the rural community with special reference to small and marginal farmers, landless labourers and village artisans with special emphasis on 'Dalits' and 'tribals';
5. emphasise the importance of techno-economic feasibility of combining credit with supply of other inputs, adequate supervision and realisation of loans advanced; and

6. stress the importance of coordination and result-oriented team work.

The other objectives are as follows:

(1) To make available credits for the above activities;
(2) To educate the rural poor about the existing credit facilities and to enlighten them as to how to avail themselves of such facilities;
(3) To create awareness among the rural poor regarding the problems of bonded and child labour and of borrowing money from the moneylenders at enormous rates of interest, and to provide them with alternative arrangements;
(4) To educate the rural poor on the various developmental programmes of the government and how to draw benefits from such programmes without becoming victims of middle men;
(5) To impart training programmes for the farmers, rural artisans and for the various functionaries of WCADL;
(6) To instil into the rural masses the spirit of self-reliance;
(7) To instil self-confidence into the rural poor to work for their own development;
(8) To educate them to invest money on productive purposes rather than on unproductive items;
(9) To bring home to the rural masses that development is to be carried out by both men and women and that development in the ultimate analysis would mean the total development of men and women; and
(10) To convey the message to the rural masses that development and liberation are to be brought about not by an outside agency but by themselves and through their own effort and struggle.

Membership

Membership in WCADL is open to all adults who accept the above aims and objectives and work for the promotion of those objectives. Whoever desires to take admission has to pay Rs 1 as admission fee and Rs 5 annual membership fee. If any member fails to pay the membership fee continuously for two years he/she ceases to be the member of the Society.

General Body and its Functions

The members of this society on payment of the annual membership fees and admission fees will form the General Body of the Association. The General Body shall meet at least once in a year, preferably on 30th November every year. The quorum of the General Body shall be two-thirds of the members on the roll. The major functions of the General Body are:

1. It elects the members of the Executive Committee.
2. It passes annual budget for the ensuing year and approves the expenditure of the previous year.
3. It approves the programme to be carried out in the succeeding year.
4. It sanctions amount to be spent on projects.
5. It appoints auditors to audit the society's expenditure.
6. It approves or ratifies the reports of the activities of the Executive Committee during the year submitted to the General Body on 30th November in the year.
7. All decisions of the General Body are made by a simple majority of votes.

Executive Board (Managing Committee) and its Functions

The General Body elects the members of the Society to form the Executive Committee. The President, the Secretary and the Treasurer of the Society will be members of the Executive Committee by virtue of their offices. There will be altogether nine members on the Executive Committee, consisting five elected members and four office-bearers.

Organisational Structure and Activities of WCADL

Structure

The central point of the structure of WCADL is the 'Sangam' in each village. The entire structure is built upon the Sangam, from

Organisational Structure and Activities of WCADL

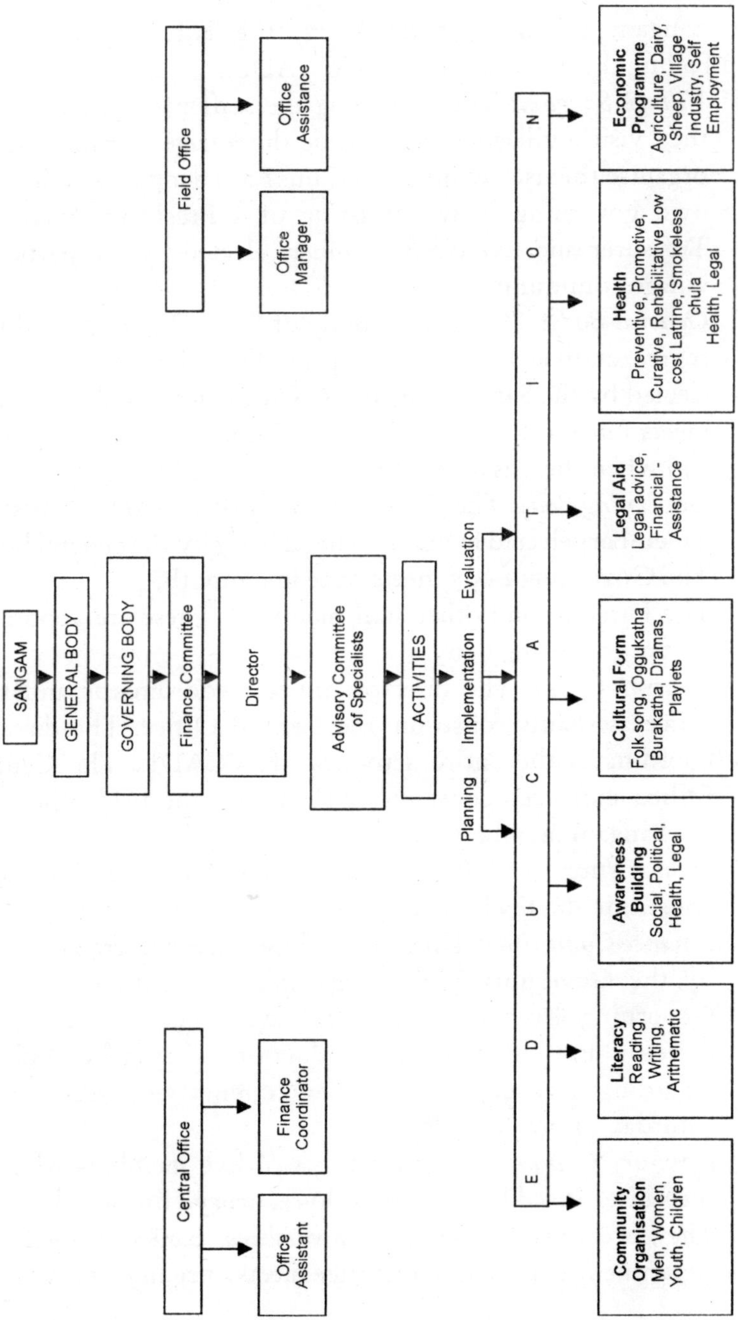

the Sangam to the General Body, the latter directing and controlling the entire activities of WCADL.

(1) *Village Sangam*: The first thing the staff members do when they visit a village is to persuade the village communities to organise themselves into a Sangam. Each Sangam will have its own governing body consisting of a President, Secretary, Treasurer and five other members elected by the particular village community.

(2) *General Body*: The General Body of WCADL consists of two representatives from each Sangam. These representatives are elected by the Sangam members. The General Body normally meets once in a year. It also meets more than once a year as and when there is a need to meet.

(3) *Governing Body*: The Governing Body of WCADL consists of 9 members elected from the general body by the general body. The Governing Body meets once in a month.

(4) The Director and other staff members: These are appointed by the governing body.

(5) *Central Office*: The director, finance coordinator and two office assistants constitute the Central Office. The director coordinates the entire activities of WCADL. The Central Office staff keep constant contacts with the field office and the Sangam members.

(6) *Field Office*: An office manager and two office assistants constitute the field office.

(7) *Finance Committee*: This consists of seven members as decided by the Governing Body, consisting of members from the Governing Body, the area and cluster coordinators, the director and the finance coordinator. They take decision regarding finance matters. This committee meets every Saturday in the field office.

(8) *Advisory Committee*: This consists of five members who are specialists in education, agriculture, dairy, finance, law etc. They are drawn from the universities, banks, government departments, etc. This committee meets once in three months.

(9) *Animators*: In every village there is an animator who conducts the literacy classes in the evening and supervises the other activities there. They are from the same village.

(10) *Cluster Coordinators*: They are responsible for the community organisation and other activities in a cluster of 7 to 10 villages. During the week they go from village to village. They are provided with ordinary bicycles. They are assisted by the animators.

(11) *Area Coordinators*: They are responsible for the activities in an area of 20 to 30 villages. They are assisted by the cluster coordinators and by the animators. They are provided with motor cycles for their conveyance.

Activities

Just as the structure of WCADL is built on the Sangam, the entire activities of WCADL are built on education.

(1) *Education*: In WCADL education means much more than mere literacy and learning. WCADL believes that the main cause of oppression and the existing socio-economic disparity is the lack of education among the oppressed groups.

(2) *Community organisation*: Material development is necessary. But human development is a must. Men, women, youth and the children of any caste, class, religious denominations must be able to live a dignified life. There should be a socio-economical, political or religious environment in which human beings can lead a dignified life. It is with this aim WCADL has 'sangam' for men, women, youths and children.

(3) *Literacy*: Due importance is given for the learning of reading, writing and simple arithematic.

(4) *Awareness building*: The existing social and economic disparity, their causes, social, political and economic and religious oppressions, etc., find a place in this education programme. The causes of ill-health, legal rights of every citizen, the existing regulations for the liberation of the oppressed, etc., also are the subject matter of the education programme.

(5) *Cultural forum*: This forum conducts folk songs, Oggukatha (one form of action song with story narrative by a group of three) dramas, playlets, etc. The cultural forum is one of the main tools in WCADL's education programme. Therefore, this has a very prominent place in all the activities of WCADL.

(6) *Legal aid*: Lack of knowledge about their rights, and the existing legislations in the country for the socio-economic emancipation of the oppressed are some of the causes of backwardness in the country. Hence, legal education and financial aid for the unavoidable court litigations as and when occasion arises are also included in the activities of WCADL.

(7) *Health*: WCADL believes in the old adage that "health is wealth". Their health programme consists of education in the preventive and the promotive aspects of health, rehabilitative programmes if and when required, promotion of low cost curatives, etc. The society also educates and helps the rural communities to build smokeless 'chullahs' and low cost latrines in the rural areas.

(8) *Economic programmes*: In the earlier stages of WCADL there was a separate fixed finance for programmes such as agriculture, dairy, sheep, village industries, and other self-employment programmes. In later years, separate finance was not earmarked for the items mentioned above. Hence, the amounts already invested on these items are collected back and any amount received is being distributed to the Sangams to meet their immediate needs as decided by the Sangams.

Development Communication

(1) *Interpersonal Communication*: For the successful implementation of any programme there should be direct contact with the community for and with whom the programmes are implemented. The more the number of intermediaries the less will be the quality of implementation. Hence, to ensure the maximum quality in implementation, WCADL staff establish direct contact with the village communities. This may be described as interpersonal communication. The interpersonal

communication is maintained in WCADL with the village communities by means of:

(a) Evening classes: In each village there are evening classes. This classes are conducted by the animator who teaches literacy, arithmetic and discusses with them several other items of importance. It is a process of mutual learning.

(b) Weekly meeting: The Sangam members in each village set apart one day for their meetings. In such meetings they discuss and plan for their development and try to find solutions to their problems. The animators, in each village, will definitely be present in such meetings. The cluster and area coordinators will try to be present at the meetings in one or more villages. These meetings are the planning and decision-making forums in each village.

(c) Fortnightly meeting: Once in two weeks the Sangam members of a cluster will meet. In such meetings they share each others views and thoughts, exchange ideas, learn from each other's experiences, and failures. Here they try to seek common solutions to the problems faced by all the oppressed groups. The staff will try to be present for such meetings and provide them with information and guidelines whenever necessary.

(d) Quarterly meeting: The Sangam representatives of an area which includes a number of clusters will meet once in three months. The main purpose of this meeting is to create and maintain solidarity between the members of the area. Here also they freely discuss the failures, improvements, their common problems and the possible solutions to their problems, etc. Such meetings have been found extremely useful to maintain the solidarity and rapport between the members of the different Sangams. This creates a family feeling between the members of the different Sangams.

(e) Annual meeting: The culmination of all these meetings is the annual get-together of all the Sangam members at the field office. This programme lasts for a full night and a day. It is a huge gathering. Thousands participate in this function. In this meeting various reports about the activities of WCADL are read out and discussions are held. Various cultural programmes staged by the different Sangam members are a special feature of this meeting.

(2) *Weekly Meetings in the Field Office*

(a) Saturday meeting: The financial committee meets every Saturday afternoon and takes decision on financial matters.

(b) Monday meeting: The early hours on Monday are spent in discussing vital issues about the functioning of WCADL. The members of the finance committee, the area coordinators and the director participate in this meeting. The decisions taken in the Saturday meetings are discussed once more in this meeting. This meeting lasts for about an hour.

By this time other staff and representatives of the Sangam assemble in the community hall. The decision taken in the Saturday meeting are discussed once more in this meeting. This meeting also lasts for about an hour.

(3) *Training and Refreshers Courses*: These are arranged for the various functionaries of WCADL for the cultural team, staff, leaders in the villages, presidents and members of the Panchayats, for the farmers and such other functionaries in the village. These programmes are conducted by the senior staff of WCADL with the help of resource persons from university and the government departments, banks, etc. The advisory committee of specialists plays a vital role in this context.

(4) *Public Meetings*: These meetings are organised on very important national days such as Independence Day, Republic Day, Gandhi Jayanthi Day on which the National Adult Education Programmes were launched, Ambedkar Jayanthi day, and on international days such as, International Women's Day, World Health Day, Workers Day, World Literacy Day, etc. The themes of these days are very much suited to the type of activities of WCADL. Hence, by

organising functions on these days WCADL conveys to the rural masses what the organisation wishes to communicate to them. The effects and impact of such functions on the rural masses have been marvellous. The organisation propose to relates the theme of such days to the day-to-day life of the masses. Hence such marvellous impact.

(5) *Mass media*: Reading of news papers and periodicals, listening to the radio, etc., are encouraged. Cassettes, cultural programmes, folk songs etc., are also used to educate the rural people and to bring about a change in their life situation.

Development Communication in WCADL

Initial Problems and Setbacks

It was some time in the middle of the year 1975 that Francis and Lucy decided to found an organisation of their choice to undertake socio-economic developmental activities for the poor and oppressed. As already stated above they had the commitment, ideology, philosophy, motivation, necessary for this purpose. But these alone were not enough to initiate the activities of such an organisation. To begin with, there should be a team of people with similar commitment, willingness to go to the people in the villages and to identify their problems. Therefore, the first problem was to search and locate a few committed people. This problem was solved to a great extent, as it was found that there were four youngsters willing to associate with Lucy and Francis. The next problem was to decide as to what kind of people to work with, i.e., to work with the poor. But then, there were poor people in all the castes and communities. Was it possible to work with all the poor people of all the castes and communities? After a prolonged and protracted discussion it was decided that it was not possible to work with all the poor people of all the communities as it would involve quite a lot of money and other resources and infrastructure facilities. Therefore, it was decided to work with the most depressed and exploited lot, namely the Dalits and the Lambada tribals. The next problem was to decide in which area to work.

Development Communication in WCADL

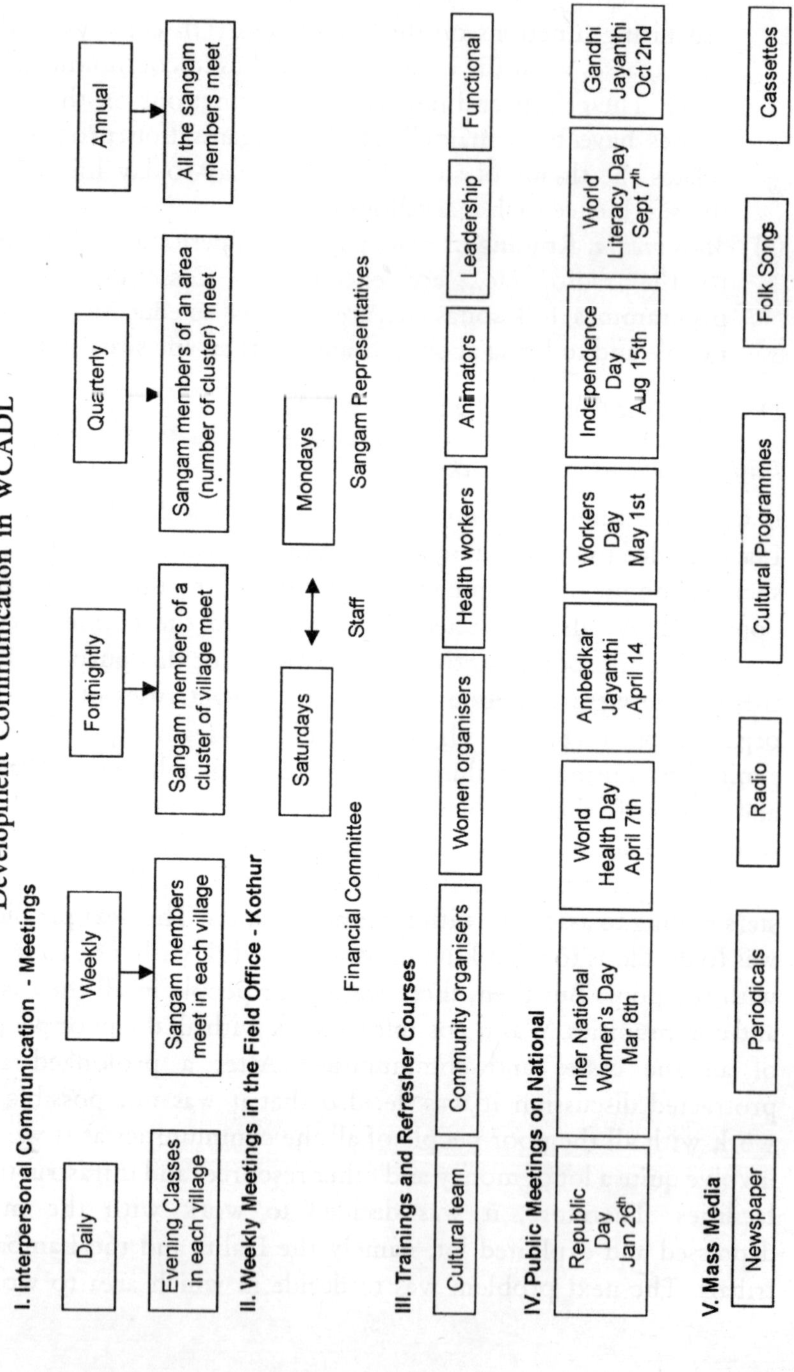

After taking into account and after a cursory discussion and study it was decided to commence the activities in Mahabubnagar district. This district was chosen because of its socio-economic backwardness and also because of the absence of any voluntary organisation in the district and also because the developmental programmes of the government were in their very initial stage.

Thereafter, the question was to decide upon the villages to initiate the dialogue with the people for their own development. Then as all the members of the team were residing at Hyderabad and there was no acquaintance with anyone in Mahabubnagar district, it was decided to initiate the dialogue with the Dalits of Thimmapur and Kothur villages as these two villages are on the national highway from Hyderabad and therefore easily accessible for the team to establish contact. The next problem was as to how to get entry into these villages as all the members of the team were new to the place and they had no antecedents of taking up developmental programmes in the nearby places which could be utilised as an introductory point. But all the same, several visits were made by the members of the team to these villages to initiate a dialogue. But all these attempts were not met with the desired results, as there were no achievements of the team in Mahabubnagar district to be presented as credentials. People in these two villages of initial contact had several misapprehensions about the team. Some of them mistook the team to be some sort of cheats who wanted to collect some money from them under the pretext of coming to develop them. They arrived at this conclusion about the WCADL team, it is said, because of their past experience. It seems at some time in the past, before the arrival of WCADL team, some people went to these villages with similar promises, collected money and vanished. The self-defence and protest of WCADL team that they were not cheats, did not carry much weight with the people. Some people mistook the WCADL team to be the members of some political party which wanted to wean them away from the then ruling party which they supported. Still some others mistook the WCADL team to be the representatives of some proselytising group. They thought so, because most of the members of the team had Christian names. Those were the days of compulsory family planning programme introduced by the Government of India. Therefore, some others considered the team to be agents of compulsory family planning who under the pretext of developing them were trying to allure them to undergo family planning. Here it may be noted that there was resistance from the people of these parts against the coercion to undergo compulsory family planning. In this context, it may be mentioned as narrated by Lucy and Francis that one day when the team visited a tribal settlement by name Rangapur Tanda, all the adult youngsters and able-bodied men and women ran away from the village because of their fear of forcing them to undergo family planning operation. But, all the same WCADL managed to gather the old ones who were left in the village and explained to them the purpose of their visit and left the village. As the WCADL team left the village, the adults and the able-bodied ones who had run away from the village came back and enquired and learned from the elders what the WCADL team had discussed with them. Once they got the message, all of them cooperated with the WCADL team, as they were in the clutches of a moneylenders from elsewhere and were looking for someone to help them to liberate themselves from the moneylenders clutches. Later on it was proved to be one of the best developed villages, which received the maximum benefit from the development programmes of WCADL. These misapprehensions and misguided judgments about the sincerity of the WCADL team would have been sufficient reasons for the team to give up hope. But it was not so with the WCADL team.

As a last resort to win over the confidence of the people, the WCADL team decided to make use of the existing institutions and the power structures in the area. In close proximity to the villages the team chose to work at a place where there is a church. The team approached the priest of the church through a friend. At first the priest agreed to cooperate. But no cooperation came from him except that he agreed to use church address in the event of registering WCADL as a society. The team was not unhappy about the non-cooperation of the priest which turned out to be advantageous to WCADL. For, if the team had taken the cooperation of the church, the people in the villages would have still misunderstood them as agents trying to convert them to Christianity. As a next step the WCADL team established contact with the Sarpanch of Kothur Panchayat, a resident of Thimmapur village, and discussed with him the willingness of the team to undertake developmental programmes in the villages under his jurisdiction. At first, his reaction was very much negative. For, he told the team that during so many years of his service as Sarpanch of the Panchayat, he had wide contacts, but never did he come across anyone who had volunteered to do something for the upliftment of the downtrodden without any vested interest. He said, instead he had come across people who exploited the poor and never went to their rescue. But all the same he did not completely rule out the possibility of cooperation. Meanwhile, the team tried to take into confidence the Dalit leaders of Kothur village and Akivanigudem, a hamlet of Kothur village. These two Dalit leaders consulted the Sarpanch and decided to extend their cooperation.

These three leaders were of the view that if WCADL was going to do something good to the poor it would be fine and welcome. On the contrary, if they failed to do anything good, the people in their villages would not lose anything. As these three leaders spoke on behalf of the WCADL team, the Dalits in the villages of Kothur, Thimmapur and Akivanigudem showed interest in listening to the team.

Before making any plan of action as to what sort of programmes were to be undertaken, the first thing the team did was to have several group discussions and meetings with the people on the streets, some times under a tree or in their agricultural fields, etc. In one such meetings the Dalit leader of Kothur village told the team, "Sirs, if you people are really interested in doing something for us, you will have to come directly to us and discuss things with us. Please do not go and sit in a house of the rich upper-caste people and call us there for discussions in their presence, as some of the Government officials do". The team understood his feelings and told him that they had not gone to any such people and instead approached them directly. It was only when they did not believe them, they went to the Sarpanch. It may be noted here that in its 27 years of existence, this was the only occasion that WCADL approached the people through the power structure of the village. In all its other activities WCADL went directly to the people, established contacts and in consultation with them and jointly with them implemented programmes.

Establishment of Sangams and the First Village-Level Planning for the Development and Liberation

After several group discussions and meetings and after being convinced about the sincerity of WCADL team, the Dalits in the three villages agreed to form into an association, i.e., a Sangam, in each village. Thereafter, micro-planning together with the Sangam members was done in the three villages regarding the programmes to be undertaken. This type of planning in the present day terminology may be called Participatory Rural Appraisal (PRA). But in those days this terminology did not exist and therefore WCADL team named the exercise as 'need survey'. During the 'need survey' people revealed a lot of their requirements. But all their proposals could not be undertaken in the first phase. The requirements were reduced into six: community irrigation wells, 30 milch buffaloes, 120 sheep and three adult education centres. Meanwhile, efforts were also made by the team to establish contacts with a donor agency by name 'Bread for the World' in Germany and also to get WCADL registered as a society under the Public Societies Registration Act.

A project proposal for Rs 1,20,000 for the implementation of the programmes planned with the people, was submitted to Bread for the World in Germany on 4, May 1976. The project proposal was approved on 16 June of the same year. On 3 June, 1976 WCADL was registered under the Public Society's Registration Act.

With this initial achievement, the WCADL team was quite happy. But all the same, there were more troubles and problems in store for them. As the project proposal was approved by the donor agency, selection of beneficiaries for the different economic programmes was done. The grounding of the first phase of the economic programme in time, and successful management of the programme would contribute a great deal for the establishment of the credentials of WCADL. But unfortunately, the project could not be grounded on time as was expected by one and all concerned. The amount approved by the donor agency could meet only a part of the economic programme. Further funds had to be raised either from a commercial bank or the State Scheduled Caste and Backward Classes Corporations. Efforts to secure assistance from the SC & BC Corporations did not meet with any success. Efforts to secure bank loans also did not bear any fruit to begin with. Several banks were approached. Here also the WCADL team faced the same problem as in getting introduced to the people of Kothur and Thimmapur villages, and the problem of being new entrants in the field of rural development without any credentials to project. Meanwhile, the beneficiaries who were selected for the programmes were becoming impatient and all the villagers were on the point of completely misunderstanding WCADL. At last, to the great luck of WCADL a friend of these teams and well-wisher introduced WCADL to a branch of a commercial bank in Hyderabad. Initially also, this bank expressed its unwillingness to sanction loans to a new organisation. But strongly persuaded by the well-wisher, the bank agreed to finance the milch animal programme and part of the sheep-rearing programme. The rest of the economic programmes were directly financed by WCADL from the money sanctioned by the donor agency. The bank gave its consent to finance the above programmes in December 1976.

Evening classes for adult learners were conducted in the three villages. Weekly meetings of the Sangam members were also being held as part of the awareness-generating education programme. The team realised that meetings conducted in each village were not enough to introduce combined interaction with the members of other villages. For this, a common place was required. Meanwhile two additional staff were recruited to supervise the programmes. All these needed some place/or roof to work under. But no accommodation was available even on a rental basis.

Participants in the programmes of WCADL could not provide any accommodation as all of them had only small thatched huts hardly adequate for them to live in. The railway station at Thimmapur had a very broad and long veranda. This veranda was the venue for the fortnightly cluster meeting of the members of the three first Sangams. There was an old unused and unoccupied building near Thimmapur railway station. The WCADL team occupied this building and it served as accommodation for the two new teams of staff. The courtyard of the building served as the venue for several meetings and discussions of WCADL until such time WCADL had its own office premises and accommodations for the staff.

As things were progressing in the right direction with WCADL, the bureaucracy in Mahabubnagar received news about the functioning of WCADL and grew suspicious about it. The suspicion was all the more because as in the case of the people of Kothur and Thimmapur villages it was for the first time that the bureaucracy in the district was facing an organisation voluntarily coming forward to do something for the poor. It was reported that the personnel from the Police Department tried to dissuade people from going to WCADL. Also the personnel from the Intelligence Department enquired about Francis and Lucy and directly interrogated Francis. At last the WCADL team breathed a sigh of relief when it got a DO letter dated 13 July, 1977 from the then District Collector, Mahabubnagar, asking Francis to meet him to discuss the developmental activities to be taken up in the district. The Collector made several suggestions and promised all the possible help. However, this could not be materialised as he was transferred soon after.

Financial Resources of WCADL

Excluding a little bit of financial assistance for the adult education programme during the year 1979 and 1983 from the Government of India, all the financial contributions for the activities of WCADL came from Germany. In Germany, as mentioned above, there is an organisation by name 'Bread for the World' which is one of the overseas development agencies of the Evangelical (Protestant) Church of Germany. Further, there is a small group of committed people in Pulheim parish of Koln district in Germany who got themselves organised to raise funds for developmental works in the developing countries. Expenses for the first phase of the project of WCADL, i.e., 1976-77, was the direct financial contribution by Bread for the World from its own resources. In 1977, WCADL sent a proposal to Bread for the World to undertake developmental activities in seven villages including the first three villages where programmes were already initiated. During this period the above mentioned Pulheim group in Germany, was looking for an organisation in the developing countries, to directly associate with. They approached Bread for the World to recommend to them an organisation to work with. Having been satisfied with the implementation of the first phase of the programme, Bread for the World recommended WCADL to the Pulheim group. Now, Rangapur village in the present day Kothur Mandal of Mahabubnagar district was one of the seven villages named by WCADL in the second phase of its project proposal in 1976-1977. The philanthropic-minded Pulheim group formed themselves into an organisation by name of Rangapur Committee, taking the name of the village Rangapur which was one of the villages mentioned in that project proposed. Ever since in Koln district of Germany, WCADL has been mostly known as Rangapur Committee. This committee was formed in the year 1977. Rev. Jorg Baumgarten was the founder president of this Rangapur Committee, and Konrad Bottcher who is a very scholarly gentle man, with a lot of enthusiasm, commitment and dedication, succeeded him. He continued in office for a long time and had to lay down his presidentship due to his deteriorating health and expired on 21, July 2003. The staff and members of WCADL placed on record the yemon services rendered by Konrad Bottcher for WCADL, through Rangapur Committee. Rev. Malchior took over from Konrad Bottcher, the presidentship of Rangapur Committee. Several members of Rangapur Committee took pains to visit some of the interior villages that too during the hottest Indian summer to see the programmes implemented by WCADL. The intention of the Rangapur Committee was not merely to raise funds for WCADL project but to have a meaningful partnership with WCADL in the process of development. They did not merely want to be a fund-raising group. But they wanted to be actively involved in the process of development.

This, they did by their occasional visits to the programme areas, to see for themselves the developments which were taking place, by interacting with the staff and members of WCADL and by inviting the personnel from WCADL to interact with the communities in Germany which contributed towards the project, etc. In short, they wanted to make sure that their efforts for the development of the Dalits in the district of Mahabubnagar were not underutilised or misutilised and to be satisfied with the implementations and the achievements and also to see that the entire amount raised by them came to the project which they adopted as their own project.

The members of Rangapur Committee in Germany are ordinary middle-class people and are engaged in their own professional occupations. Some of them are factory workers while some others are teachers and still others are engaged in different types of professions. In spite of their being fully engaged in their own professions, they found time for working for humanitarian services in the developing countries. They raised funds through various methods. Voluntary contribution by philanthropic-minded people is one way. Donating part or full of some Sunday collections in various church groups is another way. Organising food stalls during church festivals is still another way of fund-raising. Women during their leisure, knit woollen mufflers, sweaters, caps, etc., and sold them during festival days and collected money. This is still another method. Even old and retired women do this work of dress making and other activities to raise funds for development works. Francis and Lucy came across the following incident during their first visit to Germany, in 1982. During their visit they were taken to a meeting of a very old women group, who mostly were widows whose husbands died during the Second World War. After the meeting when they came out, they saw an elderly woman standing in the door stretching out her hat as a begging bowl to collect alms from the poor widow participants who mostly survived on the pension given to them by the government. Francis and Lucy had with them two DM (German money) which someone had given them. They also put that two DM in that begging bowl as this collection was for

WCADL itself. Such incidences should be an eye opener for those who squander and make ill use of money which comes to them from foreign donor agencies for developmental works in the name of poor people of the developing countries. In Pulheim, once in a month, they organise what they call 'third world' meals. This meal consists of rice, dal, etc., cooked mostly in the Indian way.

Dates for such meals is announced in the church in advance and participation from the church community members was requested. On the appointed day, the meals will be prepared and the participants will contribute a little more than the cost of the meal as they know very well that the proceeds will go for a good cause. This third world meal was initiated by the dynamic leadership of a person by name Rose Marie. During the course of her visits to WCADL she learned the Indian way of cooking. With the help of Lucy, collecting recipes about Indian way of cooking, Rose Marie published a book in German on Indian cooking. The sale proceeds of this book also went to finance WCADL projects. Besides all these, members of Rangapur committee, every year, find time to publish beautiful calendars and sell them to raise funds. These are some of the ways and means used to raise funds. It was at times, felt in certain circles in India that funds coming from the developed world for programmes in the developing world, are from the affluent of the developed world. This assumption may or may not be true. But the experience of WCADL is quite the contrary. In spite of being fully engaged in their own day-to-day activities, the members of Rangapur Committee also find time to set apart for WCADL. They also find time to meet regularly every month, to plan and discuss what to do for WCADL. They render this sort of humanitarian services not with any ulterior motive. Their motive is only to serve God by serving man. Here it may be recalled that Germany rose from the ashes of devastation in the Second World War and rose to the status of donating quite a lot of amount for humanitarian services the world over. They could do this in about fifty years of hard work and well-thought-out planning. After Japan, Germany is the second largest donor for development works in India.

Now coming back to the financial arrangements for the activities of WCADL, it may be described as follows. The funds raised by the Rangapur Committee through various means as mentioned above is pooled together in the office of Church of Koln North, from where it is sent to the office of Bread for the World. WCADL submits project proposals to Bread for the World which after approving the project, disburses the amount on an instalment basis through the branch of State Bank of India in Germany to the WCADL account in a bank in Hyderabad. This sort of project-funding continued up to 1997. From 1997 onwards, Bread for the World preferred to discontinue funding WCADL. At this critical juncture, the Church of Koln North, under the leadership of Rev. Manfred Kock, who was the then Superintendent of Church of Koln North who himself accompanied by his wife Gisella visited WCADL project several times and was quite satisfied with the performance, persuaded the Church Committee and got a project sanctioned for three years, i.e., from 1998 to 2000. The funds collected by the Rangapur Committee and deposited in the bank accrued some interest. Rev. Ernest Fey who succeeded Rev. Manfred Kock as superintendent of the Church of Koln North, in consultation with the members of Rangapur Committee agreed to sanction this interest amount for the activities of WCADL in a very limited way from 2001 to 2005, on a yearly basis, this amount will be about Rs 600,000 per year.

From 1976 almost to the end of 1985, the funds received from the donor agency were both for the administrative expenses and for taking up various economic programmes in the villages with a view to increasing employment potential and self-reliance. But from 1986 onwards, the funds received were limited to adult education, training, health care, administrative expenses, etc., and also the amount was minimal at times for various economic programmes. This is mainly because by 1986, WCADL had created a revolving fund with the amount received up to 1985. This was the amount received for investment in only about 45 villages. With this amount in the revolving process, WCADL was able to take up various income-generating and employment-oriented economic programmes in about 125 villages. It is the policy of

WCADL not to give anything free. Anything given free may work out to be a charitable act but not an act related to development. WCADL is not to take up acts of charity but to take up acts of development. But all the same, in the initial stages, money was given to the Sangam members for various economic programmes free of any interest. As years went by and as the people were advanced in their economic programmes, of late, WCADL has decided to collect a small additional amount as service charges to meet at least part of the administrative expenses.

Construction of Adult Education Training Centres-cum-Field Offices

By 1978, WCADL had established a strong base in the initial villages and had a very good rapport with the people with whom it had worked. To strengthen this rapport further, there was the need for a contact point in the village and also for the staff to stay in. As the programmes of WCADL were expanded to more and more villages, the size of staff also increased. Therefore, WCADL had to find accommodation for them to stay in the villages. There was also a need for a permanent training centre-cum-office accommodation. Hitherto, ad hoc arrangements were made to meet these needs. These needs were met in 1979 by constructing a semi-permanent structures at Kothur village. Thereafter, Sangam members from Kothur village and its neighbourhood used to come for their meetings, discussions and other requirements to this centre as and when they felt the need.

By 1985, the programmes of WCADL were expanded to another 75 kilometres from the field office of Kothur. It was not easy to monitor the activities in these distant villages from Kothur. Therefore, there was a need to have a similar set-up in a central village in this area. Some of the staff members in this area were provided with temporary accommodation in rented houses at Rajapur village, which was identified as a central village. But this accommodation was not enough for the training and office purposes. Therefore, WCADL tried to have a similar set-up in Rajapur village like the one at Kothur. For this they needed a piece of land. But the upper castes and the elite groups at Rajapur village and also the surrounding villages saw to it that WCADL did not get a piece of land to purchase. They found a threat to them in the education programmes of WCADL. As it was mentioned earlier, the policy of WCADL has been to bring about a change in the existing socio-economic structure of the village through awareness generating education programmes. Certain provisions of the Constitution of India and certain legal provisions were found handy for the education programme of WCADL. WCADL had to explain to the people in the villages certain provisions of certain laws which were favourable to the poor, especially to the labour classes. But this type of education programmes had some adverse effect on the land-holding upper castes of the villages. In addition to this, because of its conscientisation programme, the landed gentry mistook WCADL to be a radical or a terrorist group. This sort of misconceived notion about WCADL prompted the landlords in the area to effect a mental change in their attitudes and behaviours towards the members of the Scheduled Castes and to reduced their acts of atrocities against them and not to come in the way of the activities of WCADL. Therefore, it was quite natural that the teachings of WCADL were not acceptable to these sections of people in the villages. This was the reason why they thought that WCADL should not have a permanent place anywhere close to their villages.

In such a situation, the staff and members of WCADL were a bit upset and discouraged. They also made an unsuccessful attempt to occupy and obtain titles for a piece of unutilised government land. Thus, the uncertainty to acquire or rather to purchase a piece of land at Rajapur to construct a field office-cum-training centre continued. At long last the WCADL staff came to know that a person of Vaisya community who was not well-disposed to the powerful elite group of Rajapur village wanted to dispose of a piece of land belonging to him as he was in need of money. He did not want the elite in the village to know that he was going to dispose of his land. For, if they had known they would grab the land at a very cheap rate. The staff of WCADL came to know about it. Immediately they contacted Lucy and Francis who acted promptly. The sale deed was executed. It was only after the execution of the sale deed that the elite sections in the village came to know about it. They, in turn, were very much angry with the man who had sold the land to WCADL and abused him with great contempt.

Once the land was purchased, necessary steps were taken to construct a building. The construction was completed and in October 1986, it was inaugurated by the Minister in charge for Power of the Government of Andhra Pradesh. The presence of the minister for the inauguration of WCADL office, helped many Sangam members to get electricity connections to their agricultural pumping sets.

The Role Played by Sangams: Village Associations in WCADL

Sangams, being the central points, play a vital role in all the activities of WCADL. Each and every member of the Sangam, while striving for their own individual development and benefit, should give priority to the common benefit and advantages of other members of the Sangam. It is easily said than put into practice. But this is the goal towards which the members of the Sangams in the villages are expected to strive for. But all the same, one cannot overlook the individual aspirations and benefits as we live in an individualistic society rather than in a society oriented to a common welfare. The Sangams are expected to unite all the members of the oppressed classes to withstand the oppression of the elite and the rich. In the present day society, nothing can be achieved without united and coordinated efforts. It is all the more so in the case of the oppressed and underprivileged sections. The Sangams are therefore, to unite the members of the oppressed communities so that all may be helpful to each and each, may be helpful to all for working with unity for their development and for removing the causes of oppression and underdevelopment.

The removal or the minimising the causes of oppression can be done only if the underprivileged are given a chance to shape their own destiny. Planning is said to play a vital role in development. This process of planning should be based on the practical needs and aspirations of the developing communities. For this, the underdeveloped should be given a chance to spell out their needs.

The idea of village Sangams is that the developing communities should discuss and plan the various schemes for their improvement and they should themselves implement what is planned and, should be able to assess the impact of what is planned and implemented. Hence, the Sangam is for the involvement of the rural poor in the planning, implementation, monitoring and evaluation of development programmes meant for them. To resist the forces of oppression which hinder the progress and liberation of the oppressed is also the responsibility of the Sangams.

WCADL believes that community participation is the pivotal point of any development programmes. Community involvement or participation should be a process in which and by which the developing communities realise what is required for their development and then seek ways and means to achieve this goal.

The purpose of the Sangams is also the realisation of the philosophy, aims and objectives of WCADL and to make the community realise their roles and responsibilities in the process of their own development. But, it was not always hundred per cent successful for WCADL to make the participants in the various programmes, to realise this objective. Nor was it very easy. There are several reasons for this. One such reason is that basically the Indian society is structured on the caste basis and is divided on this basis. The Scheduled Castes with whom WCADL works exist on the lowest rung of the social ladder. Unfortunately, even the Scheduled Castes are divided into a number of sub-castes and they also practise different types of discrimination or untouchability. Therefore, it is not easy to achieve their unity and it makes it all the more easy for the upper-castes to exploit them. The purpose of WCADL Sangams therefore is to make the Scheduled Castes realise that their strength lies in their unity and also to make them aware that unitedly they will be in a position to oppose the age-old system of oppression to which they have been subjected to, and that they should, to some extent, give way to self-interest and to meet the common interest. WCADL members should also realise that development is not possible in isolation.

WCADL Sangams are also meant to encourage and promote true and sincere local leadership and to minimise exploitative leadership. The members of the Sangams should be in a position to settle their disputes, quarrels, etc., in their own villages by themselves instead of taking them to an upper-caste arbitrator. The Sangam members also should realise that their development depends on the proper use of the economic programmes for the maximum benefit of the maximum number of people in rotation. Such are the basic thoughts which prompted WCADL to take up organising the members of Scheduled Castes and Lambada tribals.

Meaning of Sangams as Conceived by the Members

Kucherkal village, Balanagar Mandal: During a Sangam weekly meeting in the past the staff of WCADL asked the participants as to what they meant by Sangam. One of the participants said that Sangam is a group of people to work towards the achievement of a particular objective. There should not be any difference of opinion among the members towards the achievement of their goal.

Another participant said that Sangam is to settle the disputes and quarrels that might crop up among the members, among themselves instead of taking them to an outside arbitrator.

Still another one said that Sangam means that all the members should jointly work for the increase of wages and to work against the discriminatory and derogatory practices towards SCs, etc.

Srirangapur village: A number of the participants expressed their opinions a follows: (1) Pentamma: "Sangam means, all the poor people get united as if tied up with a rope". (2) Nagamma: "Sangam means, all the poor people should contribute towards the saving fund to be utilised for the extreme needs of all the members instead of depending on moneylenders and land lords". (3) Ramaiah: "Sangam is to discuss the low wages both for bonded and casual labourers and work towards getting better wages". (4) Mallamma: "Sangam is to promote literacy and learning both for men and women". (5) Ellaiah: "Sangam is to safeguard the interests of the SCs against the oppression by the upper-castes". (6) Singaiah: "If there is a strong Sangam and if the members are united and if they have knowledge, the SCs can manage to get bank loans, and also can benefit from the programmes of the Government". (7) Ramulamma: "All the points which all of you said are very correct about the Sangam. But, unity of the members of the Sangam is very important."

In the earlier days, when WCADL staff went about discussing with the SCs the formation of Sangams in their villages in most of the villages the SCs cooperated and were willing to form themselves into Sangams for their social and economic advantage and to withstand the oppression of the upper castes. But it was not so with all the SCs whom the staff contacted. Some of the negative reactions were as follows:

(1) You fellows have come to us to get our votes. That is why you all have come straight to us without even going to the upper-castes or to any educated people.
(2) If you all have come to us to speak to us about any new religion you may please go away from here.
(3) We will think about it and inform you if we are interested in the Sangam and adult education etc., which you all speak about. Until such time do not come to our village.
(4) You people are so much interested in us because you people will have some benefits. If not, you all will not come to us.
(5) If we join your Sangam the upper-castes will push us to death.
(6) In our village we will listen to our landlords and not to any stranger.
(7) In one village, one member from the SCs said, "Our leaders (SC leaders) are afraid that if a Sangam is formed their leadership will be broken and therefore they do not want a Sangam to be formed".

Positive Changes in the Lives of SCs because of Sangams

At Kamsanpalle village, Farooknagar Mandal, during the course of a Sangam meeting, a staff member of WCADL asked the Sangam members if there were any changes in their lives after the formation of Sangam in that village. To this question all of them said that there were a lot of changes in them. When asked to spell out one of the members, Balaiah by name said that they used to go to the upper-castes to settle all their disputes and quarrels. Now they discussed and settled all their problems among themselves.

Another member, Chennaiah, said that they learned several good habits and behaviour because of the Sangam meetings.

At Chenneavelly village, Balanagar Mandal, the members of the Sangam said that their children used to while away their time in the evenings by indulging in several unhealthy practices which used to end up in quarrels among their parents. Now such things did not happen any longer. In the evenings now-a-days they attended the evening classes. In the past, adults and elderly people used to spend their time in the toddy shops, etc. They used to do any amount of physical labour free of any wages if any one offered a glass of toddy to them. Now such things did not take place.

At Lingaram village in Balanagar Mandal, the members said that there used to be a lot of quarrels and disputes among themselves. All these were settled by upper-caste leaders in the past. Now, the number of such disputes and quarrels reduced and if at all any, they were amicably settled in the Sangam meetings.

At Chinthagudem village, Farooknagar Mandal, the members said that they had changed a lot in their way of dressing, talking, etc. Untouchability and caste discrimination were being reduced gradually.

The Sangam members of Suraram village said that they had managed to receive better wages for agricultural labourers.

The Sangam members in the villages of Kucheerkal, Thirumalapur, Chokkampet, etc., also managed to get better wages through their Sangams.

The Sangam members of Ammapur village settled not only their own disputes and quarrels but also the non-SCs sought the help of the Sangam members to settle their quarrels and disputes. The Sangam in this village charged a nominal fee for such services and the money so collected was utilised for the common good of the Sangam.

Negative Reactions of Members of Upper Castes Towards the Formation of Sangam

At Eklasanpet village an upper-caste said to the staff: "If you come to our village to form Sangams we will burn your jeep". In another village, an upper caste man told the SCs: "These people are

Christians. Their aim is to make all of you Christians. At first they will not reveal their plans. Once after formation of the Sangams, etc., once all of you will be in their grip and they will convert all of you to Christianity".

Still another upper caste man told the SCs in another village: "These people were chased out from such and such a village when they went there to form Sangam. Now they have come to you. Don't listen to them and you also chase them out from your village".

Some of the Positive Reactions of Members of Upper Castes

The Public Relation Officer of Shadnagar Panchayat Samithi, stated, "I have never seen such an enlightened Scheduled Caste community anywhere". A member of an upper caste community said, "Your Sangam is very good". But you should not join the Sangam only for the sake of getting economic benefit but also to improve your social status". "Your Sangam is very good. But the activities of the Sangam should not be limited to SCs and STs alone but to the poor people of all the castes and communities", said the Vice President of Gram Panchayat of Depalli village. "Your Sangam is very good, you should not leave the Sangam" remarked an upper-caste member of Bairganpalle village. In the year 1988 WCADL conducted a survey in 151 villages to assess the opinions about WCADL beneficiaries and non-beneficiaries who mainly are from the upper cast communities and landlords against whom the education programmes of WCADL were aimed at. The outcome of this opinion poll about WCADL was quite positive except in one village where some of the members of the upper caste opined that, it could be better if WCADL desist their legal education programme because of which they face a lot of problems from the agriculture casual and bonded labour.

Some Results and Outcomes of the Work of the Village Sangams

(1) There is a certain sense of security among the SCs who hitherto felt very insecure because of the oppressions by the upper castes.

(2) Some sort of unity has been achieved not only among the SCs of a particular village but also among the SCs of a cluster of villages.
(3) Sangam members learned to represent their causes to the government officials, to the bankers, etc. Hitherto they were not so free to face any officials directly.
(4) They were able almost to dispense with the services of a middle man in such cases.
(5) They no longer needed a third party to settle their quarrels and disputes.
(6) Some of the Sangams are recognised agencies even by the non-SCs who approach them to do justice to them when they are oppressed by their own fellow members.
(7) Women members of SCs are safer as they are not ill-treated by the non-SCs as in the past because there is a powerful Sangam to support them. In some villages the non-SCs are scared of the SC Sangams.
(8) In some villages when the political leaders and government officials come, the Presidents of the Sangams are invited for discussion together with the non-SC leaders. Even the Presidents of Sangams are invited to speak from the dias and to share seats with the officials and non-SC members.
(9) Sangams in villages helped to improve the literacy status of the members.
(10) Sangams helped to improve their economic status by meaningfully participating in the economic programmes of WCADL and also helped strengthen the revolving fund of WCADL.

Education for Social Changes in WCADL

WCADL believes that education is the prerequisite for human development. This is all the more so because it is education which promotes the creative abilities in man and instil in him a positive attitude towards life. The ultimate aim of any kind of education, WCADL feels, is to effect a change in the attitudes and behaviours of the participants in the education programme. WCADL also believes that illiteracy and lack of awareness are the major stumbling blocks for the development of the oppressed. Illiteracy and lack of awareness leads to misery and poverty and therefore it is the firm belief of WCADL to get the oppressed masses out of poverty and misery and to educate them to work for a social change. Any sort of education for social change should also liberate people from the powers and forces of oppressions. Such education should also aim at distribution of the power of decision-making, removal of discrimination of women and the members of Scheduled Castes, etc. This is what is intended by the adult education programme in WCADL.

Adult Education in WCADL

As already mentioned, WCADL works for the socio-economic emancipation of the oppressed sections of society. WCADL does therefore understand very well the role which education and literacy will have to play in this regard. Before launching the adult education programme, WCADL staff made an assessment of the existing educational facilities and their performance and the actual net results of the performance of the educational services available in the area of their operation. A random survey of a few villages showed that there were single or double teacher primary schools in almost all the villages all within a walkable distance. Yet the rate of literacy among SC men, women and children of school-going age was found to be very low. The causes for such low percentage of literacy were found to be as follows:

Illiteracy Breeds' Illiteracy

Owing to their poverty and lack of means of livelihood the adult SCs were illiterate. A majority of them are agricultural labourers, marginal or sub-marginal landholders. Both men and women among them go for outdoor work to maintain the family. This prevents the children from going to school. They are forced to stay at home to take care of their siblings and to take care of home until their parents return from work. At times grown up children are also forced to work to take care of cattle, sheep, etc., of the landlords or even to work as agricultural labourers to supplement the income of their parents to maintain the family, however small their earnings and contributions are. Added to this, the attitude of the elite group in the villages is not very encouraging in the case of SC children going to school, as this would result in the shortage of child labourers to take care of their cattle and other animals. They also fear that there will be shortage of adult labourers which would result in a demand from the labourers for higher wages.

Teachers Absenteeism

Another reason is the absenteeism and lack of interest on the part of the teachers in the rural areas. Those teachers from urban and semi-urban environments, appointed in the remote rural areas very seldom visit these schools. The more unscrupulous among them run the schools by proxies. Even if any teacher opts to go to such schools there are no fixed timings for arrival to the schools, commencement of classes and dispersal. The timings are so arranged as to suit their own convenience with the result if anyone is interested to learn, they are deprived of such an opportunity.

Education Versus Job Opportunity

A third reason is the identification or the end result of education with obtaining of a white-collared job. The members of SC community feel that they are not in a position to educate their children until such time that they are able to obtain white-collared jobs. Even if they succeed in educating one or other of their children there is no guarantee in the present day world that they can obtain a job. By chance if they become school drop-outs they may not be willing to take up any manual labour in which case they become misfits in life, and might even turn out to be anti-social and pose a threat to society.

Motivation Towards Literacy Programme

In view of these causes it has not been very easy to motivate the learners, rather adult illiterates, to come to the literacy centre and learn, a majority of them being from the economically weaker sections. From dawn to dusk they work hard to earn a living. Evening or late evening they come fully exhausted and worn out. They are not in a mood to come to the literacy centre and learn.

Moreover, they do not see any immediate benefits for them in learning the alphabet. Very often the staff members who are in charge of such literacy centres are faced with questions such as: "What are we going to get from learning a few letters of alphabet?" "Are we going to become district collectors or police officers or are we going to be employed is some government offices?" Such questions are reflective of the meaning of education as very often understood by the people, namely the ultimate goal of education is to attain a white-collared job. Still some others question the staff: "If we come to the centre and learn the alphabet do we get some money with which we can overcome some of our day-to-day problems". Here the staff members had to tell them that "Yes, you will get some money". How? asked the learners. The staff had to convince the learners by saying that they would earn more money if they learned to produce better yielding crops in their fields, if they learned to get more wages from their employers, if they learned to get the bank loans, if they learned to benefit from the development programmes of the government, etc.

Some of the adult learners who are so resistant to learn are persuaded to learn to spell and write at least their names. To learn to write their names is something personal to them and therefore they showed some interest to learn. In this connection, it was also explained to them that it is very important to learn to write their names for the purpose of affixing their signatures. If they go only by their thumb impression, instead of signature, there is ample room for forgery and cheating. Then the learners themselves gave several examples of forging signatures. After learning to write their own names, they learned to write the names of the members of their families. Then they were slowly introduced to writing the names of the tools and implements with which they used to work with and also the names of the food-grains and vegetables they used to produce in their fields and those which they used to eat, etc. Thus, the learners were introduced to writing these names as they are in one way or the other personal to them and associated with their day-to-day life.

Further, the adult learners also do not restrict their learning the alphabet only to the time they attend to the literacy centre, but make use of their spare time during the day, whenever it is possible. For example, as most of the learners are agricultural workers, they work in the field but towards the mid-day when they will be resting in the field under a tree they practise writing after the mid-day meal or lunch. They are advised to make use of this time to recollect and practice the letters in the alphabet which they learned at the centre on the previous night. For practising the alphabet during such a time they do not need any writing materials like slates, pencils, etc., instead, they can practice on the mud in the field either using their index finger or a wooden peg for a pencil. Some of the learners did make use of such times to learn the alphabet. The learners were asked to learn at least one character of the alphabet per day. Some of them did learn even more than one letter per day.

In certain cases, the village leaders, presidents of local panchayats, were very cooperative in persuading the adult illiterates to go to the literacy centre and learn. Role plays, charts, 'Burrakatha', 'Oggukatha', several songs, etc., were also used to motivate them to come to the literacy centre and to improve their learning. Above all it was the income generating economic programmes which motivated the learners to come to the literacy centre and learn.

Campaign Against Illiteracy Among Children

Out of experience WCADL had come to the conclusion that the drive against illiteracy among adults alone will not solve the problem of illiteracy in the district of Mahabubnagar. Today's illiterate adults were the illiterate children of yesterday's illiterate parents. Today's illiterate children would be tomorrow's adult illiterates. Today's adult illiterates are those who either due to their poverty could not join school or dropped out after joining school. Hence, the problem of adult illiteracy should be tackled at its source, namely the eradication of illiteracy among children. The policy adopted by WCADL in this regard is to encourage the parents to send their children to school and even after enrolling them in schools parents should see to it that children do not drop out in between. When WCADL staff tried to persuade the parents to send their children to school some of the parents said, "During the day let them (ie, the children) work to earn something for their stomach, during the nights let them learn the alphabet". In spite of the negative attitudes of the parents, the staff of WCADL has succeeded to persuade many parents to send their children to schools. Wherever and whenever it was not possible to send the children to the day schools, special classes were arranged for the children in the evening before the classes for adults began. Such children were initiated to literacy in the adult literacy centres and got admission in higher classes in day schools. For examples, at Mudrarpuram village ten boys and girls were admitted to third and fourth classes after joining the hostels. These are in the age group of 11 to 16 years. Another ten children in the same village in the age group of 5 to 7 were admitted in 4th to 7th class, these instances reveal the impact of WCADL in the area.

As mentioned earlier income generating economic programmes of WCADL were an attraction for adults to come to the literacy centres and learn. Naturally those parents who sent their children to day schools preferred economic programmes from WCADL.

Instructors in the Adult Literacy Programme

Success or failure of the literacy programme depends to a great extent on the commitment of the instructors. It was not very easy to locate such committed instructors. On the whole, it was left to the learners to choose their own instructors assisted of course by the WCADL staff. As most of the literacy centres were located in the premises of Scheduled Castes dwellings, instructors should be those either from the SCs or from the other communities, willing to go to the SC habitations and to conduct the classes. Wherever SC candidates were available their services were made use of as instructors. Their job being part-time and the remuneration being comparatively low, during the day they would be engaged in other occupations. Not able to reach in time to the village to conduct classes, etc., were some of the problems faced by the instructors. In spite of such hurdles there were a band of committed instructors who worked for the literacy programme. During the monthly refresher programme, wherein some of the instructors told that they had to go from house to house to persuade the adult illiterates to come to the centre and learn. Some others said that they would remind the illiterates whenever they see them in places of their work, at the tea stall, at the drinking water wells, etc. Still others said that they would sing the songs and conduct other cultural programmes to attract the adults to the centre of learning. One of the instructors told that the learners came to the centre without the necessary writing materials such as slate and pencils. The same instructor with his own money brought some pencils and told the shopkeeper in the village to sell these things and give back the money to him whenever he sells the same. Thereafter, he instructed the learners to go to that particular shop to buy the pencils. Another instructor who faced the same problem solved it temporarily in an interesting way.

He happened to be a smoker and therefore had with him a match box with plenty of match sticks. He wrote the alphabets on the slates of the learners and distributed match sticks to all of them and asked them to practice the alphabets which he wrote on their slates with the help of the match sticks. At the end of the class, of course, he collected back the match sticks.

Aims of the Adult Literacy Programme in WCADL

(1) Literacy: to impart a minimum degree of literacy to the adults and to encourage literacy and education for children as explained above. (2) Functionality: to improve upon the existing functional knowledge of the adults in aspects such as water and soil conservation, water management by taking up crops which need less water, proper use of fertilisers, pesticides, importance of afforestation, etc. (3) Awareness: Preventive and primitive aspects of health, legal awareness, untouchability, bonded labour, minimum wages for agricultural labourers, role of women in the process of development, etc.

Activities of WCADL at a Glance

Activities of adult literacy awareness generating economic programmes and community organisation were conducted in 18 Mandals of the districts listed below:

(1) Kothur
(2) Kesampet
(3) Kondurg
(4) Balanagar
(5) Farooknagar
(6) Nawabpet
(7) Jadcherla
(8) Boothpur
(9) Mahabubnagar
(10) Thimmajipet
(11) Addakal
(12) Kilaghanapur
(13) Thadur
(14) Koilkonda
(15) Devarakadira
(16) Maddur
(17) Bijanapalle
(18) Nagarkurnool

In Ranga Reddy district: Kalvakole, Pendiala, Thuppara

Total Mandals covered	21
Total villages covered	603
Total centres	1007
Approximate No. learners participated	49,5000

Community organisation and income generating economic programme were conducted in Mahabubnagar district in 122 villages in 13 Mandals (First 13 Mandals in the above list). These programmes were conducted in three villages of the neighbouring Ranga Reddy district also

(1) Families benefited

SC families	2714
ST families	289
BC families	455
OBC families	33

(2) Total No. of families 3451
(3) No. of girls trained in tailoring 369*
(*Out of this two girls were trained as per the instruction of DRDA)
(4) No. of patients treated at the health care centre:
Rajapur = 40,863

Nature, Origin and Growth of WCADL Development Programmes and its Present Status

To begin with, the WCADL started its activities for the first time in three villages of the Kothoor Mandal. Subsequently, its activities were extended to almost all the present Mandals of Mahabubnagar district and also in the neighbouring Ranga Reddy districts.

The nature of programmes initiated may be broadly categorised as follows:

(1) Awareness development programmes
(2) Literacy and social education programmes
(3) Health, population education and environmental programmes
(4) Cultural and social developmental programmes
(5) Economic development programmes
(6) Community unity programmes through organising the unorganised with the concept of 'Sangam' which is the pivot for organising any social work.

Nature of Development Programmes

The types of programmes, their nature and their implications are as briefly discussed below.

The programmes initiated were according to the felt needs of the people which were identified in village Sangam meetings. The programmes may be designed for individuals, groups and community as a whole. Further, the programmes were also designed for short-term and long-term goals. The programmes may also vary from village to village depending on the interest, cooperation and involvement of the people of the village in general and target people and groups in particular. As already mentioned, the target groups of WCADL are mainly SCs, and STs. Besides, it has also included BCs and other castes who are considered to be poor and who have shown keen interest in the organisation, and those who could get along with the SCs.

Programmes were designed in accordance with the background of the villages and clusters and socio-economic political awareness levels of people. As such WCADL worked for the upliftment of weaker communities such as SCs, STs, BCs and women. Opportunities were also given to those who are honest, disciplined and hard working in organising the people and played an active role in implementation of programmes. Such people were also paid some salary for their livelihood if they worked full time for the organisation as organisers and in other ways.

However, it seems, the founders of the organisation Francis and Lucy Francis after their relentless long service of more than 25 years, they are not tired physically, mentally and philosophically, but they are not happy with the attitude of the funding organisations, 'Bread for the World' of Germany, and also with the attitude of the state and central governments and the role of bureaucrats who have been uncourteous to the dedicated and devoted social workers. There has been a lot of red-tapism, favouritism, corruption, indifference and scant respect for the poor and deprived sections which have become a serious hurdle for functioning of this voluntary organisation. In addition to this the role of middle men, political leaders at local and state level, the trained social workers and their attitude, the paid workers who are associated with the organisation and finally, the target people or beneficiaries and their attitude towards collective work and development of the community have become very much disturbing than ever before. It has become very difficult to seek the whole-hearted support and cooperation of the beneficiaries and non-beneficiaries in remote villages.

As such, WCADL which has worked almost in the entire district of Mahabubnagar and the neighbouring Ranga Reddy district through various socio-economic and awareness programmes, developed thousands of families with long-term and short-term benefits, has reduced the programmes and area of operation since last few years.

Now, the ongoing programmes are social education programmes, while involvement in government programmes is reduced. A few programmes, social and economic in nature, such as agricultural development and financial assistance for the responsive and well-motivated needy are organised. The staff of WCADL is also drastically reduced.

Lucy and Francis who dedicated their lives to the cause of uplifting the poor are now satisfied with limited programmes with the residual funds, due to tiresomeness of age and other unfavourable situations, though they are gifted with the wisdom of long grassroots backward village level working experience with deprived sections. But people in general and beneficiaries in particular feel that they need constant guidance and economic support of WCADL. But Lucy and Francis feel that it is difficult to carry out work as they did in the past. Further, the commitment of people particularly that of the people who are trained to work with the masses, also do not match with the spirit and temperament of devoted and dedicated service-minded people like Lucy and Francis.

There are also other valid reasons for Lucy and Francis to come to the above conclusions. First, the present day adult generation do not carry with them the patience and the social concept values of the past generation at the time when the WCADL was initiated. The present day adult generation is obsessed with the impact of television, cinema, factualism and politicisation, division of the members of the villages under the banners of ever increasing political parties. With the result the present-day generation do not have patience to sit, listen and learn from the committed social challengers. Second, the development and the educative programmes initiated by WCADL in the past 27 years are being introduced and carried out by the governments both at the centre and in the states. Hence, if WCADL is also in between, it would be the further duplication of works and unnecessary waste of money.

However, and Francis, though tired will never retire from their works. They will carry on with their works as long as they can move about. But the nature of the work will differ: at present they are seriously working out plans in collaboration with some medical doctors to start a health care centre to render health related services even specialised treatments either free or at affordable cost to them.

Notes

1. Francis, C., "Organisational Structural and Activities of WCADL", *Weaker Community's Action for Development & Liberation: Origin & Expansion*. 1976-1985, p.24.
2. Francis, C., "Development Communication in WCADL", *Weaker Community's Action for Development&Liberation: Origin & Expansion*, 1976-1985, p.28.

3

Research Procedure

This chapter deals with the research procedure in terms of the need for the study, statement of the problem, universe, nature of data, period of study, number of villages under study, types of beneficiaries, sample selection, construction of tools and techniques, methods of data collection, processing and analysis of data. Further, it also deals with the problems of data collection and limitations of the study.

Visualisation and formulation of the problem of this study has a long history. I was introduced to Mr Francis and Mrs. Lucy Francis by a liberal democrat, dynamic, rationalist, progressive humanistic thinker and academic intellectual of high ranking, Prof. Dr. F.D. Vakil, Department of Political Science, Osmania University, almost a decade ago to give a brief academic guidance to Lucy Francis who was pursuing her M.A. Sociology course at Andhra University.

As I have a passion for social work and professional inclination for sociological inquiry into human problems, I wanted to use this opportunity to enlighten myself regarding their personal and professional background and commitment. This in turn inspired me to be friendly with them and the subsequent interactions with them, have given me an opportunity of understanding not only the humble start and the glorious development of WCADL but also the professional prospects and problems of social work and the consequent wisdom of dedicated social workers in the context of change and development, particularly of the tradition bound weaker communities of Indian rural society through voluntary effort.

I must confess here that since my childhood I have a deep desire of working for the people who are helpless and I used to work for them when and wherever an opportunity came in my way. As such, I was also assessing and observing Francis and Lucy Francis not only for the purpose of this study but also to understand their lifestyle, courage and convictions and their difficulties in organising the unorganised for the latter's development with the aid and help of various national and international agencies.

From the beginning of my interactions, since I was showing interest in the cause of the poor and deprived, Francis and Lucy Francis invited me for their various organisational programmes, at times as a friend and other times as a resource person. On one of those occasions I was invited as a guest speaker in connection with International Women's Year. This was the time when the activities of WCADL were at a peak stage. On this occasion, my experience of observing the tradition bound suppressed rural men and women folk freely interacting without any inhibition and speaking on the dais occupied by high dignitaries on matters of national and international importance was really amazing, especially for a person like me who had an understanding of the weaker communities in Indian rural society.

Subsequently, I was also placed as an honorary member on the evaluation team consisting of four members. Two were from Germany, one of them was a representative of the fund gatherers at Koln in Germany and the other represented the funding agency through which aid was given to various programmes of WCADL, i.e., the 'Bread for the World'. It was a purely academic participation which has helped me to understand the complex issues of voluntary effort and its framework and methodology of evaluation.

Two of the four members of the evaluation team were from India. One of them was a professional evaluator chosen by the donor agency and was from Bangalore. The other was supposed to represent the actual voluntary organisation that is, WCADL, which had chosen me as their representative in the evaluation team. It was a non-remunerative, unpaid honorary professional role that gave me an opportunity of studying the people of deprived sections of backward villages of Mahabubnagar district and also the role of NGOs, specifically WCADL which had been working for more than two decades by that time for the upliftment of downtrodden and the weaker communities of the rural society. Further, it gave me an opportunity to understand the problems of the weaker communities, i.e., target groups, the role, structure and functioning of WCADL, and the objectives of sponsors of the programmes or donor agencies which aid and help people through voluntary organisations to improve the conditions and the standard of living of the weaker communities, and their other goals and methodological issues while evaluating the work of voluntary organisations striving for the development of the downtrodden communities and the people of backward rural society. Further, it also provided me with an understanding of the fund gatherers in other countries like Germany and the agencies through which fund is given, i.e., 'Bread for the World', the terms and conditions imposed on voluntary organisations of the under-developed countries and the point of view of fund receiving organisation, like WCADL. My exposure to the programmes, their nature and the types, structure of the organisation and the method of organising the people, the problems and prospects of the people, the effect of the programmes, etc., gave me new insights. Likewise, I was able to understand the development and change which had taken place in the lives of the people. It also gave me an opportunity of understanding the evaluation methods of voluntary work, methodological issues and the point view of the parties concerned and the various agencies and the people as partners in the process of change and development.

At this point of time, due to my academic interest I took a decision on my own, to make an objective study of the voluntary social work by this rural development organisation, i.e., WCADL, led by the dedicated couple for almost more than two decades of long struggle. Further, the problems of the target people in availing themselves of programmes conducted by WCADL in the process of their upliftment, the role of government, bureaucracy, general population, the social workers of the organisation and finally the role of beneficiaries were multifaceted which had to be understood on the basis of an objective scientific procedure. This was so because of the growing importance of the role of NGOs all over the world in mitigating human suffering more than ever before. The role of the governments had been marginalised due to the long experience of failure in achieving the objective goals of development during the past three decades.

This problem which has a very long history in the academic sphere of human development has not been studied adequately. A comprehensive study in this direction would have enabled voluntary organisations, donor agencies, academics, politicians, planners and administrators to be more effective while planning and implementing their programmes for mitigation of human suffering.

Universe

The universe of the study consists of all kinds of beneficiaries of the various programmes designed in the various villages of Mahabubnagar district since the beginning of the WCADL organisation, i.e., since July 3, 1976. Further, it also includes the opinion of donor agencies in the form of their correspondence and appraisal reports, government programmes, the opinion of bureaucrats, public opinion in general and beneficiaries' opinion in particular, since it is a complex multifaceted problem. This study is mostly based on opinion survey. However, for activities and other details of the programmes utilised, organisational data were available in the form of records and reports.

Nature of Study and Types of Data

The nature of study is longitudinal and the data are of quantitative and qualitative, of abstract and concrete and of primary and secondary nature. Secondary data were collected from various sources such as Memorandum of Association of WCADL, its annual reports, evaluation reports, office records, news reports, academic journals, books, articles and census reports, etc. The study is mainly based on objective assessment of beneficiaries on the efforts made by WCADL, its impact on the target communities and people in terms of development and change. As such, detailed interviews were duly conducted to draw all kinds of information such as the socio-economic background of the respondents, the nature and types of programmes implemented and the development and change among weaker community people like women, SCs and STs. About 350 were scheduled for various villages and after scrutiny 304 were used for data analysis.

Methods of Data Collection

Methods of data collection included observation, group discussions, case studies, historical and evolutionary approach and survey method. Structured interview schedules were administered to collect information from the selected respondents, such as socio-economic demographic data, association with the WCADL, causes and consequences of awareness and social, cultural and economic and political development of various sections of the society.

Study Period

The duration of field work was from 20 November, 1999 to 24 September, 2000 and subsequently a number of field visits were made to verify facts and to update the data. This period consisted of field visits to gain acquaintance of the area the general public and their beneficiaries and their problems in particular. Further, these visits helped to understand the voluntary organisation and its strategies, plans and programmes and the role of paid workers in working with the people. The actual data were collected from 16 July, 2000 to 24 September, 2000.

The number of villages visited for the field studies were about 36 and 304 beneficiaries were selected on random basis for the detailed study.

The respondents of the study are beneficiaries who belong to the various social groups such as SCs, STs mainly, BCs and other sections that are poor and marginal in size. In this study adequate importance is given to women to understand their opinion since they played a crucial role in the process of development and change as partners in decision-making. Certain programmes were also exclusively developed and implemented for the upliftment of women. Hence, a considerable number of women beneficiaries were also chosen at random for the detailed study.

The actual study is based on analysis of primary and secondary data collected through formal and informal means, that is, through various reports and records of WCADL and also on the data collected through group discussions, case studies, observations, etc. But the concrete information collected through structured interview schedules is from 304 beneficiaries who belong to 36 villages or hamlets of six Mandals in Mahabubnagar district, Andhra Pradesh.

The respondents chosen at random from all the 36 villages belong to diverse socio-economic background in terms of caste, tribe, sex, age, education, occupation, land ownership, income, etc.

Construction of Tools and Techniques

A checklist of items regarding the village background such as, caste composition, occupational structure, general problems of the area and specific problems of the weaker communities was also used.

Further, a concrete structured interview schedule was prepared and administered among 350 respondents for the collection of qualitative and quantitative data and after scrutiny, 304 schedules were found suitable for analysis.

The schedule consisted of questions regarding the beneficiaries, socio-economic and demographic background, their relation to WCADL in terms of period of association, reasons for association, type of involvement, nature of assistance received, conditions of assistance, problems in implementation of the programmes, assessment of desired change and development, and nature of socio-economic development.

The data have been processed on the computer to generate uni-variate, bi-variate and cross-tabulation tables for the selected questions for the analysis in relation to the objectives and hypotheses specified and finally findings were listed and generalisations were made.

Problems and Limitations of the Study

This study, though well-conceived, had its starting problems due to lack of financial support except for the conveyance and courtesies provided by the voluntary organisation under study during the period of data collection. Just as any serious research study is faced with difficulties in data collection in seeking the cooperation of the respondents we too had problems of data collection and those of processing and programming which posed a constant and serious problem.

With regard to the problems of data collection, finding the respondents at day time was the main problem. It was difficult to reach the remote villages and hamlets of the backward Mahabubnagar district in early mornings. Further, to stay during the night to catch hold of the respondents was also a problem due to the prevalence of alcoholism and the sporadic violence of organised and unorganised groups. Added to this, it was also difficult to find accommodation and basic facilities in the villages which are scattered and far off from one another.

Further, seeking the cooperation of the beneficiaries was also a big problem. The beneficiaries doubted the investigators motive behind seeking information. They also tended to suppress information in relation to their income, loans, habits, cultural practices, etc., as well as their views regarding the role of WCADL and its organisers and functionaries of various levels.

Moreover, they were very inquisitive of the use of the study. Their apprehension could be that this study was conducted by the donor agencies to check the activities of WCADL. It might go against the continuation of the activities, which they did not relish. Further, it was also difficult for them to comprehend the various aspects of the study, viz., the respondents, attitudes and views about WCADL, their goals of life and the problems related in realising them.

4

Socio-economic Profile of Mahabubnagar District and the Beneficiaries of WCADL

This chapter is devoted to the study of the inherited socio-economic and cultural conditions of the people of Mahabubnagar district and the social profile of the beneficiary respondents. This part of the study becomes significant because it provides the basis of understanding development and change, the backdrop of the general, social conditions that prevailed before the voluntary effort, and the changes brought about afterwards. Further, any study normatively or otherwise cannot reach every beneficiary and assess the change that has taken place in the life of each individual beneficiary due to the effort of the voluntary organisation (here WCADL). As such a sample of respondents, i.e., about 304 beneficiaries, has been identified in order to understand their opinion regarding the change and development that has taken place in the lives of weaker communities as a result of the effort of WCADL. In addition, the study has also considered the opinion of the sample of beneficiaries on the professional and personal skill and integrity of the authors of the voluntary organisation, WCADL, in fulfilling their aims and objectives.

Socio-economic Profile of Mahabubnagar District

In this section an effort is made to present the historically inherited socio-economic and cultural conditions of Mahabubnagar district such as geographical location, rainfall, and landholding pattern, economic exploitation, caste and social inequalities, dominant castes and communities, cultural practices, the position of traditional occupations and employment opportunities, poverty and unemployment, indebtedness, money lending, etc.

The above conditions impelled and motivated WCADL to choose to work in Mahabubnagar district of Andhra Pradesh, focusing special attention on the socio-economic development of the Dalits and Lambada tribals as mentioned in the preceding chapters. This district was chosen because it is very much underdeveloped socially, economically and in several other aspects. This is one of the 72 drought-prone districts in the country and one of the five drought-prone districts in the state of Andhra Pradesh. This district is predominantly agricultural. In general, success or failure of agriculture depends mainly on two factors namely, the type of soil and the proportion of rainfall. These two preconditions for the success of agriculture are lacking very much in this district, the normal rainfall in the district being 721 mm which is the lowest in the region and is too inadequate to sustain normal crop growth. Red soil which is of very low quality is predominant in about 80 per cent of the villages. Only in about 20 per cent of the villages in the district, there is black soil of high quality. On the basis of climate, rainfall, and soil and other characteristics, the entire district is classified as a dry farming zone. A major portion of the district is identified as a drought affected areas. Not withstanding the adverse atmosphere in the district, it is felt that the people of the district are sturdy and industrious. Given the necessary assistance and encouragement, they will not lag behind in their efforts to overcome poverty, illiteracy, and ill-health and can make serious efforts to withstand the various kinds of injustice and exploitation to which they are subjected and therefore victimised.

The other socio-economic situation in the district was all the more deplorable. Mahabubnagar district was part of the erstwhile state of Hyderabad ruled by a Muslim ruler (Nizam), while the majority of the people were Hindus. The rural poor, it is said, at that time were the worst victims of exploitation by the Razakars (Nizam's private army), Deshmuks and the landlords. These Deshmuks were the revenue tax collectors serving under the rulers. Owing to the infertility of the soil and the unsteady nature of the monsoons, agriculture was not a profitable occupation in the district. In addition to all these, exorbitant taxes imposed and compulsorily collected on the meagre agricultural produce further aggravated the lack of interest on the part of the farming community to take up agriculture. This was so in spite of the fact that a majority of the people including members of the weaker sections possessed land. Resource crunch to invest in agriculture was another reason for the farmers to lose interest in agriculture. In a situation of uncertain returns due to unsteady monsoons they hesitated to seek credits to invest on agriculture.

When such a situation was prevailing, small and marginal farmers, especially members of Dalit and tribal communities, left their land vacant and opted to work either as casual labourers or as bonded labourers, under one or other big farmer who had the resources to cultivate his land, or they migrated to cities in search of livelihood. Agricultural daily labour being only seasonal, most of these unfortunate people opted to be in bonded labour because in this system there was seeming permanency of employment in spite of unlimited number of working hours and very low remuneration. They preferred to be something, to have something instead of being non-entities having nothing. In the absence of opportunities for employment and in a situation of surplus labour, labour became very cheap. In a situation of unfertile soil and unsteady monsoon and in the absence of any other assured water sources for agriculture, land also became very cheap. Industrialists and upper caste farmers from other parts of the state and the country exploited the situation to the maximum. Industrialists purchased lands at very cheap rates, making use of the cheap labour available and raised wine gardens. Upper caste farmers, mainly from the coastal regions of Andhra Pradesh came and purchased land of black soil, undertook various types of agriculture and established their colonies. At present, the land of wine gardens gave way to several kinds of industries.

Local moneylenders and the rich peasants exploited the situation, to the maximum extent to their advantage. The latter made use of the situation to keep the poor under bondage, by giving them petty loans and extending some other kinds of minor help. They exploited the situation by lending small amounts of money at exorbitant rates of interest. Even after the nationalisation of some of the major banks, the rural poor could not get access to bank credit, except in very isolated cases that too with the help of a middleman. The process, of course, was time consuming and expensive, and therefore many of the poor did not venture to seek a bank loan. Even if any one succeeded in getting loan, the amount received after deducting all the expenditure incurred in getting it, would not be enough for the purpose for which the loan was sought, with the result that the borrower would invest the money on some other unproductive activity and consequently he would not be in position to repay the loan and this would make him ineligible for further bank loan.

Ill-health, illiteracy, etc., were rampant. While affected with one or other ailments people took recourse to some magical practices for treatment. No medical facilities were available. School-going habit among children was very much negligible. Parents preferred to send their children to take care of cattle and sheep of rich farmers instead of sending them to school, because in this practice they found that children, though in a very small way, could supplement the earnings of their families. In this backward district, the development programmes of the government at that time were only in the initial stages. Incidentally, WCADL was the first voluntary organisation in the district to attempt a comprehensive and integrated approach towards human development.

Socio-economic Profile of Beneficiary Respondents

This part of the study deals with the socio-economic profile of the beneficiary respondents such as sex, age, caste, occupation, education, religion, marital status, family size, type of family, income of the family, etc.

As already mentioned, 304 respondents were chosen at random for the study from six Mandals of 36 villages and settlements, scattered in far-off places. They belonged mostly to SC and ST communities. A few of them were also BCs. A considerable percentage of women were also chosen as respondents in view of their active participation in the programmes of WCADL and equal importance given by WCADL to men and women in the development process. The respondents were chosen at random in about 36 villages and settlements, which have been actively associated with the organisation.

Table 4.1

Sex of the Beneficiaries

Sex	*Number*	*Percentage*
Male	231	76
Female	73	24
Total	304	100

The above table depicts the sex of the beneficiaries. Out of 304 total beneficiaries 231 (76%) are males and 73 (24%) are females. It is clear that out of four beneficiaries three members are male and one is female.

Table 4.2

Age Distribution of the Beneficiaries

Age (in years)	*Number*	*Percentage*
20-30	19	6.3
31-40	99	32.6
41-50	102	33.6
51-60	56	18.4
61-70	25	8.2
71 & above	3	1.0
Total	304	100.0

In spite of the emphasis of the organisation to involve women equally in the process of development, only 25 per cent of the beneficiaries are females.

The above table indicates the age distribution of the respondents. Almost one-third of the beneficiaries are in the young age, i.e., 31-40 years age group. Another one-third of them are in the middle age, i.e., 41-50 years. Among the remaining beneficiaries, a substantial number of people about 18.4 per cent and 8.2 per cent are in the age groups of 51-60 and 61-70 years, respectively.

It may be noted that most of the beneficiaries are in young and middle age groups. It may be inferred that young and middle age groups are very active and are of appropriate age to adopt new and innovative methods.

Table 4.3

Social Status of the Beneficiaries

Social status	*Number*	*Percentage*
Scheduled Castes	228	75.0
Scheduled Tribes	54	17.8
Backward Castes	22	7.2
Total	304	100.0

The above table shows the social status, i.e., community background of the beneficiaries. Most of the respondents, i.e., 75 per cent are SCs. A considerable number of beneficiaries, i.e., 54 (17.8%) are STs. A negligible number of people, i.e., 22 (7.2%) are BCs and others.

Thus, it may be noted that most of the beneficiaries are SCs and a significant number of the beneficiaries are STs while a negligible number of beneficiaries belong to BCs and other communities. Further, it may be stated that most of the deprived and socially backward are SCs and the above table also indicates that three out of every four respondents belong to SCs.

Table 4.4 depicts the sub-caste background of the beneficiaries. There are 208 (68.4%) beneficiaries out of 304 who belong to SCs sub-caste, Madiga. A negligible number, i.e., 20 (6.6%) of the total beneficiaries belong to the SCs sub-caste Mala. A considerable number of beneficiaries, i.e., 54 (17.8%) belong to STs (Lambada tribe) while the remaining, i.e., 22 (7.2%) are BCs belonging to various sub-caste groups.

Table 4.4

Sub-caste of the Beneficiaries

Sub-caste	*Number*	*Percentage*
Madiga (SC)	208	68.4
Mala (SC)	20	6.6
Lambada (ST)	54	17.8
Others (BCs)	22	7.2
Total	304	100.0

Therefore, it may be stated that most of the beneficiaries belong to the Madiga SC sub-caste and a considerable number of people belongs to STs sub-caste, Lambada. A negligible number of people are Malas (SC) and other backward castes. Thus, this study included a fair representation of the people who belong to the weaker communities.

Table 4.5

Occupation of the Beneficiaries

Main occupation	*Number*	*Percentage*
Agricultural labour	178	58.6
Manual labour	12	3.9
Agriculture	102	33.6
Attached labour	2	0.7
Bonded labour	1	0.3
Tenant cultivator	1	0.3
Petty Business	1	0.3
Private service	2	0.7
Government service	2	0.7
Self-employment	1	0.3
Others	2	0.7
Total	304	100.0

The above table presents the occupational background of the beneficiaries. A majority of the beneficiaries, i.e., 178 (58.6%) have agricultural labour for their main occupation. Among the remaining, a significant number of beneficiaries, i.e., 102 (33.6%) are engaged in agriculture as their main occupation. About 12 numbers (i.e., 4%) are manual labourers.

On the whole, it may be noted that most of the beneficiaries are working as agricultural labourers and a significant number of beneficiaries are working as agriculturists and very few people are working as manual labourers.

Table 4.6
Subsidiary Occupations of the Beneficiaries

Sub-occupation	*Number*	*Percentage*
Nil	108	35.5
Agricultural labour	2	0.7
Agriculture	167	54.9
Caste occupation	6	0.3
Attached labour	1	0.3
Bonded labour	1	0.3
Yearly servant	2	0.7
Tenant cultivator	1	0.3
Vegetable vender	8	2.6
Petty business	2	0.7
Private service	1	0.3
Government service	1	0.3
Others	4	1.3
Total	304	100.0

The above table depicts the subsidiary occupations of the beneficiaries. A majority of the beneficiaries, i.e., 167 (54.9%) have agriculture as their subsidiary occupation. This means that their main occupation is agricultural labour or manual labour. It is a common feature that in most of rural families and particularly in lower community, there is more fragmentation of landholdings. People who have small pieces of land with or without irrigation water facility, will be cultivating it occasionally, whenever it is feasible in terms of good rains, etc. As such they depend mostly for their livelihood on agriculture or manual labour and also engage themselves in agriculture seasonally.

Interestingly, slightly more than one-third of the respondents, i.e., 108 (35.5%) are not engaged in any subsidiary occupation. This indicates that either they do not have any piece of land of their own or any other vocation connected to their skill. It may be mentioned here that, in the process of present development, their traditional occupations have been losing their importance as they are being replaced by machine-made mass production.

In this connection, it may be seen that more than half of the beneficiaries have agriculture for their subsidiary occupation, whereas slightly more than one-third of the beneficiaries have no subsidiary occupation whatsoever.

Table 4.7

Educational Background of the Beneficiaries

Education	*Number*	*Percentage*
Illiterate	156	51.3
Literate	114	37.5
Primary	20	6.6
Middle	7	2.3
Secondary	6	2.0
Others	1	0.3
Total	304	100.0

The above table reveals the educational background of the beneficiaries. As can be expected slightly more than half of the respondents are illiterates. There are about 114 (37.5%) who are literate. Among the remaining beneficiaries 20 (6.6%) studied up to the primary school level, 7 (2.3%) studied up to middle school level, 6 (2%) have studied in secondary school while only one member studied up to others category, i.e., a technical course after school education.

Thus, it may be stated that slightly more than half of the beneficiaries are illiterate which is the normal feature of the Indian rural scenario.

Table 4.8

Religious Background of the Beneficiaries

Religion	*Number*	*Percentage*
Hindu	293	96.4
Muslim	2	0.7
Christian	9	3.0
Total	304	100.0

The above table depicts the religious background of the beneficiaries. Out of 304 respondents, almost all, i.e., 293 (96.4%) beneficiaries belong to Hindu religion. Among the remaining people only two and nine beneficiaries belong to Muslim and Christian religions respectively.

Thus, it is clear that most of the beneficiaries are Hindus and this reflects the common feature of Indian society.

Table 4.9

Martial Status of the Beneficiaries

Marital status	*Number*	*Percentage*
Married	294	96.7
Unmarried	5	1.6
Divorced	2	0.7
Separated	3	1.0
Total	304	100.0

The above table shows that almost all the beneficiaries, i.e., 294 (96.7%) are married and only 5 (1.6%) are unmarried, while the divorcees are 2 (0.7%) and the separated are 3 (1.0%).

On the whole, it may be concluded that almost all the beneficiaries are married.

Table 4.10
Family Size of the Beneficiaries

Family size	*Number*	*Percentage*
2-3	41	13.5
4-5	107	35.2
6-7	104	34.2
8-9	36	11.8
10 and above	16	5.3
Total	304	100.0

The above table depicts the family size of the beneficiaries. It may be noted that 107 families (35.2%) have 4-5 members each in their families followed by 104 (34.2%) of the families with 6-7 members each. About 41 (13.5%) of the beneficiary families have 2-3 members each. Further, about 36 (11.8%) of the beneficiary families have 8-9 members each and 16 (5.3%) families have 10 and more members each.

Thus, it may be stated that most of the families consist of more than five members each as their family size. This is also a reason for their backwardness, ignorance and poverty. This is a common feature of communities of lower strata in rural India.

Table 4.11
Type of Families of the Beneficiaries

Type of family	*Number*	*Percentage*
Nuclear	225	74.0
Joint	79	26.0
Total	304	100.0

The above table shows the family type of the beneficiaries. As can be noted from the table, 225 (74%) out of 304 beneficiaries live in nuclear families while 79 (26.0%) live in joint families.

On the whole, it may be noted that almost three-fourths of the beneficiaries live in nuclear families and one-fourth of them are in joint families. Thus, it can be seen that most of the beneficiaries belong to nuclear families.

Table 4.12

Land (Dry + Wet) Ownership of the Beneficiaries

Size of land ownership	*Number*	*Percentage*
Landless agricultural labourers	16	5.3
Marginal farmers (0 - 2.5 acres)	160	52.6
Small farmers (2.5 - 5.0 acres)	105	34.5
Medium farmers (5.0 - 10.0) acres)	21	6.9
Large farmers (10 acres and above)	2	0.7
Total	304	100.0

The above table reveals the distribution of dry and wet land ownership of the beneficiaries. It is interesting to note that most of the beneficiaries own a piece of each which is mostly dry and rural possess a few guntas of wet land. An insignificant number of people, i.e., 16 (5.3%) who have no land depend on agricultural labour.

Among the total beneficiary respondents slightly more than half of the respondents, i.e., 160 (52.6%) are marginal farmers who have land below 2.5 acres each and slightly more than one-third, i.e., 105 (34.5%) beneficiaries are small farmers each owning 2.5 to 5.00 acres of land.

Among the remaining an insignificant number of the beneficiaries, i.e., 21 (6.9%) are medium farmers each having 5-10 acres of land while large farmers who have above 10 acres each are only 2 (7%).

Therefore, it may be stated that most of the respondents possess some piece of land, whatever worth it may be, but the least number of beneficiaries own medium and large size land. But a majority of the beneficiaries are marginal farmers. A significant number of the beneficiaries are small farmers. This fact indicates the importance of the direction in which the voluntary effort has to be made for the development of these people who are bonded to the earth.

Table 4.13
Wet Land Ownership of the Beneficiaries

Size	*Number*	*Percentage*
No wet land	294	96.7
Marginal farmers (0 - 2.5 acres)	8	2.6
Small farmers (2.5 - 5.0 acres)	2	0.7
Total	304	100.0

The above table depicts the wet land ownership of the beneficiaries. It is very interesting to note that most of the beneficiaries, i.e., 294 (96.7%) out of 304 do not own any wet land. Among the remaining, only 8 (2.6%) possess below 2.5 acres of wet land whereas just two respondents (0.7%) possess below 5 acres of wet land.

Hence, it may be stated that most of the weaker sections, i.e., SC and STs do not posses any wet land which certainly determines their economic and social power in the village. In Indian villages, generally the source of income is wet land and therefore whoever owns more wet land enjoys more socio-economic and political power.

Table 4.14
Beneficiaries Family Income per Month

Income (per month)	*Number*	*Percentage*
Rs 500	7	2.3
Rs 501 - 1000	47	15.5
Rs 1001 - 1500	62	20.4
Rs 1501 - 2000	61	20.1
Rs 2001 - 2500	39	12.8
Rs 2501 - 3000	27	8.9
Rs 3001 - 3500	10	3.3
Rs 3501 - 4000	12	3.9
Rs 4001 - 4500	16	5.3
Rs 4501 - 5000	14	4.6
Rs 5001 & above	9	3.0
Total	304	100.0

The above table indicates the monthly family income of the beneficiaries. Surprisingly, almost an equal number of beneficiaries, i.e., 62 (20.4%) and 61 (20.1%) belong to income range of Rs 1001-1500 and 1501-2000 per month respectively. About 47 (15.5%) of the beneficiaries, fall in the income group of Rs 501-1000. Further 39 (12.8%) beneficiaries are in the income group of Rs 2001-2500.

Thus, it may be noted that most of the respondents are in the income group of Rs 501-2500 while a negligible number of people are in all the income groups from Rs 2501-5001 and above.

In spite of 25 years of WCADL work, the income levels of the people have not risen substantially and this may be due to various other reasons such as, the increase of the members in the family and their growing needs, high cost of living, increase in the cost of agriculture investment such as chemical fertilisers and other items. For example a pair of plough animals in 1976 cost about Rs 2000. The present cost of the same is about Rs 15,000. In addition to this the growing ambitions and aspirations of the poor and the middle class to imitate the elite groups could be another reason.

5

Beneficiaries' Relationship with WCADL

The success of any voluntary organisation working for the weaker sections depends on establishing a good relation with the target people in the chosen area. It is also a fact that the poor are always sceptical. They live in an environment which would be constrained for free interaction with people other than those of their own caste and class. Normally, they would not think that they are equal to others. They prefer to live in their own world rather than to mix with others considered to be unequal and misbehaving. Further, they consider other's identity to be superior to their own.

This kind of attitude of the weaker sections is misconstrued, sometimes as an attitude of 'self-respect' and sometimes as 'culture of poverty'. In fact it is a culture of respecting others as advanced men and achievers due to their past background and the so-called god-given gifts. They believe in the theory of 'karma' to be responsible for their suffering or helpless condition. Further, it is a sociological fact that people in human history lived in groups similar to them and prefer to meet and interact more with who live in conditions similar to theirs. Hence, the consciousness levels of people are also a natural reflection of their conditions. In this context it is worth recalling the theory of knowledge proposed by Karl Marx. He stated that "consciousness of the people is conditioned by their conditions". There is also a theory counter to the above, viz., the mind also has the capacity to think beyond conditions. It means that the human mind can think freely beyond conditions. In human history men who shaped the world or those who conquered the world were men of imagination and were beyond their conditions. If we observe the history of those, who made history in the world, belongs to poorer sections or from poor families. Hence, conditions cannot be a hindrance to self or community development. However it is a reality in the Indian rural society, people belonging to weaker sections are mostly from lower castes. They have been either deliberately or otherwise kept out of the mainstream for development since ages.

Conditions have been so created and continuously practiced that the poor and lower caste people, even after 56 years of India's independence, believe that they are not equal to others and other castes. This belief or attitude of theirs towards themselves and others has become a major hurdle for their development. Consequently, even today, there is an alarming social situation in Indian rural society that a number of inhuman atrocities are perpetrated freely and openly on those who work for change and freedom. Due to the power of money and muscle and political power nothing will happen to those who violate the law and create invisible fetters in the society. It is an ironical situation in India that majority voters belong to the lower castes and classes whereas leaders, gundas (anti-social element) in all fields are invariably from upper castes.

Hence, development and human rights are denied to righteous persons and the poor in a largest democratic country in the world. Against the above scenario this part of the study makes an attempt to understand establishment of good relations with the target population by the development organisation.

This chapter discusses the beneficiaries interaction, in terms of its origin, and type involvement, their socio-economic conditions before and after the interaction, programmes implemented, involvement in decision-making of the organisation with regard to programmes, type of social change, conditions, availing of programmes, problems of the beneficiaries, if any, in availing themselves of the programme, etc.

This discussion is crucial for the study of understanding the organisation's work for the upliftment of weaker section of society because it indicates the actual style and functioning of WCADL and its nature of interaction and approach towards the target people. It also depicts the constraints, if any, in the process of beneficiaries availing themselves of the programmes designed for their objective development. The data pertaining to this discussion is presented in a tabular form, analysed and interpreted below.

Table 5.1

Respondents' Relation with WCADL

	Number	*Percentage*
As members	296	97.4
As non-members	8	2.6
Total	304	100.0

The above table shows the beneficiaries' relation with WCADL, namely, whether they are members of the village Sangams organised by WCADL or they are working in the organisation as organisers of skilled or unskilled workers.

The data show that out of 304 respondents almost all, i.e., 296 (97.4%) are members of the village Sangams organised by the WCADL. An insignificant number, i.e., 8 (2.6%) are non-members of the village Sangams. It may be stated that even those eight respondents may not be formal members of the organisation but might be related to the regular member of the organisation.

Table 5.2

Respondents Type of Membership

	Number	*Percentage*
Primary members	291	95.7
Executive member	1	0.3
Employees	3	1.0
Members and employees	1	0.3
Others	8	2.6
Total	304	100.0

The above table depicts the type of membership of the respondents in WCADL. Out of 304 respondent beneficiaries almost all, i.e., 291 (95.7%) are primary members of village Sangams and only one is an executive member and another one is a member employee. Among the remaining, 3 (1.0%) are employees and 8 (2.6%) are neither employees nor member of the organisation.

Table 5.3

Designation of the Employee Respondents

	Member	*Percentage*
Driver	01	0.3
Coordinator	03	1.0
Others (NA)	300	98.7
Total	304	100.0

The above table depicts the number of respondents who are working with WCADL. The data shows that out of 304 respondents, only four people are paid workers in the organisation. Among the four working respondents, three are working as coordinators and one is working as driver.

It may be stated that in comparison with the past when WCADL was working in a larger area for various socio-economic programmes, a large number of people were working. In view of the declining financial aid from various agencies, national and international, like government and 'Bread for the World' the present strength of the staff has drastically declined.

Table 5.4

Salary Structure of Employee Respondents

Salary (per month)	*Number*	*Percentage*
Rs 1201-1300 (Coordinators)	3	1.0
Rs 1401-1500 (Drivers)	1	-
NA	300	99.0
Total	304	100.0

The above table reveals the salary structure of the employee respondents who are working in the organisation. A point to be noted here is that the management used to claim that those who had no education and skill but were sincere among the Sangam members were chosen for full-time work as per their talent. Subsequently, required personal guidance and training was given to them to perform their given duties. A limited monthly salary was paid to them, which would enable them to meet some of their basic needs.

Though the above table shows the initial salary structure for the employees but the data show that the organisers are paying Rs 1900 per month for coordinators and the drivers are paid Rs 2000 per month, which was normally corresponded with daily wage rates of the local area. In this regard, the management felt that it was reasonable salary for the employees if not higher as it is not normally possible to pay higher salaries in a voluntary organisation.

However, the workers had a feeling that they were not paid satisfactorily according to the work done. But they had work satisfaction. As such, it maybe seen that both the views are reasonable. However, as per the general and local conditions, the workers deserved more than what they were paid.

Table 5.5

Reasons for Association with WCADL

	Number	*Percentage*
AID and help	30	9.9
All joined and I joined	107	35.2
Organised to join	54	17.8
For better living	32	10.5
To improve awareness	30	9.9
To get interest-free loans	20	6.6
For survival	6	2.0
Don't know	17	5.6
Not applicable (general public)/ Non-members	8	2.6
Total	304	100.0

In any development organisation, identification and involvement of genuine individuals and families in development programmes is a difficult task. Normally, those who deserve to be helped are unaware of the organisation and its programme. Even if they are aware, it is difficult for them to cross the social and community barriers of the village to reach the development organisation. In the case of lower castes and women, this is much more difficult. Hence trained social workers, were to seek the help of community leaders, village elders to identify the potential beneficiary to be involved in the organisation. It is also an established fact that the Indian village people mostly depend on their community or caste leaders rather than on their own or officials whenever there is a context of dealing or involving with outsiders. Hence, it was felt necessary to understand the reasons that prompted the beneficiaries to establish relations with WCADL.

Table 5.5 depicts the beneficiary respondents reasons to associate with the organisation. Out of 304 beneficiary respondents, about one-third of them, i.e., 107 (35.2%) stated that they had associated with the WCADL because all the members of the community were joining, and they too joined. A substantial number of people, i.e., 54 (17.8%) stated that they were organised to join to be social workers of the organisation with the help of the opinion leader of their caste and community. Further, about 32 (10.5%) stated that they joined the WCADL for a better living.

Among the remaining, 30 (9.9%) in each category, expressed that they joined WCADL to seek aid and help to improve their awareness respectively.

An insignificant number of beneficiaries, i.e., 20 (6.6%) and 6 (2.0%) stated the reasons for their joining WCADL for interest-free loans and their survival respectively.

Thus, it may be stated that every one person out of three persons joined the organisation without any idea but they joined the organisation since others were joining. A significant number of beneficiaries stated that they joined for aid and help, were organised to join WCADL to receive aid and help for better living and to improve their awareness.

From the above analysis it may be noted that the people who belonged to weaker communities did not have any clear idea as to why they joined the organisation, but they would go along with their community members or follow the other members of the community or their leaders.

Table 5.6

Respondents' Family Members' Association with WCADL

	Number	*Percentage*
Alone	101	33.2
Other member	179	58.9
Other members	16	5.2
NA	8	2.7
Total	304	100.0

The above table provides data regarding the association of respondents' family members with the organisation. It can be noted that out of 304 respondents a majority 179 (58.9%) stated that their other members of family were also associated with the organisation. That is a beneficiary's spouse son or brother might also associate with the organisation. Among the remaining 101 (33.2%) respondents stated that they alone joined the organisation while 16 (5.2%) respondents stated that members of their family also joined organisation and therefore they too followed suit.

On the basis of the above data it may be stated that a majority of the respondents other members of the family were also associated with organisation. It means that the organisation encouraged the other members of the family to join the organisation to change the whole family. This approach of involving or encouraging other family members in the development organisation is essential because unless all the family members have an understanding of their needs aspirations and means to fulfil them it will not be possible to seek their cooperation for the development programmes.

Table 5.6.1

Respondents' Fathers' Association with WCADL

	Number	*Percentage*
Yes	35	11.5
No	173	56.9
NA	96	31.6
Total	304	100.00

The above table depicts the proportion of association of the respondent's fathers with the WCADL. It can be noted that out of 304 respondents, there were 35 (11.5%) fathers who are associated with the organisation. A majority of the beneficiaries, 173 (56.9%) stated that their fathers were not associated, probably for various reasons such as old age, functional inability etc. A significant number of respondents, i.e., 96 (31.6%) stated that this question was not applicable to them due to various reasons like the demise of their father.

Table 5.6.2

Respondents' Wives' Association with WCADL

	Number	*Percentage*
Yes	120	39.5
No	80	28.5
NA	96	31.6
Total	304	100.00

The above table depicts the position of the beneficiary respondents' wives' association with WCADL. Out of 304 respondents about 120 (39.5%) respondents' wives were also associated with the organisation. Among the remaining, 96 (31.6%) stated that this question was not applicable to them and 88 (28.5%) stated that wives were not associated so. It is interesting to note that nearly 40 per cent of respondents allowed their wives to be associated with the organisation, which is pertinent as it shows the position of involvement of women in the development process. It can therefore be stated that this organisation succeeded in involving the poor women in their development efforts.

Table 5.6.3

Respondents' Brothers' Association with WCADL

	Number	*Percentage*
Yes	26	8.6
No	182	59.9
NA	96	31.6
Total	304	100.00

The above table depicts the respondents' brothers' association with the organisation. Out of 304 respondents, a significant number of respondents' brothers, i.e., 26(8.6%) were associated with the organisations. The association of brothers could be for various non-explicable reasons.

Table 5.6.4

Respondents' Sons' Association with WCADL

	Number	*Percentage*
Yes	25	8.2
No	183	60.2
NA	96	31.6
Total	304	100.0

The above table shows the respondents' sons' association with the organisation. Out of 304 respondents, only 25 (8.2%) of their sons were associated with the organisation and this is understandable because a majority of their sons are minors and children

Table 5.7

Proportion of Benefits Received

	Number	*Percentage*
Yes	276	90.8
No	20	6.6
NA	8	2.6
Total	304	100.0

The above table depicts the position of respondents receiving the benefits from the organisation. Out of 304 respondents, most of them, i.e., 276 (90.8%) stated that they were benefited by the organisation. Among the remaining respondents, 20 (6.6%) stated that they were not so benefited. Only 8 (2.6%) respondents stated that it was not applicable to them. It means that they did not belong to the organisation or were members of general public.

Table 5.7.1

Respondents' Opinion on Benefit of Financial Aid

	Number	*Percentage*
Yes	276	90.8
No	20	6.6
NA	8	2.6
Total	304	100.0

The above table shows the number of respondents who received the benefit of financial aid. The data show that almost all 276 (90.8%) of the respondents stated that they had received financial aid.

Table 5.7.2

Respondents' Opinion on Benefit of Education

	Number	*Percentage*
Yes	243	79.9
No	53	17.5
NA	8	2.6
Total	304	100.0

From the above table it can be noted how many of the respondents received the benefit of education from the efforts of WCADL. Out of 304 respondents, 243 (79.9%) stated that they had received the benefit of literacy education through night and informal schools.

Table 5.7.3

Respondents' Opinion on Benefit of Awareness Programmes

	Number	*Percentage*
Yes	267	87.8
No	29	9.6
NA	8	2.6
Total	304	100.0

The above table provides information on the benefit of awareness development programmes received by the respondents. As can be seen 267 (87.8%) out of 304 respondents, i.e., most of them were benefited by awareness development programmes which constitute the essential component of any voluntary organisation. It is obvious that people who are not aware of their rights are normally backward. Such people follow the traditional superstitious and unhealthy social practices in solving the problems of their day-to-day life and health problems. As a result of the efforts of the organisation, the people in the sample are normally adopting right and approved ways of living, such as marriage at right time, treating women as equal partners of life and using scientific medicine for ill-health instead of depending upon folk medicine, spiritual practices and magic to ward off evil spirits, ghosts, etc.

Table 5.7.4

Respondents' Opinion on Benefit of Guidance

	Number	*Percentage*
Yes	254	83.6
No	42	13.8
NA	8	2.6
Total	304	100.0

The above table shows the impact of guidance from WCADL for the benefit of the respondents. Out of 304 respondents, 254

(83.6%) stated that they were benefited by the guidance given by the organisation in relation to various problems. This is a very important aspect of any voluntary effort. Normally, most of the backward people need guidance in solving various problems such as socio-economic cultural and educational nature. Hence, the success of any voluntary organisation depends on its ability in guiding and helping the people in such a way that they can help themselves and to make use of their skills and resources rather than simply depending on aid and help in terms of finance and material goods such as fertilisers, pesticide etc.

Table 5.8

Respondents' Opinion on Terms and Conditions of Financial Aid

	Number	*Percentage*
No condition	161	53.0
Repayable	92	30.3
1% interest	13	4.3
Others	10	3.2
NA	28	9.2
Total	304	100.0

The above table reveals the opinion of the respondents on the conditions and terms for seeking economic benefits from the organisation. Out of 304 respondents, a majority, i.e., 161 (53%) stated that there were no conditions for seeking financial aid. Field observation and the records showed that the financial aid was given to the people in their difficult times through village Sangams. It means Sangam membership is a must. Further, in fixed time, a few informal conditions were also imposed, for example the loan was repayable soon after the people obtained the crop yield and defaulters would not be helped in future unless the money was paid back. If anyone became a defaulter, it would be the responsibility of the village Sangam to recover the money. Normally, if one or a few fail to abide by the conditions, all the other members would not be given any financial aid until the entire dues were cleared by the village Sangam. Likewise, the collection of loan money from the members was the responsibility of the village Sangam. It is a collective responsibility of the Sangam members. Even after this, if some failed to repay, it would be noticed that those people were expelled from the Sangam.

Among the remaining respondents, one-third, i.e., 92 (30.3%) stated that the loan taken was repayable while 13 (4.3%), said at 1 per cent interest and 10 (3.2%) cited other conditions whereas for 28 (9.2%) it was not applicable. Thus, it may be concluded that a majority of the beneficiary respondents stated that there were no serious conditions for getting financial aid from revolving fund for agricultural and other needs, except obligatory repayment after the crop season.

Table 5.9

Respondents' Opinion on Frequency of Financial Benefit

	Number	*Percentage*
Once	34	11.2
Twice	39	12.8
Thrice	25	8.2
Four times	24	7.9
Many times	149	49.0
Other way	25	8.3
NA	8	2.6
Total	304	100.0

The above table reveals the frequency of financial and other types of benefits received by the respondents from the organisation. Out of 304 respondents almost half of the members, i.e., 149 (49%) stated that they got various benefits many times from the organisation. Only those who received once are 34 (11.2%) and those received twice are 39 (12.8%). An insignificant number of people reported to have received three and four times. But almost half of the beneficiaries received financial and other type of assistance many times.

Table 5.10

Respondents' Opinion on Change in Lifestyle

	Number	*Percentage*
Yes	286	94.1
No	10	3.3
NA	8	2.6
Total	304	100.0

The above table provides data on the opinion of the respondents with regard to the change that had taken place in their lifestyles due to the effort of the organisation. Out of 304 respondents, almost all, i.e., 286 (94.1%) stated that there was a lot of change in their lifestyles. Among the remaining respondents, 10 (3.3%) and 8 (2.6%) stated that there was no change and "do not know", respectively.

However it may be noted that most of the respondents stated that there was a substantial change in their lifestyle due to the effort of the organisation. This fact also coincides with the observations made in the filed study.

Table 5.11

Kinds of Change in Lifestyles of Respondents

	Number	*Percentage*
Change in agriculture	43	15.0
Change in standard of living	83	29.0
Change in socio-economic status	159	55.5
Others	1	0.5
Total	286	100.0

The above table shows the kind of change that had taken place in the lifestyles of the respondents who stated clearly that there was change in their lifestyles. A majority of the respondents, i.e., 159 (55.5%) out of 286 who claimed that there was a change stated that there was a change in their socio-economic status. Among the remaining, 83 (29.0%) and 43 (15.0%) stated respectively that there was change in their standard of living and agricultural practices, such as dairy development. Therefore, it may be noted that the majority of the respondents agreed that there was change in lifestyles and socio-economic status due to the effort of the organisation.

Table 5.12

Change in the Family Life of Respondents

	Number	*Percentage*
Yes	286	94.1
No	10	3.3
NA	8	2.6
Total	304	100.0

The above table reveals the opinion of the respondents in relation to change in their family life. Out of 304 respondents, 286 (94.1%), i.e., most of the respondents opined that there was a change in their family life due to the organisation's effort. Among the remaining beneficiaries, 10(3.3%) and 8 (2.6%) stated that there is no change and "do not know", respectively.

Thus, it may be noted that most of the respondents agreed that there was change in their family life. The term 'family life' is an abstract concept. But, in this context, it means an improvement in interpersonal relations such as better understanding, mutual respect for each other, and striving for common goals, etc.

Table 5.12.1

Type of Change in Respondents' Life

	Number	*Percentage*
Personal development	26	8.5
Improved economic conditions	166	54.6
Improved social conditions	32	10.5
Better health and education	60	19.7
NA	20	6.7
Total	304	100.0

The above table provides the details of change that had taken place in the life of the respondents. A majority of the beneficiaries, i.e., 166 (54.6%) stated that there was an improvement in their economic condition. A significant number of beneficiaries, i.e., 60 (19.7%) stated that their condition of health and education improved. Among the remaining, 32 (10.5%) stated that there was an improvement in their social condition while 26 (8.5%) of the respondents reported improvement in their personal development. Therefore, it may be concluded that more than half of the respondent benefited economically.

Table 5.12.2

Other Changes in Respondents' Life

	Number	*Percentage*
Economic change	26	9.1
Social change	140	49.3
Overall change	20	7.0
Improved unity	43	15.1
OK	55	19.5
Total	284	100.0

The above table shows the type of other changes that had taken place in the life of those who stated that there was change. It can be seen that 140 (49.3%) out of 284, almost half of the respondents stated that there was a change in the social life of their families. This is a very significant fact. The aim of the organisation was also to develop the people socially. Among the remaining, 43 (15.1%), 26 (9.1%) and 20 (7.0%) stated respectively that there was a change in terms of better unity in economic life and overall change. Further, 55 (19.5%) of them stated that the conditions were normal. Therefore, it may be stated that half of the respondents opined that there was a change in their social life. The observation in the field also supports the above findings. There was lot of mobility among the people and inter-personal relations like caste restricted relations in the past.

Table 5.13

Respondents' Conditions before Interaction with WCADL

	Number	*Percentage*
Good	5	1.6
Normal	271	8.9
Bad	264	86.8
OK	8	2.6
Total	304	100.0

The above table provides data pertaining to the living conditions of the respondents before their association with WCADL. It is very important to consider and understand the change that had occurred in the lives of the people due to the effort of the organisation. The data shows that out of 304 respondents, a large majority, i.e., 264 (86.6%) revealed that their living conditions were bad before their association with the voluntary organisation.

Among the remaining respondents, 27 (8.9%), 5 (1.6%) and 8 (2.6%) respectively reported that their living conditions were normal, good and OK.

From the above analysis it may be concluded that most of the respondents agreed that their conditions were bad before their association with WCADL. Thus, it is a significant point to note that the conditions of the respondents improved due to the effort made by the voluntary organisation.

Table 5.14

Present Condition of the Respondents

	Number	*Percentage*
Good	226	74.3
Normal	54	17.8
Bad	1	0.3
No change	15	4.9
OK	8	2.6
Total	304	100.0

The above table provides the opinions of the respondents in regard to their present living conditions. The data shows that out of 304 respondent, most of them, i.e., 226(74.3%) stated that their present living conditions are good.

Among the remaining, 54 (17.8%), 15 (4.9%), 8 (2.6%) and 1 (0.3%) stated respectively that their present living conditions were normal, without change, OK and bad.

Thus, it may be said that most of the respondents present that living conditions improved in comparison with those in the past and this was due to the effort of the voluntary organisation.

Table 5.15

Respondents' Awareness of the Programmes of WCADL

	Number	*Percentage*
Educational programmes	9	3.0
Dairy development programmes	52	17.1
Financial assistance programmes	9	3.0
Agricultural needs (assistance)	214	70.4
Other programmes	9	3.0
Don't know	11	3.6
Total	304	100.0

The above table gives the details on the awareness of the respondents in regard to the major programmes implemented by WCADL. Out of 304 respondents, 214 (70.4%) stated that agricultural development programmes were implemented. Among the remaining respondents, a significant number, i.e, 52 (17.1%) reported that dairy development programmes were implemented. An insignificant number of people, i.e., 9 (3%) each identified respectively educational and financial assistance programmes to have been implemented.

However, it may be concluded that most of the respondents mentioned that the voluntary organisations implemented the programmes of agricultural developments such as community irrigation wells and irrigation pumps, daily development programme, and fertilizers and pesticides which were implemented by the voluntary organisation for the development of rural poor.

Table 5.16
Social Status of Respondents

	Number	Percentage
All people benefited	11	3.6
Scheduled Castes benefited	246	80.9
Scheduled Tribes benefited	37	12.2
Scheduled Castes and Scheduled Tribes benefited	2	0.7
Others benefited	8	2.6
Total	304	100.0

The above table shows the social status of the respondents. Out of 304 respondents, 246 (80.9%) stated that the Scheduled Castes (SCs) people were the highest proportion to have been benefited by WCADL.

Among the remaining, the next highest, i.e., 37 (12.2%) were Scheduled Tribes (STs) who were benefited. Only 11 (3.6%) stated that all categories of people were benefited in the village.

Thus, it may be noted that most of the beneficiaries of the programmes of the organisation were from the SCs and STs.

Table 5.17
Type of Benefits Received by Respondents

	Number	Percentage
Economical	168	55.3
Social	108	35.5
Agriculture	9	3.0
Others	19	6.3
Total	304	100.00

The above table provides data pertaining to the type of benefits received by the respondents who were mostly SCs and STs. Out of 304 respondents, a majority, i.e., (55.3%) stated that they were benefited economically. Among the remaining, 108 (35.5%) stated that they were benefited socially, and 9 (3%) benefited in agriculture needs. Hence, it may conclude that a majority were benefited economically and socially, which was the main goal of the development organisation.

Table 5.18

Respondents' Opinion on Programmes

Beneficial to people	*Number*	*Percentage*
Yes	294	96.7
Can't say	2	0.7
NA	8	2.6
Total	304	100.0

The above table reveals the opinion of the respondents whether the programmes implemented were really beneficial to the people. Out of 304 respondents, almost all of them, i.e., 294 (96.7%) stated that the programmes implemented really benefited the people.

Table 5.19

Respondents' Opinion on Programme Decision-Making

Programmes were decided by the people	*Number*	*Percentage*
Yes	299	98.4
No	5	1.5
Total	304	100.0

The above table depicts the opinion of the respondents in regard to their involvement in the decision-making process of the programmes. Out of 304 respondents almost all, i.e., 299 (98.4%) stated that the people, i.e., members of the village Sangams were involved in democratic discussions to arrive at the consensus on various issues of the implementation of programmes.

6

Programmes of Economic Development: Problems and Prospects of Self-Reliance of the Weaker Communities

This part of the study mainly deals with the economic development of the target people, the number of programmes initiated by WCADL since its inception, type of economic programme implemented, the number of beneficiaries of the programme, sources and the quantum of money spent, approach and the strategy adopted for implementation of the programme, and also elicits the experience of the beneficiaries. Further, this part also explains the opinion of the beneficiary respondents in relation to the various issues of developmental programme of the target people's involvement.

As mentioned by the organisers in their year-wise reports, "excluding a little bit of financial assistance for the adult education programme during the years 1979 and 1983 from the Government of India, all the financial contributions for the effort of WCADL came from Germany". WCADL used to receive financial contribution, from three agencies through the main funding organisation, 'Bread for the World' in Germany, which is one of the development agencies of the Evangelical (Protestant) Church of Germany. Expenses for the first phase of the project of WCADL, that is, during 1976-77, were met by 'Bread for the

World'. Subsequently, project-wise funding continued up to 1998. From 1998 onwards 'Bread for the World' preferred to discontinue funding WCADL. At this juncture the Church of Koln North sanctioned a project for three years, i.e., from 1999-2001 and it is being continued in a minor scale up to 2005.

Francis (1996: 14-15),[1] while highlighting some of the economic development programme of WCADL and their impact on rural poor particularly SCs and STs, states:

> It is the policy of WCADL not to give anything free, for anything given free, especially in the development process will not only contribute towards development but also at times might turn out to be counter-productive. Hence the policy of WCADL is that any amount invested on productive items should come back for further re-investment in the same villages for the same beneficiaries or other beneficiaries, or in other new villages. In short, with regard to the income generating economic investments WCADL follow the policy of revolving fund pattern.
>
> Thus, the development process initiated in three villages gradually got expanded to several villages. Economic and education programmes were extended to 121 villages and education without economic programmes to another 886 villages by 1994. In these 121 villages, several economic programmes were undertaken as per the needs of the people. These consist of new irrigation wells, desalting and deepening of the existing irrigation wells, supply of pump sets, seeds, fertilisers, plough bullocks, land reclamation, water conservation, milch cattle, sheep, fruit and vegetable vending, leaf plate and mat making, brick making, grocery shops, fair price shops, etc. Two tailoring centres were also started to train young women. These activities are backed up and followed up by conscientising education programmes. All these income generating activities were undertaken with a view to generating employment and to improving the economic status of the participants and finally to bringing down poverty rate to a certain extent.
>
> Thus, WCADL is in the field of poverty eradication and employment generation for the past 27 years in the rural areas. A

lot of changes have taken place in the lives of the rural poor especially in the lives of SCs and STs, several of these categories of people are making a good use of the development process initiated by WCADL, without seeking any additional loans from the conventional lending agencies. They have improved their financial position and constructed their own permanent houses in the place of their temporary houses, purchased more land, repaid their existing loans, conducted marriages of their sons and daughters, have been able to eat better nutritious food, maintain clean and healthy environment in the villages and maintain good health. Besides all these, migration to the cities got reduced and there is an improvement in the number of school-going children, both boys and girls.

The Economic Conditions and Programmes of Development

Economic Conditions

As has already been mentioned in the earlier pages of their report, WCADL commenced its activities in a socially and economically underdeveloped area, viz., Mahabubnagar district in the state of Andhra Pradesh, India. The agro-climatic conditions which prevailed in the area were quite unsuitable for the small and marginal agriculturists to take up profitable farming. In the absence of unreliable and unsteady monsoon, nature of the soil, it is said that, "agriculture is a gamble in the district". As a result, people especially from the SCs and STs preferred to leave their land uncultivated and to opt as casual or bonded labourers under those who had the facilities to produce, namely the fertile land with assured water supply, or to migrate to the cities and to far away places in search of employment. The wages paid by the landlords in those days, both to the casual and bonded labourers were very much nominal as the labourers were in plenty and the job opportunities were very much limited. Many among the SCs and STs borrowed money from the rich farmers, local money-lenders and also from the cooperative credit societies. But they were not in a position to pay back the borrowed amount. The persons or institutions from which they borrowed money were harassing them for repayment. The poor in this area at that time were almost in a desperate state. WCADL was the first voluntary organisation to take up developmental works in this area and to come to the rescue of these helpless people.

In view of the then prevailing situation in the area, WCADL's main concern was to help the people to confine to their own lands, in other words, to help them to develop their land and to produce some useful crops there. Livestock development was taken up as an allied sector of agriculture development. Later on, some sort of village industries were taken up. In consequence, debt redemption had also to be taken up as a necessary corollary to the other matters of economic development. This was an unforeseen matter which cropped up in the beginning. The economic development programmes in WCADL were categorised into agriculture, live-stock, and debt redemption and village industries. These programmes emerged out of the felt needs of the people, finalised as decisions after repeated and prolonged discussions and planning in the village Sangam meetings.

Programmes of Economic Development

Francis and Lucy Francis in their unpublished report (1976-1990)[2] entitled "An Experience in Working with Rural Poor" described some of the important economic programmes and their impact on the rural poor. The prominent among those programmes implemented are as follows:

Agriculture

Digging of new community irrigation wells, deepening of the existing wells, pump sets, land reclamation, seeds, fertiliser, pesticides, sprayers, plough bulls, fruit trees, etc., come under this programme.

Community irrigation wells

Water is one of the most important requirements for raising good crops. Hence, top priority was given to digging of new irrigation wells and revitalising the existing ones by means of deepening, desilting and in-well drilling. Side walls of wells in soft and black cotton soil were strengthened with reinforced concrete walls. Excavation of wells normally began in the month of December and ended by the second week of May. During this period there was no rain and therefore there would not be much work in the fields and the labour class did not have any work and therefore they would migrate to other places in search of work. The organisation insisted that the wells should be dug by the participants themselves instead of entrusting this work to a contractor. They so insisted because if the participants themselves did the work they would feel that it was their own, and also they got work in their own fields in the lean agricultural season, there was no need to migrate to other places in search of work, and further the cost of excavation would be much less than what a contractor would charge. So far, 250 new wells and revitalising of 77 old wells were undertaken. Water supply was satisfactory in almost all the wells. A surface bore well with submersible pumping set irrigated about 15 acres of land at Kothur Thanda just in front of the WCADL office at Kothur.

Pumpsets

Before the initiative of WCADL, water lifting in this area was being done by means of leather buckets tied to a rope connected to a pully driven by bullocks. This was a strenuous operation for the bullocks, and time-consuming for the labourers who operated and the water supply by this operation was not commensurate with the strain and the time spent on this. To overcome this situation WCADL introduced 'diesel' engines. These engines were purchased in bulk and were supplied at the wholesale rate to the participants of the irrigation wells programme until 1980. During this period there was a gradual increase in the cost of diesel which became unbearable for the small and marginal farmers. Therefore, WCADL stopped purchasing and supplying diesel engines and switched on to electric motors. Diesel engines were replaced by electric motors wherever power supply was available. During the diesel engine period, the staff of WCADL got trained in the maintenance and repairs of such engines and the same knowledge was transferred to engine owners. Now they are educated in the maintenance and minor repairs of electric motors. In the initial stages of change over from the diesel engine to electric motors the staff had to help the people to go to the office and to do the needful in getting power supply. Now the staffs do not do that. Instead, the people themselves are able to do the same for themselves. One SC lady from Edulappllay village had to go to the electricity office for power supply to her well. The officer did not pay much attention. In the end she sat in front of the officer and threatened him that she would commit suicide in front of him if he did not arrange power supply to her well. The officer immediately made arrangements for power supply to her well. So far, a total number of 325 pump sets have been installed.

Pipelines

It so happens that a well is dug at a low level depending on the availability of water, whereas the land to be irrigated lies at an elevated area. In such a situation, unless alternative arrangements are made it is not economic to have a well. This problem was solved by arranging pipe lines from the well to take water to the highest point and from there to be distributed to the entire land. For this purpose cement pipes were used in the earlier stage, but now plastic pipes are being used. Ten such units have been arranged for irrigating the areas which are at higher levels than that of the irrigation wells.

Land reclamation

Most of the lands in question were either left uncultivated or put to use only for dry farming purposes. In either case the lands were not levelled or bunded and therefore were unsuited both for irrigated farming and dry farming. During the monsoon, the top fertile soil of such lands is washed away thereby undermining the fertility of the soil. Such lands were badly in need of bunding and levelling to prevent soil erosion and to retain the rain water for enhancing the fertility of the soil. Hence, soil conservation and land reclamation programmes were undertaken in about 1250 acres of land by the organisation and its participating members. In the present day development term the above practice is known as watershed development. Such a programme of the government reached Mahabubnagar only by about 1994 or so. This means WCADL was much ahead of government in the process of development of the poor.

Ploughing animals

The weaker sections especially the SCs and STs, were not in a position to own their own plough bullocks. Now that they have irrigation wells, their lands have been reclaimed and made cultivable, they needed to have their own ploughing animals. These animals were not only useful for the ploughing operations but also contributed organic manure for the crops. This requirement of the people has been fulfilled by making arrangements for the purchase of 1,250 pairs of ploughing animals/bullocks.

Supply of high yielding varieties of seeds

With the assured water supply and other infrastructure facilities of agriculture, the weaker sections were in a position to take up farming in high yielding varieties of seeds. Hitherto, only the landlords and the affluent sections in the village were in a position to take up this sort of farming. In the early stages of the working, WCADL had to purchase and supply such seeds. WCADL purchased and supplied 125 kg of high yielding varieties of various kinds of seeds. Thereafter, the people themselves knew the locations where such seeds were available and were able to purchase the seeds for themselves.

Supply of fertilisers

High yielding varieties of seeds require chemical fertilisers to supplement the organic manure. There is a difference of rate in the retail and the wholesale purchase. In the wholesale purchase rate one can save about Rs 3 per bag. Hence, WCADL purchased lorry loads at the wholesale rates in the pre-monsoon season and stored them in their godowns and distributed the seeds to the Sangam members. Moreover, the prices for fertiliser shoot up during the monsoon season. But the Sangam members were not affected by the monsoon season price rise. About 7,250 bags of chemical fertilisers were purchased and distributed to these farmers. WCADL not only purchased and supplied fertilisers but also instructed the users in the moderate use of chemical fertilisers and to take recourse to the use of more and more organic manure. The member farmers were also instructed in the preparation and use of compost manure. The ill-effects of the use of high dose of chemical fertilisers and the impact of on the health of human beings and animal life were also explained to them by WCADL.

Pesticides

High yielding varieties of agriculture cannot escape the use of pesticides. In this case also the people were instructed in the moderate use of the same, the impact of it on human and animal life, the precautions to be taken while handling such harmful substances, etc. In the early stages, WCADL was purchasing and supplying these items. Now as the farmers have gained experience by doing as per the directives given to them, they themselves are in a position to purchase and handle them.

Sprayers

Ninety-five sets of spraying equipment were supplied and the Sangam members were trained in handling these sets. There was a government scheme in 1987 to supply some spraying equipment at subsidised rates to the weaker sections. But the weaker sections were not in a position to purchase them. In the absence of required number of purchasers from the weaker section the scheme would go to the elite groups. In this situation, WCADL purchased about 75 per cent of such sprayers and stocked them and later on distributed them to the weaker sections when they were in need of them.

Bullock carts

Transporting facilities especially in the farming and harvesting operations are in a low gear in the rural areas. The affluent sections use tractors and tillers for this. But the weaker sections are not in a position to avail them of such transporting facilities in their farming operations. Hence, bullock carts are the poor man's transport in the farming operations such as transporting the manure to the field, the agriculture products either to their home or to the market, etc. At times these carts are used to transport people in groups to the nearby pilgrimage centres, on the occasions of marriage, etc. Most often, this is the only transport available to take serious patients to the hospitals. Owners of such carts can also earn some money by doing hire services. So far finances were made available for the purchaser of 59 such bullock carts with the efforts of WCADL.

Fruit trees

The idea of growing more and more useful trees has been gaining momentum due to WCADL's education process. The organisation promoted and inculcated the idea of taking up tree plantation not only for the mere preservation of ecological balance but also for supplementing the nutritious aspect. For this purpose fruit trees such as guava, mango, pomegranate, etc., were found to be useful. So far the organisation has purchased and distributed about 3,000 saplings of fruit trees of various varieties.

Livestock

Agriculture alone does not provide full time occupation to the small landholders especially among the SCs and STs. This alone does not boost up their economic condition. Moreover the landless among them are not covered by the agricultural programmes. Hence, livestock development was undertaken by WCADL for supply of cross-bred variety of buffaloes and sheep.

Cross-breed milch buffaloes

In each household there are one or two cows of nondescript varieties. These are highly uneconomical as the milk yield is very low. The organisation tried to educate the people about the non-feasibility of rearing such animals and therefore to replace them with cross-bred milch buffaloes. Prospective participants of this programme were taken batch by batch to the dairy farm of the Agriculture University. There they saw for themselves the feasibility of rearing cross-bred milch buffaloes, the various kinds of green fodder, etc. This prompted them to rear this kind of animals and to cultivate green fodder, etc. So far the organisation has supplied 1,395 such animals. In the early stages, these animals were purchased in a market at Hyderabad, where these animals were brought from coastal regions of Andhra Pradesh. Now the people themselves go to the market, select the animals, bargain the price. Here they have the satisfaction of selecting the animals of their own choice. In a similar government programme, the officer from the department concerned, the bank officer, etc., together do the purchase and bring the animals to the village and distribute them by lots. In this method the people do not have the satisfaction of having the animals of their own choice. In the dairy programme WCADL tried to involve the banks and the government department. Somehow their involvement did not result in any extra benefit to the participants and therefore the organisation had done away with this practice. As years went by the medium size animals were not available at Hyderabad market and therefore, at present the people are going to the coastal regions of Andhra Pradesh and are purchasing the animals from there. Before the purchase of the animals the people are instructed to see that they have sufficient green and dry fodder and to make arrangements for the sale of milk. In the beginning, WCADL staffs took the lead in making all these arrangements. But now all these are being done by the people themselves.

Sheep rearing

The Kurba community, one section of the shepherd community, has the knowledge of sheep rearing. Besides them some of the SCs and STs are used to sheep and goat rearing. Some of these people expressed their desire to have sheep and goats. However, WCADL restricted the supply of this item to 45 units, each unit consisting of 20 females and one male.

Village Industry

Woolen blankets (Gongadis)

The Kurba community takes up gongadi-making (hand woven woollen blankets) as a part-time occupation. For this they use the wool from their own sheep and also purchase it from others. When necessary women actively participate in the cleaning and the spinning operations while men alone do the weaving. This sort of rough and very strong quality woolen blankets are in great demand in rural areas. Villagers use them to protect themselves from the inclemency's of weather in all seasons.

So far finances were arranged for 93 such units through WCADL's effort.

Brick-making

Brick-making is an operation undertaken in the slack agricultural season especially in summer when the agricultural labourers are otherwise unoccupied. As construction works are picking up, there is always a great demand for bricks. If properly managed, this is a profitable occupation which was in the past monopolised by contractors. Now many from the SCs and the STs are engaged in this work. So far 25 such units were financed by WCADL.

Slipper-making

The soft, fine factory-made sort of footwear is impractical on the thorny stony surfaces and the rough roads in the villages. They need strong and rough footwear. This sort of footwear is made in the villages by the local slipper makers. Such slippers find market in the villages weekly fairs. Each pair of such slipper costs about Rs 30 to 35 and even more when made on special orders and of special quality. So far WCADL has financed about 45 such slipper-making units.

Crane service

Now-a-days cranes are mobilised in mud-lifting operations of well excavations. One of the Sangam members in a village, an unemployed youth, was able to find a living when he was provided with a crane. Initially, WCADL was not very sure of the success of this item. But all the same, the Sangam members recommended it on a trial basis though they themselves were not sure about its economic feasibility. Therefore, one such weight lifting crane was purchased. In practice it was found to be economically not as feasible as it did not provide a full time occupation, though it is definitely a feasible item. In fact this crane unit was not a failure and did not end in utter loss.

Stone cutting

Like bricks, stones are also in a great demand for construction works especially in summer season. This also provides employment in slack agricultural season for the labourers. Stones are to be cut and stocked. During the cutting and storing operations the labourers need money for their sustenance. In the past, they used to borrow money from the contractors and used to supply stones at lower rates as demanded by the contractors. This ended in a great loss to the labourers. To overcome this situation, five such stone cutting units were financed by WCADL in the past.

Musical instrument

Musical instruments are used in the village during marriages and certain festivals. Normally it is the barber community which does this. The SC Sangam members in one village took a fancy to learn this and requested money for purchasing one set of such musical instruments. This request was complied by WCADL.

Bicycle repair shop

Next to the bullock cart somewhat easily available transport in the villages is the ordinary two-wheeler, i.e., bicycle. In many villages adjacent to the highways, there are cycle taxi and cycle repair shops. Such shops serve both the owners and the customers in the sense that the owners most often and also unemployed youth earn something either by repairing or by renting them out. The customers can utilise this facility by getting their cycles repaired or hiring one for their transport needs. Realising the need and as per the people's requests, WCADL has made finance available for four such units.

Grocer's shop

Grocery items are the daily requirements of everyone. Very often, in remote and small village shops which sell such items are not to be seen. This need was felt by some of the Sangams and decided to have such shops in their villages. Some persons came forward to manage such shops. The required finances were made available by WCADL to eleven grocer's shops in eleven villages.

Fair price shops

Normally fair price shop owners are from well-to-do sections. Recently the state government decided to entrust few such shops to members of the SCs. But it so happens that SCs do not have the required capital for the initial investment, which runs into thousands. In this situation what happens is that the officials in collusion with the affluent sections, propose an SC whose name is found only in the official records whereas for all practical purposes, the shop is owned by someone from a well-to-do section, though in theory it is owned by an SC. This again perpetuates the exploitative system and the SCs are deprived of their rights to own a shop for the benefit of their own community. Three village Sangams who had the chances to have their own fair price shops put forward their requests for initial investments. These requests were complied with by WCADL.

Fruit vending

There are some people who hire fruit trees only for fruits for one or more fruit-bearing years. Trees like tamarind, mangoes, and guavas come under this category. They bargain and hire these trees when they are in the flowering stage. Such purchasers need to pay the major portion of the amount in advance before the fruits are sold. Some of the Sangam members have been engaged in this business. So far finances were made available to ten such groups by WCADL.

Barber shop

In the caste ridden Indian society, barbers in the villages do not render services to the SCs. In two such villages the SCs themselves opened their own barber shops and in two other villages two barber youth came forward to open such service shops wherein services are rendered to all irrespective of caste. Thus, caste discrimination at the two service centres owned by these youth barbers is slowly disappearing. WCADL has financed four such units so far.

Vegetable vending

Women purchase vegetables from the producers and go about in the village carrying them as headloads and sell them. At times they sit in a convenient place in a village where more people are likely to come and purchase. Most often they go about in the villages and sell. So far about 75 such units have been financed by WCADL.

Sewing machines

Training in tailoring is imparted to young women. This provides them with part time employment in the rural set up. So far 45 sewing machines have been supplied by WCADL to the women in the study area.

Leaf-plate making

Leaf plates are in a great demand for serving food in functions like marriages, pilgrimage dinners, etc. Both men and women collect the leaves and dry them in the shade and stitch them together. While they go about collecting the leaves and during the stitching they need money for their needs. Usually they borrow money during this period from the businessmen who advance them money. If they borrow money from such businessmen they will have to sell the products only to them at the prices fixed by them. This will end in a great loss to those who work hard to produce such plates. To overcome this unhealthy situation, the Sangams in such villages recommended advance of money to such people for their consumption needs. So far about 175 such units have been financed by WCADL.

Mat-making

Mats are the poor men's beds in the villages. Many do not know how to produce such mats. For this, leaves of one kind of palm tree are cut and dried and then split into small pieces and are woven into a mat. Though no capital investment is needed for this mat making operation they need money for their consumption needs during their work. Incidentally toddy is also tapped from the same kind of trees. But the number of such trees is being reduced. Therefore, the mat weavers say that now the owners of such trees do not allow them to cut the leaves free of cost as in the past. Anyhow, so far they have not purchased leaves for weaving mats. WCADL has made finances available for the consumption needs of 25 families engaged in mat-weaving.

Housing

Construction of houses is not on the priority list of WCADL. Their policy is to improve the economic status of the people mainly by increased agricultural production, dairy, sheep rearing and village industries, etc. Such that, people themselves will be in a position to build their own houses. There are several examples in several villages where people have changed their thatched huts into tiled houses, each house costing about Rs 30,000 to Rs 40,000 after they improved their economic status. Only on two occasions WCADL directly intervened in the housing programmes. One occasion was in 1981 during a cyclonic storm when some houses were damaged. On this occasion, WCADL made finances available for the repair of 100 houses. Another occasion was that under the government housing programme the beneficiary participants were not in a position to deposit their share of the cost of the houses meant for them. Those Sangam members who were not in a position to pay such share approached WCADL and finances were made available to 230 such beneficiary participants to pay their share of deposits in the construction of their houses.

Financial operations

WCADL takes special care with regard to the planning and implementations of the economic programmes. WCADL insists that the economic programmes should reach the really poor and needy. There should not be any misappropriation or malpractices. The finances should be made use of for the purpose for which they are taken, and the participants in the programme should benefit and should repay the loans without interest, to the revolving fund of

WCADL to be reutilised for their own future needs and for others who are in a similar helpless position.

Conditions for Taking up Any Financial Programme

Any economic programme in a village should be preceded by education to all community organisations at least for a period of one year. Both husband and wife of a family should be active members in all the activities of WCADL such as adult literacy, Sangam meetings, follow the directions of WCADL and observe the principles of health and hygienic, etc. During the one year period the participation of each family in the activities of WCADL will be closely observed.

Members of the family including husband, wife and the adult sons and daughters for themselves should first of all plan and assess the priority economic needs of their family and should present the same in the weekly Sangam meetings. The priority needs of each family thus presented in the weekly meetings of each village will be discussed in common by all the participants and common decisions would be arrived at as to what programmes are to be taken up on the basis of priority of needs. Here, the aim of WCADL is to bring home to the rural people that family is the basic unit of planning for development. After assessing the priority needs in the weekly Sangam meetings they will be presented in the form of a report in the weekly meeting with the WCADL field office either on Mondays at Kothur or on Tuesdays at Rajapur office, depending on the villages which come under these two offices. With these reports the staff members visit the villages from where requests for finance are made. Reports from the Sangam members and the assessment of the same by the staff members, etc., will be taken up by the finance committee on every Saturday and their decisions will be informed to the Sangam members on the following Monday. In this process the Sangam members concerned will receive the reply within a week. Subsequently, finances will be arranged for the items which are decided upon. Thereafter, it is the duty of the Sangam members to see the proper functioning of the programmes and for the maximum benefits to the participants.

Revolving Pattern of Finance

From 1976 to 1981 'Bread for the World' gave money for the various items under the economic programmes. Thereafter, money was received from 'Bread for the World' only to expand administrative items and education programmes. This does not mean that since 1981, WCADL has not undertaken any economic programmes, instead the amount that was received from 1976 to 1981 is being revolved for further economic programmes. Till recently, the amount that was invested in each village, when it was repaid, was deposited in a bank in the name of each village Sangam to be operated and reutilised for the same village. Thus, there were separate accounts in the name of about 65 village Sangams. Later on, there arose the need for money in new villages where so far no economic programme has been undertaken. At this juncture, some Sangams were not willing to part with any part of their money which was invested in their villages. Therefore, a decision was arrived at, in consultation with all the Sangam members to reduce the number of accounts into four for the four areas of operation. Thus the money in each account will be utilised for the benefit of all the villages either new or old that come under each area. Table 6.1 shows amount sanctioned from 1976 to 1990.

Cooperation with the Banks

For some time, WCADL had arranged bank loans for the poor among the SCs, STs and BCs for milch animals and sheep rearing schemes, by offering 33 percent of the total loan as collateral security and WCADL as guarantor for the entire loan amount. This resulted in the banks taking no responsibility with regard to the collection of dues and the entire burden of repayment fell on WCADL. This had become an additional burden to the WCADL as they had to approach the banks directly and in case they failed to secure bank loans, their needs are taken care of from the revolving fund of WCADL.

Table 6.1

Details of Amount Sanctioned by BFW to WCADL from 1976 to 1990

Project Number/ Year	Economic programme	Education community organisation	Office equipment/ stationery	Vehicles travels	Health	Office building	Adminis-tration	Audit fee evaluation legal aid etc.	Total
2459/1976	1,56,000	24,000	7,000	-	-	-	14,000	-	201000
2810/1977	7,13,182	96,150	21,000	92,000	-	-	31,400	14,973	968705
3128/1979	10,37,624	1,75,895	26,000	36,400	42,700	94,040	50,000	5,000	11467659
3700/1981	6,11,400	6,79,900	1,50,000	1,64,597	92,800	-	1,35,000	1,07,00	1940697
Emergency 1981	1,25,000	-	-	-	-	-	-	-	1,25000
7602/1982	-	-	-	71,878	-	-	-	-	71878
4560/1984	-	10,27,400	1,18,000	2,44,400	40,200	-	1,65,600	1,50,000	1745600
4923/1985	-	-	5,000	1,75,409	-	4,26,800	-	-	607209
986	9,00,000	(Drought Relief)	-	-	-	-	-	-	9,00000
05506/1987	1,68,200	15,73,680	1,52,400	5,30,280	2,13,000	-	2,48,400	3,50,000	32,35960
9773/1988	-	-	-	1,67,600	-	-	-	-	1,67600
Total	37,11,406	35,77,025	4,79,400	14,82,564	3,88,700	5,20,840	6,44,400	6,26,973	11431308

Cooperation of the State and the Central Governments

On 13 July, 1977, the then District Collector Mahabubnagar, M.T. Gopal Rao, wrote to Mr Francis to meet him on 26 July, 1977 for a discussion on the activities to be undertaken by WCADL in this district. Though Mr Francis met the Collector on the appointed day, the proposed meeting could not take place as the Collector was busy with some unforeseen engagement. The discussion therefore was postponed to 7 August, 77. On this day the collector was given a detailed report of the functioning of WCADL. After this he promised to extend full support to the activities of WCADL. He agreed to release margin money and subsidy to the participants of milch animals, sheep rearing and community irrigation-well programmes. As there were not many organisations in the district at that time, he also advised WCADL to expand its activities to more number of taluks in the district and promised to give temporary accommodation for WCADL's office either in the Zilla Parishad office or elsewhere in the government buildings. Shortly after this, the Collector was transferred and all his promises could not materialise. But all the same, an amount of Rs 60,922 was made available to 111 participants of milch animals and sheep rearing scheme from 1976 to 1978. Under the National Adult Education Programme, WCADL received from the Government of India Rs 25,000 in 1979, Rs 97,190 in 1983 and Rs 30,000 in 1984.

Opinion of Beneficiaries on the Impact of Economic Development Programmes

This part of the study examines the impact of the economic development programmes on the target people and the experience of beneficiary respondents. It is obvious that most of the voluntary organisations in contemporary times are designing their programmes comprehensively for the all-round development of the target groups. In other words, this approach is called integrated approach for the upliftment of weaker communities of the society.

It is not mere bringing awareness among the poor but also designing various strategies and programmes to meet various types of their needs. In their effort for the socio-economic, political and cultural advancement weaker community's voluntary organisations have to initiate suitable programmes should involve of target people by providing various kinds of aid and help to the deprived in their pursuit of survival so that they can develop some assets needed for them in accordance with their skills and aspirations. This is a very crucial role to be played by any voluntary organisation that aims to develop the deprived and suppressed communities. As such, this part of the study discusses the efforts made by WCADL, for the economic development of the target people through various kind of programmes, in terms financial assistance provided, the type of assistance, caste, kind of assistance, conditions of assistance, the position of indebtedness of beneficiaries, how much and in what form, etc.

Further, it also deals with the position of providing assistance regularly, if there was no assistance, reasons thereof, the present condition of the people in terms of self-reliance, the measures suggested by the respondents for the improvement of effective functioning of WCADL, problems for better service of WCADL, confidence of target groups in regard to their future position for self-reliance, etc.

Table 6.2

Beneficiaries who Received Financial Assistance

	Number	*Percentage*
Yes	230	75.7
No	70	24.3
Total	304	100.0

The above table shows the position of the respondents who received financial assistance from the economic programmes of the organisation.

The data show that 230 (75.7%) out of 304 received financial assistance from the economic programmes of WCADL for various needs. Mostly, they received the assistance for the agricultural activities, self-employment or for any other subsidiary occupation as reflected in the office records of WCADL.

Thus, it may be noted that three-fourths of the respondents received financial assistance from the economic programmes of the organisation for their various needs. As such, it may be concluded that most of the respondents needed help from the organisation through the programme of financial assistance, as finances pose a serious problem to the downtrodden people in Indian villages. The factors of general economic condition of the weaker communities are the lack of capital, assets, credibility and credit facility in the market.

This organisation rendered good services for the weaker community people, particularly SCs and STs, through its programmes of economic assistance.

Table 6.3

Purpose for which Assistance Given

	Number	*Percentage*
Financial needs	28	12.7
For health needs	26	11.3
Buy livestock	17	7.4
Pumpset	32	13.4
Fertilisers	10	4.3
To buy land	22	9.6
Agriculture needs	43	18.7
House construction	26	11.3
Marriage and others	15	6.5
Others	11	4.8
Total	230	100.0

The above table presents the respondents' opinion on the purpose for which they sought financial assistance from WCADL. The data reveal that the respondents received financial assistance mostly for agricultural practices and related activities, such as buying livestock, purchase of pumpset, fertilisers to the extent of 43.8 per cent of the respondents. A considerable number of the respondents, i.e., 17.8 per cent have taken financial assistance for health needs and for the purpose of marriage and other ritual purposes.

Thus, it may be stated that nearly half of the respondents received financial assistance from WCADL for the agriculture related activities. Table 6.3 depicts the various agricultural needs of the respondents as well as family needs such as health, marriage, buying land and other financial needs.

Table 6.4

Conditions for Financial Assistance

	Number	*Percentage*
Free loan	235	77.3
Repayable with 1% interest	40	13.2
Others	29	9.5
Total	304	100.0

The above table depicts the conditions prescribed by the voluntary organisation while providing financial assistance to the respondent in the form of loans. It is evident from the above table that 235 (77.3%) out of 304 respondents reported that they availed free loans from WCADL. About 40 (13.2%) respondents stated that they availed loans on repayable condition with 1 per cent expenditure cost. It may therefore be stated that most of the respondents received financial assistance on repayable condition without interest.

Most of the respondents revealed that the financial assistance was provided on the basis of repayable condition from the organisation soon after they got their crops. This is a good programme to help the poorer section of the society and make them self-reliant. It is a well known fact that the poor in villages are normally caught in the debt-trap and are indebted to money-lenders due to heavy interest rates. It is very difficult for the poor to come out of such indebtedness and in the process they sell off their land, etc. The best way of helping the poor is to help them with financial assistance in their pursuit of livelihood specially those who pursue agriculture as their occupation. It must be stated that the organisation has done a commendable job in this context.

Table 6.5

Penalty for Violation of Conditions

	Number	*Percentage*
Penalty	48	15.8
No penalty	241	79.3
Can't say	15	4.3
Total	304	100.0

The above table reveals the respondents' opinions with regard to the penalty imposed on them by WCADL in the case of their default in the repayment of the financial assistance.

It is clear from the above table that 241 (79.3%) out of 304 respondents reported that WCADL did not impose any penalties on the default of the repayment of the financial assistance provided by WCADL. But, it was observed in the field survey that there were some people in some villages who became willful defaulters of repayments, the organisation used to pressurise them through the village Sangams for repayment. In spite of the pressure, if they failed to pay back for certain reasons, they were excluded from the Sangam activities and were disqualified for further assistance. Such people were entertained for assistance only as and when they cleared the earlier dues.

Table 6.6

Type of Penalty

	Number	*Percentage*
No further assistance	22	45.8
Black-listed	18	37.5
Any others	6	12.5
Total	48	100.8

The above Table 6.6 presents the opinion of the respondents with regard to the type of penalty imposed by WCADL on those who have availed financial assistance and failed to pay it back.

The above data show that 22 (45.8%) of out of 48 respondents reported that no further assistance was provided to those beneficiaries who were defaulters. A considerable number of respondents opined that the beneficiaries were blacklisted in case they became defaulters. It means they were not given any further assistance. But field observation showed that the defaulters were pressurised by the members of village Sangams to repay the loan. Even if one member of the village Sangam failed to repay, the other members were not given further assistance. This was the reason why the people who paid back the financial assistance were unhappy. It is an important aspect for understanding collective responsibility through cooperative societies. In rural India there is an ample of evidence of failure of cooperative movements.

Table 6.7

Spouse Availed Assistance

	Number	*Percentage*
Yes	239	78.6
No	65	21.4
Total	304	100.0

The above table reveals the position of the respondents whose spouses availed themselves of financial assistance from WCADL. It is evident from the Table 6.7 that 239 (78.6%) out of 304 respondents reported that their spouses also availed themselves the financial assistance from WCADL in their difficulties. A considerable number of people 65 (21.4%) stated that their spouses did not seek any financial assistance.

It may therefore be stated that many of the respondents' spouses also received assistance from the voluntary organisation for various purposes. This approach certainly goes a long way to improve the status of women. The women who had no direct credit facility in the past are now receiving financial assistance from WCADL.

Table 6.8

Type of Assistance to Spouse

	Number	*Percentage*
Cash	69	22.7
Kind	49	16.1
Assets	38	12.5
Assistance	30	9.9
Guidance	26	8.6
Any other	27	8.9
NA	65	21.4
Total	304	100.0

The above table provides data on the type of assistance provided by WCADL to the spouses of the respondents. It is clear from the above table that 69 (22.7%) of the respondents revealed that their spouses took financial assistance in cash whereas 49 (16.1%) of the respondents revealed that their spouses took financial assistance in kind. A few of the respondents reported that their spouses received the assistance in the form of assets. Some other respondents also stated that their spouses took guidance from WCADL. On the whole it may be noted that large number of respondents reported that their spouses received the financial assistance from WCADL in cash or kind.

Table 6.9

Present Indebtedness of Respondents

	Number	*Percentage*
Yes	207	68.1
No	97	31.9
Total	304	100.0

Table 6.9 reveals the present position of indebtedness of those respondents who received financial assistance from time to time from WCADL.

It may be noted from the above table that 207(68.1%) out of 304 respondents stated that they were indebted to WCADL, whereas 97 (31.9%) respondents mentioned that they were not so indebted. From this, it may be inferred that many of the respondents reported that they were indebted to WCADL. Further, it may be inferred that many of the respondents regularly took financial assistance from the organisation to meet various needs.

Table 6.10

Quantum of Assistance

	Number	*Percentage*
Up to Rs 1000	56	27.1
Rs 1001 - 2000	93	44.9
Rs 2001 - 3000	6	2.8
Rs 3001 - 4000	15	7.2
Rs 4001 - 5000	8	3.8
Rs 5001 and above	29	14.0
Total	207	100.00

The above table depicts the quantum of amount of financial assistance received by the respondents from WCADL. The data indicate that a large number of the respondents, i.e., 93 (44.9%) out of 207 respondents revealed that they had received the financial assistance in the range of Rs 1001-2000. Whereas 56 (27.1%) of the respondents revealed that they received financial assistance to the extent of Rs 1000. Thirdly, of the remaining respondents a significant number, i.e., 29 (14%) agreed that the quantum of assistance they received was about 5001 and above.

From the above analysis it may be stated that among the people who had received financial assistance a large number, nearly half of them received financial assistance to the extent of Rs 1001 to Rs 2000. Thus, it may be inferred that the quantum of the financial assistance given to the respondents in monitory terms seems to be very meagre. This shows the poor conditions of the people and their level of dependence on WCADL.

Table 6.11

Respondents' Opinion on Timely Financial Assistance

	Number	*Percentage*
Yes	142	46.7
No	162	53.3
Total	304	100.0

The above table provides information on the opinion of the respondents who received financial assistance from WCADL whether it was timely or not.

It is evident that 142 (46.7%) out of 304 respondents stated that they had received assistance from WCADL as and when they were in need. Whereas 162 (53.3%) out of 304 respondents said that they did not receive the assistance from WCADL as and when they needed.

Thus, it may be concluded that slightly more than 50 per cent of the respondents revealed that they did not receive assistance as and when they needed. But 46.7 per cent of the respondents stated that they received the assistance from WCADL as when they needed. It may be inferred that it is difficult for WCADL to provide assistance as and when they required assistance. It may be due to various reasons such as shortage of funds and recovery from the beneficiaries, etc. Further, institutional loaning is not possible to provide in difficult situations but it was provided for income generation and productive purposes and this is the limitation of any voluntary organisation.

Table 6.12 reveals reasons for not providing financial assistance by the voluntary organisation in times of need. It is clear that 10 (6.2%) respondents out of 162 opine that this was so as they were not members of WCADL while 32 (19.7%) respondents said that they did not approach for financial assistance and 36 (22.2%) respondents admitted that they were declared defaulters, of the remaining 31 (19.1%) stated that they would get assistance if all approach the WCADL. Finally, 22 (13.6%) stated that they could not get such assistance since they had already availed themselves of this opportunity.

Table 6.12

Reasons for not Providing Financial Assistance in Need

	Number	*Percentage*
Non-member	10	6.2
Not contacted	32	19.7
Due to default	36	22.2
If all come we get	31	19.1
I did not receive as my family got it	22	13.6
Organised but not paid we developed by ourselves	20	12.4
Others	11	3.6
Total	162	100.0

Table 6.13

Respondents' Present Position of Self-reliance

	Number	*Percentage*
Yes	186	61.2
No	72	23.7
Can't say	46	15.1
Total	304	100.0

Table 6.13 above reveals whether the respondents were self-reliant or not after getting financial assistance from WCADL.

As can be noted from the table that 186 (61.2%), out of 304 respondents, revealed that they became self-reliant after getting financial assistance from WCADL, whereas 72 (23.7%) of the respondents stated that they did not become self-reliant. Only 46 (15.1%) expressed uncertainty regarding their position of self-reliance.

It may be noted that more than half of the respondents (61.2%) revealed that they had become self-reliant after getting financial assistance regularly from WCADL. But only 23.7 per cent of the respondents reported as they did not become self-reliant and still they depended on WCADL for financial assistance.

Thus, it may be inferred that most of the respondents still need to be supported through financial assistance and this reflects a major economic problem in rural India especially in the context of the development of Dalits and weaker sections.

Table 6.14

Reasons for not being Self-reliant

	Number	*Percentage*
Continuous help required	37	51.3
Loan on interest	34	47.2
Don't know	1	1.5
Total	72	100.0

The above table presents data pertaining to the reasons expressed by the respondents for not becoming self-reliant even after getting financial assistance from WCADL. It is clear that 37 (51.3%) out of 304 respondents felt that they needed regular help of financial assistance from the organisation and 34 (47.2%) respondents stated that they had received loan on interest. Thus it may be noted that almost all the respondents needed continuous financial assistance, free of interest and penalty for default which was not available from any other organisation. Lack of financial resources is a serious problem for Dalits for not becoming self-reliant.

Table 6.15 above presents the first set of suggestions given by the respondents for better working of WCADL in the upliftment of the target people. It is clear from the table that 43 (14.1%) out of 304 respondents suggested that WCADL should provide individual assistance. rather than assistance tied up with the group. Next 45 (14.8%) recommended need-based assistance, while 53 (17.4%) respondents felt that WCADL should extend timely assistance. Sometimes assistance was not given in time, but in a delayed way. Further, 37 (12.2%) respondents expressed that the unity of

Table 6.15

First Set of Suggestions for Better Functioning of WCADL

	Number	*Percentage*
Individual assistance	43	14.1
Need based assistance	45	14.8
Timely assistance	53	17.4
Unity of members	37	12.2
Unbiased help	23	7.6
Provision of more finance assistance	32	10.5
Unbiased decision	20	6.6
Others	24	7.9
Don't know	26	8.6
NA	1	0.3
Total	304	100.0

the members was difficult to achieve and unity was a condition for getting financial assistance from WCADL and lack of unity was a hindrance. Further, they felt that unbiased help, more financial assistance and unbiased decision, were required to improve the better working of WCADL. Thus, it may be concluded that financial assistance through Sangam has become a hurdle for assistance because the need of the members and the time of assistance might not coincide. Individual approach and recognition could be appropriate to serve better target people more effectively and for better working of WCADL.

Table 6.16 above provides data on the second set of suggestion by the respondents regarding a better performance of WCADL.

The table reveals that 32 respondents suggested that the organisation should extend or provide financial assistance individually. Further, 39 (12.8%) respondents felt that it should provide need-based help while 32 (10.5%) respondents recommended that it should provide timely assistance while 38 (12.5%) respondents suggested that it should provide financial assistance without insisting on condition of unity of the members. Finally, 46 (15%) of respondents felt that the WCADL extended biased help. Thus, it may be noted that the second category of suggestions were also more or less the same as those expressed in first category.

Table 6.16

Second Set of Suggestions

	Number	*Percentage*
Individual	32	10.5
Need-based help	39	12.8
Timely assistance	32	10.5
Unity of numbers	38	12.5
Biased help	46	15.1
Finance for more loan	32	10.5
Biased decisions	23	7.6
Others	31	10.2
Don't know	31	10.2
Total	304	100.0

Table 6.17

Problems for Getting Better Services from the Organisation

	Number	*Percentage*
No unity	38	12.5
No repayment	40	13.2
Not convinced	37	12.2
Elders' decisions	50	16.4
How to approach	49	16.1
Not recognised	33	10.9
Others	27	8.9
Don't know	30	9.9
Total	304	100.0

Table 6.17 furnishes data on the various problems of the respondents in making use of WCADL in a better way.

As can be seen from the table, 38 (12.5%) out of 304 respondents that there was no unity among the beneficiaries. Among the remaining 40 (13.2%) respondents felt that repayment the financial assistance to be a problem while 37 (12.2%) respondents stated that convincing the organisers for financial assistance was a big problem. Further 50 (16.4%) respondents' opinion that elder's decision posed a problem for better use of financial assistance from WCADL.

Table 6.18

Respondents' Confidence of Leading Self-reliant Life

	Number	*Percentage*
Yes	97	31.9
No	162	53.3
Can't say	45	4.8
Total	304	100. 0

Table 6.18 above depicts the position of the respondents' confidence in relation to their leading a self-reliant life.

From the table it is clear that 162 (53.3%) out of 304 respondents, i.e., more than half of the respondents expressed their view that as the beneficiaries they were not self-reliant whereas 97 (31.9%) respondents stated that they had become self-reliant after receiving financial assistance from WCADL from time to time.

Thus, it may be noted that a majority of the respondents opined that they could not become self-reliant while a significant number of beneficiaries expressed that they became self-reliant. A few respondents were not certain about their self-reliance. From the above analysis it may be inferred that a majority of the target groups are yet to reach the stage of self-reliance. Hence, WCADL is required to work further with greater energy to reach the poor in the process of development so as to make them self-reliant.

Table 6.19 provides data in respect of the various reasons by the given respondent why they could not achieve the state of self-reliance. Among 162 respondents who had felt that they did not attain self-reliance, the highest number, i.e., 39 (24%) stated that they could not achieve self-reliance due to lack of fixed assets. Among the remaining, rain was the reason for failure 34 (20.8%), misuse of assistance given for 29 (17.8%) and uncertain crops 23 (15%) are the major reasons for their failure to attain self-reliance.

Table 6.19

Reasons for not Attaining Self-reliance

	Number	*Percentage*
Uncertainty of crops	23	15.0
Rain failures	34	20.8
Misuse of funds	29	17.8
No fixed assets	39	24.0
Lack of hardwork	15	9.2
Others	12	7.0
Can't say	10	6.2
Total	162	100.0

Thus, it may be noted that those respondents who could not achieve self-reliance stated that they lack fixed assets which would be helpful in need, failure of rain and uncertain crops to be the major reasons for not attaining self-reliance in economic terms.

Notes

1. Francis, C., "Poverty Eradication through Employment Generation in WCADL", *Indian Poverty Eradication Foundation, Bulletin*, Vol. 1, July-September 1996, pp. 14-15.
2. Francis, C., "An Experience in Working with Rural Poor", WCADL report 1976-1990, p. 277.

7

Voluntary Effort: Social Development and Changing Social Life of Weaker Communities

This part of the study deals with the socio-cultural and political development of the weaker communities as a result of the voluntary effort of WCADL organisation under the leadership of C. Francis and Lucy Francis who have been working very hard for the development of weaker communities specially SCs, STs and women of rural village people for more than two decades. This part of the study consists of three sections. The first section discusses social development in terms of the target people's changing social conditions of the weaker communities through the educational, social and health awareness programmes. The second sections deals with the target people's changing values and cultural practices such as belief in honesty, hard work, belief in God, belief in black magic, types of treatment taken for health problems etc. Further, the third section examines their political development in terms of participation in political parties and their awareness about parties, ideology, and knowledge about village Sarpanch, MLA and MP and the services expected of them for the village community, etc.

Y.V. Rao and C. Francis (1993: 625-651),[1] in their article "Action Oriented Adult Literacy and Education in WCADL", highlighted the importance of adult education and the aims and objectives of the adult education programmes which are implemented by WCADL and its achievements.

The authors stated that WCADL's goal was to "struggle for the eradication of illiteracy and social evils such as superstition, untouchability, gender discrimination to help the poor to help themselves, to reach the goal of self-reliance, etc." Its unique approach of educating people was interpersonal approach which is different from the approach sponsored by the government and village functionaries like Sarpanch, Patel, Patwari in which the entire programme depends on the whims and fancies of the village elites. But WCADL adopted the interpersonal approach by meeting the people wherever and whenever they are available including in their fields and motivating them to make use of the adult literacy programmes by involving all the members of the family irrespective of their age. Women are all also encouraged to learn in literacy centres and also in centres specially organised for women.

C. Francis and Lucy Francis (1976-1990)[2] in their report "An Experience in Working with Rural Poor" explained that "WCADL believes that education is the prerequisite for human development because it is education which promotes the creative abilities in man and instils in him a positive attitude towards life. A human being cannot be treated as a mere participant in production of material values. No doubt, this is required for his survival, but a harmonious development of human personality with enriched and health culture is essential for an individual to become an enlightened member of the human society". They further stated that "education is adjustment to higher values... The ultimate aim of any kind of education is to effect a change in the attitudes and behaviours of the participants and in the prevailing system in the country... Illiteracy and lack of awareness are causes of their backwardness and are the major stumbling blocks for the development of the oppressed".[3]

WCADL therefore feels that education in social change leads first and foremost the masses to the power of decision-making. But unfortunately it slipped into the hands of the elite groups and further strengthened their hands in oppressing the weaker sections.

At present, the Panchayati Raj system in Andhra Pradesh boasts of having so many SC and ST presidents and members. But in reality most of such SC and ST presidents and members are dummy candidates. Behind each one of them, there is a powerful upper-caste man who makes use of this dummy candidate to his own kins and hence his own men's advantage and to the disadvantage of the dummy candidates and their kinsmen. Hence, within the present framework of the Panchayati Raj system the poor cannot expect to have the power of decision-making for their development unless they become conscious of their rights and duties, the causes which keep them away from coming closer to the decision-making process. They should be in a position to discuss and reflect on all these matters and should be able to react in the proper way.

Through the process of education development, WCADL aims at making the oppressed communities realise that the elite group which is a mere minority has succeeded in keeping them uneducated, unorganised and dependent on them for every needs of life and that the whole affairs is being so cleverly managed by them in such a way that the oppressed ones are made to look upon the oppressors as their saviours.

The second fundamental aspect in the process of education is to work towards an equitable distribution of the resources of the country which will help the oppressed community to improve the quality of their life which can pave the way for them to have an opportunity to share the power of decision-making, thus education is for the empowerment of weaker sections.

There were changes in the case of dominant and oppressing groups from Mughals to colonial and free India. But, there is not much tangible change in the life of the oppressed classes. In certain cases their condition has further been deteriorated. Criminal atrocities on them are on the increase. All these are due to the lack of unity and awareness among the oppressed classes. These thoughts gradually found place in the education programmes of WCADL. These aspects are the living realities of the life of the oppressed.

Such realities are being reflected upon the community in a dialogical form in the non-formal educational process of WCADL and reacted upon by the community and not by any particular leader of that community alone.

Any sort of education for social change must also be liberative; liberative from the powers, forces and evils of oppression of the depressed and the have-nots. As liberative education is the one which is promoted by WCADL, all these issues in one way or the other or in one form of other are discussed, reflected and acted upon in as far as it is possible in the working situations of WCADL. In the final analysis, WCADL felt that any from of education for a social change should aim at the distribution of power of decision-making, sharing of resources of the country by the oppressed groups, elimination of other social evils such as untouchability, oppression and discrimination of women and to encourage and promote collective leadership from among the oppressed communities. This is the ultimate goal of our non-formal educational process.

Approach

Apart from this kind of persuasions and motivations, charts, cultural programmes like, songs, role plays, dramas, 'burrakatha', 'oggukatha', etc., are also made use of to make the literacy programme more and more attractive to the learners. Those villages where WCADL undertook economic programmes, preference was given to those who had made a good use of the literacy programmes. At times, economic programmes served as motivating factors for the learners. Cooperation of the village leader, Panchayat President and other village officials was also solicited to persuade and motivate or even to compel the illiterate to go to the centres and learn. In very many cases they extended their cooperation for the success of the literacy programmes. Inter-personal communications, meetings, training programmes; lessons related to their day-to-day life also have contributed to a great deal for the success of these education programmes.

C. Francis and Lucy Francis in "A Profile of WCADL" (pp. 9-10)[4] highlighted some of the achievements through adult education programmes as follows:

To most people, the word adult education means proficiency in alphabets and numerals and the efficiency in reading and writing and in doing arithmetics. But in WCADL, adult education means improvement in knowledge which will help the learners to develop and liberate themselves to lead a real human life. Apart from literacy and numeracy, learners are made aware of the causes of poverty, the existing laws of the country, preventive, promotive and curative aspects of health, hazards caused by alcohol addiction and smoking, environmental hazards caused by the polluted environment, agricultural improvement such as dry farming, water conservation, organic farming, compost manure, moderate use of chemical fertilisers, importance of tree plantation, saving habits, unity among the poor, etc.

From 1976 onwards, adult education programme was conducted in 630 centres in 550 villages of the Mandals of Kothur, Farooknagar, Kesampet, Kondurg, Balanagar, Nawabpet, Jadcherla, Boothpur, Mahabubnagar, Koilkonda, Thimmajipet, Addakal, Ghannapur, Devarakadira, Maddur, Thadur, Bijanapalle and Nagarkurnool. About 51,600 adults participated in the literacy programme in the past. The adult education programmes also included an effective campaign against child illiteracy. WCADL believed that adult illiteracy had to be tackled at the child level as today's child illiterate would be tomorrow's adult illiterate. WCADL was of the firm opinion that the failure of the implementation of the constitutional provision of compulsory primary education was responsible for the innumerable adult illiterates in the country.

Awareness Generation Programmes

As part of adult education programmes, there were a number of other awareness programmes initiated such as awareness about legal education, Bonded Labour Abolition Act, Minimum Wages Act, eradication of untouchability, land reform regulations, land title without possession of land, why development programme did not reach the poor?, awareness on clean and healthy environment, promotion of soil and water conservation and rain fed farming, etc.

Legal Education and Assistance

Legal education based on the Fundamental Rights in the Constitution of India formed part of the legal education programme in WCADL. The learners were instructed to have some awareness on the provisions of the laws prohibiting untouchability, child marriage, bonded labour, on the provisions of Land Reforms Act, Minimum Wages Act for agricultural labourers, etc. The legal education programme helped to create some sort of awareness among the upper castes that the practice of untouchability in public places was forbidden by law and among the Scheduled Castes (SCs) that they had a right to be treated as equal citizens of the country. It also helped the agricultural labourers to claim and get better wages, helped many bonded labourers to liberate themselves from the clutches of landlords and to benefit from the release and from the rehabilitation programmes of the government.

Community Health Care

As has already been pointed out, health education is part of the adult education programme. This consisted mainly of education in the preventive and indigenous curative aspects. All the staffs were well instructed on these issues. Special emphasis was laid on the eradication of superstition and superstitious practices in the preventive and curative aspects of health.

For curative purpose, WCADL maintained small health care centre at Rajapur, started in 1986. This is being managed by three trained health workers. Once a week a doctor by name Dr. C.H. Madhusudhan visits the centre. A lot of patients irrespective of their caste and class visit this centre for their curative needs. They come from as far as 60 to 70 kilometres of distance. This is in spite of the fact that the organisation did not make any publicity about their health care centre. Several chronic cases rejected by other doctors were being cured here. A total of 40,863 patients were treated for their various ailments, as on June 1995.

One-Day Eye Camp at the Kothur Centre: On 24 July, an eye camp was organised at the Kothur centre with the help of an eye surgeon Dr. Vital Rao and Dr. Madhusudhan who were closely associated with WCADL. Two hundered patients attended the camp and 30 of them needed surgery while 24 of them needed glasses for their sights. Surgery was conducted at Sarojani Devi Eye Hospital, Hyderabad. Arrangement was made with an optician to supply glasses at subsidised rates at Kothur village. On the whole this was a successful attempt that satisfied all the participants.

Awareness on Clean and Healthy Environment

Action-oriented education in the preservation of ecology has been one of the activities of WCADL. Several seminars and training programmes were organised for this purpose. Special meetings and programmes were conducted on the World Environment Day, World Earth Day, and World Forest Day, etc. People were instructed to stop the indiscriminate felling of trees and plants. They were encouraged to grow more trees for the promotion and preservation of human, animal and vegetative lives and for maintaining ecological balance. Every year a lot of saplings were collected from the nurseries and distributed in the villages. Farmers were introduced to the Horticulture Department of the State Government to avail themselves of the facilities available with them.

Social Development

This section deals with the social development of the beneficiary respondents in terms of conditions of social deprivation, the types of deprivation, prevalence of casteism, reasons for casteism such as poverty, illiteracy, lack of political power, etc., and WCADL's effort in adult and social education, building unity among the poor and poorer sections, improving cleanliness and health, education, avoiding bad habits and encouragement, cooperation in the pursuit of livelihood, etc.

Further, it also deals with the sociability or otherwise of the beneficiaries in general functions, and the reasons thereof, etc. It also examines the respondent's awareness in regard to family planning, practice and methods of family planning, reasons for not practicing family planning, educational status of the children and the reasons for lack of education practice of gender equality, awareness levels of the respondents in regard to marriageable age of girls and boys, etc.

Table 7
Social Deprivation of the Respondents

	Number	*Percentage*
Yes	15	4.9
No	289	95.1
Total	304	100.0

The above table indicates the degree of social deprivation of the respondents. It is very interesting to note that almost all, i.e., 289 (95.1%) respondents stated that they were not deprived socially as in the past. However, an insignificant number, i.e., 15 (4.9%) stated that they were deprived socially. It could be for any other reason but not necessarily social environment or caste status of the respondents. However, it may be noted that due to the efforts of WCADL, the social conditions of weaker communities had improved drastically in terms of social interaction among the various castes without any feeling of superiority or inferiority in relation to the common issues of the village.

Table 7.1
Type of Social Deprivation

	Number	*Percentage*
Not allowed into temple	15	100.0
Not treated fairly	13	86.3
No equal respect	15	100.0
Humiliated	13	86.3
Insulted	14	93.3
Discriminated	15	100.0
Exploited	11	73.0
Suppressed	11	73.0
Total	15	-

Among the 15 respondents out of 304 who stated that they were deprived socially, identified various forms of social deprivation. Almost all of them mentioned that they were not allowed to enter the Hindu temples while thirteen of them stated that they were not treated fairly by the upper caste people. Further, in regard to social respect and equality, all the 15 respondents stated that equal respect was not given to them. Further, 13 of them stated as they were humiliated in various occasions of daily interaction. Fourteen stated that they were insulted. Fifteen of them stated that they were discriminated whereas eleven of them stated that they were suppressed and exploited respectively.

Table 7.2

Reasons for Social Deprivation

	Number	*Percentage*
Casteism and poverty	15	100.0
Lack of education	14	93.3
Lack of political power	13	86.3
Backwardness	13	86.3
Total	15	-

The above table provides on various reasons for the respondents social deprivation. Fifteen out of fifteen respondents stated that casteism and poverty were the reasons for social deprivation. Further, fourteen of them stated lack of education as the reason, thirteen of them stated lack of political power, thirteen of them who stated that as they were living in backward conditions and they were subjected to social deprivation.

Table 7.3 reveals the opinion of the respondents on the various kinds of programmes initiated by WCADL for the social development of weaker communities. Out of 304 respondents, as many as 296 (97.4%) stated that WCADL organised adult educational programmes. The next programme was cleanliness improvement mentioned by the 293 (96.4%). Other programmes, which were mentioned by most of respondents, were health by

287 (94.4%) and development of unity among the weaker community people by 280 (92.1%).

Table 7.3

Types of Social Development Programmes of WCADL

	Number	*Percentage*
Educational	296	97.4
Develop the unity	280	92.1
Cleanliness	293	96.4
Health	287	94.4
Removal of bad habits	126	41.4
To develop cooperation	124	40.8
Total	304	

Further, 126 (41.4%) out of 304 stated that WCADL made an effort in removing bad habits and 124 (40.8%) out of 304 respondents stated WCADL worked in building up cooperation and unity among the people of village community people in general and weaker community people in particular which is a crucial factor for the development of underdeveloped.

Table 7.4

Respondents' Opinion on Social Freedom

	Number	*Percentage*
Mixing freely with others	304	100
Not mixing freely with others	Nil	Nil
Total	304	100

Any development organisation's first task is to understand the socio-economic conditions of the target people and then to design the programmes which would enable them to participate in the programmes voluntarily without any kind of hindrances to get benefited by the programmes. Hence, data were collected to understand the opinion of the respondents in regard to their freedom in the context of development process sponsored by WCADL.

Table 7.4 depicts the position of social freedom of the beneficiary respondents. Normally, in Indian villages, there is not much of social freedom for interaction among the people of different castes. But this table shows that 304 out of 304 (100%) i.e., all the respondents, stated that they were mixing freely with one another without any caste barriers due to the effort of WCADL. This is a significant contribution of WCADL which created a free, fair and healthy social environment which is the basic environment required for the target people to develop socially.

Table 7.5

Awareness of Family Planning

	Number	*Percentage*
Aware	304	100
Not aware	0	0
Total	304	100

The above table shows details of the respondents' awareness about family planning. Out of 304 respondents, all, i.e., 100 per cent respondents stated that they were aware of the family planning programme. This is a remarkable achievement in the field of population education. This was due to population education programme of the organisers. All the respondents came to know the unlimited growth of population was a big hurdle for the development of poor families and also of the society at large. Hence, they realised that family planning programme was a must. The respondents aware of the family planning programmes, were also practicing some or the other methods of family planning. Hence, it can be stated that the effort made by WCADL in bringing awareness among the poor people about the problems of large family and over population and the happiness of small family was fully successful.

Table 7.6 presents the number of respondents who were practicing family planning. Out of 304 respondents three-fourths, i.e., 230 (75.7%) stated that they were practicing family planning. Only about one-fourth of the respondents, i.e., 74 (24.3%) were not practising family planning. The reasons might be old age, younger in age, illness and need for one more child, etc. Therefore, it may be pointed out that three out of every four of the respondents were practising family planning. It was clearly due to the awareness and population education programmes initiated by WCADL.

Table 7.6
Practice of Family Planning

	Number	*Percentage*
Practising	230	75.7
Not practising	74	24.3
Total	304	100.0

Table 7.7
Practice of Family Planning Methods

	Number	*Percentage*
Tubectomy	140	60.8
Vasectomy	49	21.6
Natural control	19	7.3
Others	22	9.3
Total	304	100.0

The above table shows the various methods of family planning practiced by the respondents. It can been seen from the table that 230 (70%) out of 304 respondents stated that they were practicing family planning in some way or the other. Among those who were practicing family planning, 140 (60.8%) was practicing tubectomy. It means women were more practicing it than the men. Among the remaining respondents only 49 (21.6%) were practicing vasectomy and 19 (7.3%) natural control followed by 22 (9.3%) who were practising other methods.

Thus, it may be noted that this development organisation succeeded in improving the awareness of the people about family planning, especially among the women.

Table 7.8
Respondents Educating their Children

	Number	*Percentage*
Yes	241	79.3
No	63	20.7
Total	304	100.0

The above table indicates the position of the respondents in respect of educating their children. It is clear from the table that most of the respondents were educating their children. Out of the 304 respondents 241 (79.3%) stated that they were showing interest in educating their children, despite their poverty and lack of minimum basic facilities. This attitude of respondents towards education of their children has to be attributed totally to the efforts of WCADL and its social and educational programmes.

Table 7.9
Reasons for not Educating Children

	Number	*Percentage*
Poverty	16	25.4
No children	20	31.7
Care of small children	18	28.6
Additional income	9	14.3
Total	63	100.0

The above table indicates the various reasons expressed by the respondents for not educating their children. Out of 63 number of respondents who were not educating their children, 20 (31.7%) stated that they had no children. Among the remaining respondents, 18 (28.6%) stated that they were not sending their child to school because the child had to take care of the younger children. Among the remaining, 16 (25.4%) mentioned poverty and 9 (14.3%) mentioned generation of additional income by their children as reasons for not sending their children to school.

Table 7.10

Parental Attitude in Treating Sons and Daughters Equally

	Number	*Percentage*
Yes	240	78.9
No	64	21.1
Total	304	100.0

The above table reveals data on gender bias. Interestingly, most of the respondents, i.e., 240 (78.9%) out of 304 stated that they were treating their sons and daughters equally. Only 64 (21.1%) respondents mentioned that they were not treating their sons and daughters equally.

As such it may be concluded that due to the social education given by WCADL in the context of gender equality, most of the respondents were not showing gender discrimination and they were treating their sons and daughters equally.

Table 7.11

Reasons for Gender Bias

	Number	*Percentage*
Male dominance	23	35.9
Patrilineal family	15	23.4
More work and earnings	10	15.6
Assertion	9	14.2
Any other	7	10.9
Total	64	100.0

The above table presents data on the reasons for gender discrimination in the case of 64 respondents who admitted that they were not treating their sons and daughter equally. One, out of the three respondents, i.e., 23 (35%) out of 64 stated that the reason for gender bias was traditional because Indian society, specially rural society, is a male-dominant society. Among the remaining 15 (23.4%) stated the reason to be patrilinial family system and for 10

(15.6%) the reason was more work and higher earnings of men for the family.

Thus, it is clear that the reasons for gender bias specially in respect of discrimination against women traditionally were the subordinate position of women and the advantage of earning position of men.

Table 7.12

Respondents' Awareness of Marriageable Age

	Number	*Percentage*
Aware	251	82.6
Not aware	53	17.4
Total	304	100.0

The above table shows the respondents awareness in regard to marriageable age of their boys and girls. Out of 304 respondents most of them, i.e., 251 (82.6%) stated that they were aware of marriageable age of girls and boys. An insignificant number of people, i.e., 53 (17.4%) of the respondents stated as they were not so aware. Marriageable age is an important aspect of rural social life. People generally arrange marriage for girls at an early age soon after puberty. Mostly this is below 15 years of age. Medically as well as socially it is not a healthy practice. Hence, the Government of India fixed the age of marriage for boys and girls 21 and 18 years respectively. If anyone violates the rule they are punishable under law and such marriage will become void. Hence, there is a need for the people to understand the benefits of this law.

It is clear from the data that most of the respondents were aware of marriageable age of their girls and boys. This is a significant achievement on the part of the WCADL organisers. Generally, people who belong to weaker communities and poorer sections prefer child marriages. This practice leads to so many socio-economic and cultural problems. This unhealthy social practice was almost given up due to the social education programmes of the WCADL.

Table 7.13

Awareness of Boys' Marriageable Age

	Number	*Percentage*
Right answers	228	75.0
Wrong answers	23	7.6
Can't say	53	17.4
Total	304	100.0

The above table furnishes data on awareness of the respondents on the proper marriageable age of boys. Most of the respondents out of 304 respondents, i.e., 228 (75%) mentioned the correct marriageable age of boys. But an insignificant number of respondents, i.e., 53 (17.4%) out of 304 did not mention the correct marriageable age for boys.

Therefore, it may be stated that most of the respondents among the weaker sections were now aware of the appropriate marriageable age of boys and this awareness was due to social education programmes conducted by the organisation.

Table 7.14

Awareness of Marriageable Age of Girls

	Number	*Percentage*
Right answers	229	75.3
Wrong answers	73	24.0
Can't say	02	0.7
Total	304	100.0

The above table depicts the respondents awareness in regard to the proper marriageable age of girls. It is clear from the table that 229 (75.3%) out of 304, mentioned the correct marriageable age of girls, whereas, about 73 (24%) of the respondents did not mention the correct marriageable age of girls.

From the above analysis it may be stated that contrary to the general lack of awareness among villagers in rural India, the beneficiary respondents had the right kind of awareness in respect of the marriageable age of boys and girls because of the social education programmes organised by WCADL.

Changing Values and Culture

This section examines the social values and cultural practices of the beneficiary respondents. To understand this aspect, a few selected questions related to their value system and cultural pattern were asked. The questions asked were on their belief in honesty, hard work, faith in God, and attitude towards educating their children, belief in black magic, health practices and reasons for their present suffering if any.

An attempt is also made to understand the changes in the cultural practices of the weaker communities. If there was any change, it is considered as the result of the long social education imparted by WCADL in contrast to the past. The main goal of any voluntary organisation is not only to provide economic aid and help to the weaker sections but also to alter or change their attitudes, habits and cultural practices of life if they are unscientific and detrimental to their progress in life and to their better living.

As such this part of the study is significant in the context of changing values and culture which may enable the tradition-bound weaker community to adopt new, modern and scientific methods for better ways of living. This is the main objective of any development organisation.

Table 7.15

Belief in Honesty

	Number	*Percentage*
Belief in honesty	269	88.5
No belief in honesty	12	3.9
Can't say	23	7.6
Total	304	100.0

Table 7.15 indicates the beneficiary respondents' belief in honesty. This question is more pertinent to understand the people's belief in honesty which reflects their lifestyles which

corresponds to the beliefs and goals. Hence, it becomes pertinent for the voluntary organisations to understand the values and cultural patterns of the respondents in order to change their function according to the set goal.

The above table reveals that 269(88.5%) out of 304 respondents have expressed the opinion that they had believed in honesty and only 12 (3.9%) stated that they had no faith in an honest way of living. Thus, it may be noted that most of the respondents had faith in an honest way of living and this value-orientation may be attributed to the effort of the organisation.

Table 7.16

Belief in Hard Work

	Number	*Percentage*
Belief in hard work	251	82.6
No belief in hard work	24	7.9
Don't know	29	9.5
Total	304	100.0

The above table reveals the belief of the respondents in regard to hard work. Most of the respondents, i.e., 251 (82.6%) out of 304 selected that they had belief in hard work.

Among the remaining people about 29 (9.5%) and 24 (7.9%) respectively reported that they did not know and had no belief in hard work respectively.

On the whole it may be concluded that a majority of the respondents had their belief in hard work. Again this practical attitude may be due to the social education given by WCADL with an expression of hard work which is essential to build a healthy and strong society.

The dominant feature of all backward societies and also a predominant feature of Indian villages is that, most of the people are God-fearing and God-centred. It is a fact that in rural India most of the people associate themselves with God-centred rituals from birth to death and there are a number of rituals practiced in the context of processes of production such as agriculture which is the major occupation. Also people perform a number of rituals related to the activities of agriculture from sowing to harvesting of crops.

Table 7.17
Belief in God

	Number	*Percentage*
Yes	263	86.5
No	35	11.5
Don't know	6	2.0
Total	304	100.0

The above table reveals that most of the respondents, i.e., 263 (86.5%) out of 304 believe in God and several rituals in various stages of life. Thus, it may be noted that in spite of rational teachings of the organisation, the people still had faith in God and they still practiced certain rituals. However, faith in God and the related rituals need not be due to either ignorance or intellectualism, but it is a super-social phenomenon which people inherit in their consciousness irrespective of education and economic development.

Table 7.18
Belief in Black and White Magic

	Number	*Percentage*
Yes	13	4.3
No	291	95.7
Total	304	100.0

It is a universal fact that the more is the socio-economic backwardness, the more is the belief in supernatural powers and the related superstitions and ritual practices. In rural India also most of the people believe in black and white magic and religious rituals to solve their problems, specially health problems. The study area, i.e., Mahabubnagar district in Andhra Pradesh is popularly known for this kind of ritual practices.

Interestingly, due to the effort of WCADL through social and health education, 291 (95.7%) out of 304 respondent stated that they had no belief in black and white magic and other kind of ritual practices in the pursuit of resolving their problems (Table 7.18).

Table 7.19

Visiting Hospital for Health Problems

	Number	*Percentage*
Yes	66	21.7
No	238	78.3
Total	304	100.0

Normally, in rural India, especially weaker communities use folk medicine and black magic in times of ill health. It is due to various reasons they may not have faith in scientific medicine, not being aware of new medical practices and they may not afford the expenditure for medical treatment. Further, they are also exposed to a system of medicine which is easily available at less cost and they can easily approach the village doctor who has been known to them for a long time.

The above table indicates that only 66 (21.7%) out of 304 respondents were visiting the government hospital while the remaining 238 (78.3%) were getting treatment from private doctors and through traditional practices like folk medicine, etc.

Table 7.20

Reasons for their Present Condition

	Number	*Percentage*
God	60	19.7
Fate	238	78.3
Self	6	2.0
Total	304	100.0

Table 7.20 above shows the reasons given for their present conditions of existence. Most of the respondents, i.e., 238 (78.3%)

stated that they remained victims of suffering due to their fate. Among the rest of 60 (19.7%) and 6 (2%) God and self are the reasons for their suffering respectively.

Voluntary Effort and Political Development

This section of the study aims at understanding the political awareness, participation and attitude of the respondents which is a crucial factor and an important aspect for the success of democracy. In India, most of the weaker communities could not understand the spirit of democracy due to their illiteracy and ignorance. This socially backward condition has been perpetuated for a very long time. This kind of ignorance increased further due to the suppression under the feudal set-up; consequently, the political participation of the weaker sections in a democratic polity without fear has remained a mirage even after 60 years of Indian independence. As such, voluntary effort in this sphere is also needed to make the poorer sections of the society to become aware of their rights and privileges, and also to build a healthy and educated society.

Hence, of late, the Indian planners, academicians and administrators felt that there should be an effective role of weaker citizens in a democracy, in all its institutions. It is possible only with the aid and help of voluntary organisations to build a meaningful democratic political system in India. As such it was very much felt in recent times that the role of NGOs in a civil society is of paramount importance. Accordingly, this section attempts to discuss the role of WCADL in developing political and civil consciousness among weaker communities in the backward regions, i.e., Mahbubnagar district of Andhra Pradesh.

For this purpose respondents' membership in political parties, if they were members, their knowledge of ideology of the parties, awareness of their Sarpanch, MLA, MP and their political parties, etc., have been considered. Further, an attempt is made to elicit opinions of the respondents in regard to their receipt of any benefit from such leaders, types of benefit received, etc.

Table 7.21
Membership of Political Party

	Number	*Percentage*
Yes	77	25.3
No	227	74.7
Total	304	100.0

The above table reveals the position of respondent's membership in different political parties and their political affiliation. As the Indian political system is based mostly on illiterate and ignorant voters, it is very fluid and loose in character and the mass bases of different political parties are also mostly illiterate and ignorant population who lack any spirit of democracy, self governance, etc. It may be due to the past political legacy and severe socio-economic political inequalities in the various sections of the society in the form of caste groups.

The above table reveals that only one-fourth of the respondents, i.e., 77 (25.3%) out of 304 were members of some other political party or the other and most of the respondents, i.e., 227 (74.7%) were not members of any political party. This shows that most of the respondents were not members of any political party. Thus, it may be noted that Indian politics is not based on, and not guided by, ideological understanding and direction.

Table 7.22
Membership in Different Political Parties

	Number	*Percentage*
TDP	30	39.0
Congress Party	32	41.5
BJP	9	11.7
Others	6	7.8
Total	77	100.0

Table 7.22 above depicts the position the respondent's political party affiliation and membership in various parties.

Among the total 77 respondents who stated that they had membership in various political parties, 32 (41.5%) had membership in Congress, 30 (39%) in TDP, 9 (11.7%) in BJP and 6 (7.8%) in other parties.

It is interesting to note that the largest numbers of respondents had membership in the Congress Party. That is the general political feature of weaker sections in rural areas was that they were associated with the Congress Party. Illiterate and ignorant people generally voted with the sentiment rather then with reasoning and fact. Most of the weaker sections generally and traditionally had been voting for the Congress Party since the first General Elections after Independence. They did not shift their loyalty. In spite of TDP ruling for more than 15 years, this party could not succeed in increasing its electoral base among the weaker sections, specially among the SCs in comparison with the Congress Party.

Table 7.23
Knowledge of Party Ideology

	Number	*Percentage*
Right	97	31.9
Wrong	202	66.4
Don't know	5	1.6
Total	304	100.0

The above table reveals the knowledge of the respondents in relation to the ideology of the popular political parties such as Congress Party, TDP, BJP and Communist Parties irrespective of their membership. Only one-third of the respondents, i.e., 97 (31.9%) out of 304 mentioned correctly the ideologies of the various parties. Among the remaining 202 (66.4%) there was no proper knowledge of the ideologies of various political parties.

It means in spite of 25 years of social education by the organisation, the weaker communities could not understand the ideologies of various political parties. This shows the necessity of the voluntary organisation to work with the rural weaker communities further to improve their political understanding along with economic development essential for the survival of the democratic system itself. Religion and politics are very sensitive issues in India, more especially in villages. If voluntary organisations indulge in discussing these issues in villages it would undermine their very existence. Hence, WCADL kept away from these two issues.

Table 7.24

Awareness about Sarpanch

	Number	*Percentage*
Right	301	99.0
No	3	1.0
Total	304	100.0

The above table depicts the awareness of the respondents in regard to their village Panchayati Board, Sarpanch.

It is clearly evident that almost all, i.e., 301 (99%) out of 304 respondents, stated that they were aware of their village Sarpanch. This means that they knew who their Sarpanch was and what his name was.

Table 7.25

Awareness of Sarpanch's Political Party

	Number	*Percentage*
Right	298	98.0
Wrong	6	2.0
Total	304	100.0

The above table shows the respondents' awareness in regard to the Sarpanch's political party affiliation.

It is evident from the table that 298 (98%) out of 304 respondents rightly stated about their Sarpanch's political party affiliation. Thus, it may be noted that almost all the respondents were aware of their village Sarpanch's political affiliation.

Table 7.26
Awareness of their MLA's Name

	Number	*Percentage*
Right	243	79.9
Wrong	3	1.0
Don't know	58	19.1
Total	304	100.0

It is generally felt that most of the villagers and more so the weaker sections, generally are not aware of their MLA's name and his political party affiliation, etc.

The above table reveals that about 243 (79.9%) respondents mentioned their MLA's name correctly. Among the remaining, 58 (19.1%) stated they did not know and only 3 (1%) gave a wrong answer.

Thus, it may be stated that most of the respondents were aware of their MLA's name. This awareness may be due to the effort of the WCADL which inculcated the habit of knowing of their leaders in social education classes. Normally, this is not the feature of rural population.

Table 7.27
Knowledge of MLA's Political Party

	Number	*Percentage*
Right	217	71.4
Wrong	3	1.0
Don't know	84	27.6
Total	304	100.0

The above table indicates the knowledge of the respondents in relation to their MLA's political party. Out of 304 respondents, 217 (71.4%) gave the right answer. Among the remaining people 84 (27.6%) and 3 (1%) respectively stated that they did not know and gave wrong answers.

Thus, it may be noted that most of the respondents had the right knowledge about their MLA's political party. This improvement in awareness may be attributed to the effort of WCADL, which is otherwise absent in rural people in India.

Table 7.28
Knowledge of MP's Name

	Number	*Percentage*
Right	105	34.5
Wrong	3	1.0
Don't know	196	64.5
Total	304	100.0

The above table reveals the beneficiary respondents knowledge in respect of their MP (Member of Parliament). Interestingly, out of 304 respondents only one-third of the respondents, i.e., 105 (34.5%) rightly mentioned the name of their MP. But, a large number of them, i.e., 196 (64.5%) stated that they did not know and only 3 (1%) gave a wrong response.

Hence, it may be concluded that more than half of the respondents stated that they did not know their MP's name. This shows not only the ignorance of the respondents about their MP but also their lack interaction with MP and vice versa.

In spite of social education by WCADL for more than two decades, people were not clear about the name of their MP. This political reality not only reflects the ignorant state of the people but also the political system and leadership which could not influence their own voters to the extent of knowing their names at least.

Table 7.29
Knowledge of MP's Political Party

	Number	*Percentage*
Right	88	28.9
Wrong	3	1.0
Don't know	213	70.1
Total	304	100.0

The above table indicates the respondents' awareness about the party affiliation of their MP. Out of 304 respondents only 88 (28.9%), slightly more than one-fourth of the respondents had correct knowledge of their MP's political affiliation.

Among the remaining people, 213 (70.1%) stated that they did not know their MP's political party and only 3 (1%) gave a wrong response. Thus, it may be noted that most of the respondents did not know the political party affiliation of their MP.

Table 7.30

Benefits from Leaders

	Number	*Percentage*
Yes	68	22.4
No	236	77.6
Total	304	100.0

Normally, in a democratic society, people seek the help of their elected leaders in solving their personal and community problems. In this context it can be observed from the above table that only 68 (22.4%) of the 304 respondents stated that they were benefited from their leaders and the remaining 236 (77.6%) stated they did not get any benefit from their leaders.

Thus, it may be noted that most of the respondents were not at all benefited by their elected leaders in spite of civil rights awareness camps organised by WCADL.

Table 7.31

Types of Benefit

	Number	*Percentage*
Helped our family	18	26.3
Helped our village	16	23.5
To get a job	13	19.3
To get a scheme	12	17.3
Others	9	13.3
Total	68	100.0

The above table shows the type of benefit received by the respondents from their elected leaders. It is clear from the table that the leaders helped respondents, 18 (26.3%) in family matters 16 (23.5%) in village matters, 13 (19.3%), in getting jobs, 12 (17.3%) in getting schemes sanctioned and 9 (13.3%) in other kinds of benefits.

Thus, it may be noted that a minority of the respondents who received help from their elected leaders, received help in their family affairs and village affairs. This is a very insignificant contribution of leaders in terms of work done.

Notes

1. Y.V. Rao and C. Francis in their article "Action Oriented Adult Literacy and Education in WCADL", 1993, pp. 625-651.
2. Francis in their report "An Experience in Working with Rural Poor" 1976-1990.
3. Ibid., 1976-1990.
4. C. Francis and Lucy Francis, "A Profile of WCADL", pp. 9-10.

8

Development of Rural Women through Voluntary Effort

This part of the study deals with the voluntary effort for the development of rural women, especially in relation to weaker communities such as SC, ST and BC communities. Voluntary effort and development of rural women has been a fascinating field of interest for not only developmental organisations but also for the government, planners, administrators and academics. This changing trend is due to the increasing realisation of the fact that it has become difficult even for the rural masses to maintain the families without utilising the inherent tremendous capacities of rural women in productive and creative processes – this is a well known fact. However, it is a well-established fact that rural women specially the weaker community women are always and at all times playing a supporting role to the men in the production and decision-making process, unlike the other category of women, i.e., those belonging to upper castes and landed gentry in rural scenario and affluent women in urban setting.

The role of weaker community, rural women in all activities of production besides various kinds of services such as those of domestic servant, house keeping, child rearing, cooking, washing clothes, vegetable gardening, plantation, continuity of social customs and traditions, recreation, fairs and festivals, numbering and her socialising role of all the family members to maintain the status and esteem of the family are some of the very crucial roles for the comprehensive understanding of any voluntary effort in rural development in general and changing status of rural women in particular.

The role of women in rural development in India has been the focus of sociological enquiry since 1976, when Delhi School of Economics initiated studies in all the countries of subcontinent such as India, Pakistan, Bangladesh and Sri Lanka with the support of overseas government, i.e., Great Britain. Since then, there has been a tremendous endeavour to boost women studies and women scholars to initiate a number of studies in relation to women of all communities such as urban, rural, tribal – to examine women's changing status, role, role conflict of political, bureaucratic participation and social role in changing the scenario of Indian society on the one side and consequent crisis and conflict and various atrocities against women and their new challenges on the other. Yet the changing status and the role of Indian women has been an ever-green subject for sociological enquiry. It is due to women's strength as a social section which constitutes half of human population, above all they are the source of human life, human happiness, and continuity of human chain and existence. Usha Rani and P. Jay Ram Reddy (1998:36),[1] in their article on "Women in Rural Development", while quoting the world economic profiles of women, stated that women represent population of 30 per cent in official labour force and perform 60 per cent of all working hours but receive 10 per cent of world income. The condition of women is ever gloomy and therefore an evergreen field of interest for scientific enquiry since the role of women has been always changing to the changing conditions and needs of human society. Whatever may be women's real socio-economic position and status in human history, in India, they have been given a prominent role and status in all activities of family and community life besides their suppressed condition in real life in dark times. If anyone wants to understand the present status and the role of women of any community of Indian society, it is necessary to understand their traditional and changing role and status in various stages of human history.

It is a stretch of imagination that what had been the position, role and status of woman in pre-civilised society, i.e., in the state of nature. Her life had been always in terror and insecure. If we examine the subsequent stages of human life, specially, the plight of women in India, there is evidence that the position of women in the Vedic period was if not superior to man, but equal in respect to men. There is also evidence in the Vedic times that she was participating in warfare, property was inherited from mother to daughter, the family system was matrilocal and matrilineal and there were not many superstitions and customs where women were disassociated from cultural life. Hence, most of the problems of modern times which are manifested manifold in regard to women, were unknown to the Vedic women. But the position of the woman dangerously deteriorated in the Middle Ages and she was considered as a property of man and was sold in open markets. She was not given the least human rights, let alone equal and civil rights. She was considered as a commodity which is meant for enjoyment of man.

This kind of position was institutionalised and various forms of social customs and practices were initiated against women such as 'sati', child marriages, institutionalisation of prostitution in various forms like Devadasi, Dasi, Parvati, Jogini, etc. But, in the modern period, due to the dawn of scientific thinking all over the world, more so in India, and due to the efforts of the greatest social thinkers and social reformers of India such as Raja Ram Mohan Roy, Mahatma Gandhi, Sarojini Naidu at the all India level, Kandukuri Veeresa Lingam Panthulu, Gurujada Appa Rao and Durga Bai Deshmukh at the state level, tried through their reformistic approach to raise the status and position of women. Because of their relentless effort, the position and status of women has been drastically changed socially, culturally but in practice local customs and traditions are yet dominating the social milieu of Indian women in general and A.P. women in particular.

However, the post-independence Indian government has initiated various measures to uplift and empower the women on par with men by providing constitutional declaration and directions against discrimination of anyone on the basis of caste, class, creed, race, sex, region, religion, etc. Women can take part in all walks of public life such as polity, bureaucracy, economic, social spheres, etc. But, the real situation is that even after 60 years of India's independence the position of women in all parts of the country in all communities has not changed much. Though there is a significant change in urban affluent sections but the role and status of women in tribal and rural context is much the same, besides the mechanisms of protection in caste councils and joint families. The true spirit of protecting the weak in all communities among women specially could not last long due to various other external forces which are playing an important role in the organisation of all communities in contemporary times. The position of women in contemporary times specially tribal and rural women is like *na gharka na ghatka* which means neither is there protection for women in family or in society. Still, the age-old systems of suppression against women prevail on the one side but they are asked to play a modern role for the convenience of man and family on the other. As such their position and role has become vulnerable and sandwiched between the two polarities of traditional suppression and modern roles. Woman is the silent sufferer of all forms of suppression. Of late, her space of living has been drastically narrowed due to deforestation, fragmented community and family life. Declining importance to their manual labour and traditional supporting role to their husbands in caste occupation forced the rural women to leave their place of origin and proceed to far off, unknown places of 100 to 1,000 miles away as contract and bonded labourers. This shift of place of living has become easier due to increased transportation facility. As a result, women who felt secure in their place of origin and locale, due to some economic conditions are now forced to live often in unknown places. They return to native places for the occasions of birth and death ceremonies and marriages. In this context the Telugu progressive writer, Goreti Venkanna highlighted the plight of Mahabubnagar SCs and STs communities in his song describing the declining natural habitats of rural people and increasing migration to various parts of the country. It is due to personnel problems of Mahabubnagar weaker community that they leave their native places seeking livelihood and they are popularly known as 'Palamoor labour'. Old women are left at home to their fate to ill health and social seclusion by their sons and daughters. Further, there are a number of atrocities perpetrated on women in their work place on the basis of caste and sexual harassment, dowry deaths while bride burnings are also frequently reported. Besides, problems of ill health and occupational hazards, discrimination and social evil practices such as Parvathi, Banamathi, Jogini, etc., also subject them to endless suffering.

Against the above historical and realistic backdrop of the changing position and status of rural women in general and the weaker community women in particular, this part of the study aims at understanding WCADL's effort for the development of weaker community women belonging to SCs, STs and BCs. The approach of the voluntary organisation, i.e., WCADL, towards upliftment of weaker community rural women has its unique inherent advantages in terms of leadership and strategies and programmes. Unlike the other voluntary organisations, the uniqueness of WCADL is placing leadership in the hands of well matched couples in terms of aims and goals on personal and organisation levels. The lifestyle of Lucy and Francis reflects their conviction and commitment to the cause of the poor.

As already stated in the methodology, the couple having the Catholic Christian Malayali background, inherently if not professionally, have a human approach in organising the poor and the deprived sections for their betterment, especially in the rural area. They laid a special emphasis on equal importance for women and men in development and sometimes gave more importance to women in all their programmes of development.

This is a challenging task for the organisers of any voluntary organisation since the levels of understanding, the living conditions of the people are primitive and dominated by tradition. Paid professional workers may not have the spirit of service and the zeal to work hard in the interior villages with women folk belonging to SCs (Madiga and Mala), STs (Sugalis) and BCs. WCADL has the privilege of having. Lucy Francis as its founder, a social worker who has a lot of spirit and commitment to service; she provided real strength for the organisation. As a result, WCADL could overcome the difficulties in organising the women folk with commitment and a service motive through the participatory approach of development. Normally, weaker community women in rural areas are not available in day time at home. If anybody wishes to organise them it is possible only early in the morning or late in the evening. It is very difficult to catch hold of them in certain seasons like sowing and harvesting. This is the time when most of the women will go to the field early in the morning to do the work of sowing, planting, weeding and harvesting, etc. These women are faced with tremendous pressure of work and role conflict of fulfilling their family obligations like taking care of children, husband, relatives visiting now and then, and any other dependents like old parents and in-laws and their health problems etc. They have to cater for everyone with their limited income of family labour. It is very difficult for them to stay at home normally. At the most, they may be available at home now and then when nature does not permit them to go to the field in times of heavy rains, etc., or when they are not able to find work during certain days or seasons. In such circumstances, WCADL under the leadership of Lucy Francis, organised the women folk remarkably by going to the agricultural fields, and to the homes of women folk repeatedly day and night for motivating them towards the chosen areas of their development. Lucy Francis would go to the agricultural fields, to the kitchen rooms, as and when women were available, sit with them, talk to them, understand their problems, their approach towards solving the problems, their aims and aspirations of life, and constraints, if any etc., even late in the night, to motivate them to participate in the organisational activities such as adult education programmes, health and environmental awareness, population education, social and political awareness programmes; she enlightened the women folk in health camps on various diseases, their effects and treatment, social and evil practices and their negative effects, bad habits such as smoking and drinking alcohol, civic duties, constitutional rights, character building and moral values on settlement of disputes, abolition of bonded labour, child labour, importance of women education, value of nutritious food, importance of training in skilled occupation like stitching, shoe-making, basket-making, saving habits, importance of unity and cooperation for the benefit of self and community, etc.

It was a very difficult task in the initial stages for Lucy Francis to handle and change the tradition-bound illiterate and ignorant rural women but she was able to succeed in mobilising all categories of women, specially those from the weaker communities to attend Sangam meetings of the village and the fortnightly or monthly meetings of all villages in the field office. The present author had the opportunity of witnessing one of those meetings when these women were able to speak from the public platform about various problems and issues in relation to women in particular and social issues in general, at the meetings of international importance such as International Women's Day, May Day, etc.

A number of developmental programmes were initiated by the organisation since its inception, i.e., from 1976 onwards. The records and oral interviews with the organisers, especially its leaders like Mrs. Francis and Mr. Francis show that WCADL, initially started its activities only in three villages as mentioned earlier which were extended to many other villages later on. Within a few years, educational and economic programmes were organised simultaneously in 121 villages. Only educational programmes, i.e., adult education through night schools, were organised in another 886 villages by 1994. There were certain educational and economic programmes, conducted specially for women. Educational programmes through night schools were organised only for women with the help of women teachers. The other programmes conducted were economic programmes like milch cattle, sheep rearing, making of leaf plates and mats, brick-making, grocery-selling, vegetable-vending, running fair price shops, shoe making, besides helping in agricultural activities, health problems and social education programmes for the socio-economic and political advancement of weaker community women of rural society.

Further, a number of young girls were trained in tailoring in the two main centres of WCADL, i.e., Kothoor and Rajapur nearly 100 km away from each other. Even today, this activity is still continued by tailoring teachers appointed by WCADL. This is a good opportunity for the young and unfortunate women of weaker communities who were divorced from their husbands or who became widows and who had the initiative to learn and earn and wished to lead a decent way of living. For them, these tailoring centres have provided an opportunity to learn tailoring and pursue tailoring as an occupation. It was witnessed in the field that many Scheduled Caste (SC) and Scheduled Tribe (ST) women were benefited a lot by these training programmes. Some ladies were also trained in midwifery and nursing, and they used to serve in the medical service centre of WCADL where a senior MBBS doctor Dr. C.H. Madhusudhan used to serve once a week and hundreds of patients, including men and women were given treatment for various chronic health problems at a minimum maintenance cost. Besides these programmes, social education programmes, on health and hygiene, civil and political rights, awareness programmes, health and environmental education programmes were also organised. Further, several programmes of income generation were organised to suit the requirements of weaker community women. As such, women were encouraged in various fields of activity without discrimination and without disturbance to their routine activity.

Training Programmes for Women

Since WCADL believed in human power and realised that a lot of it was being wasted without being utilised, particularly in rural society and more so among weaker community women, deprived of their legitimate position and rights due to the age old practice of traditions and customs and ignorance, the organisation encouraged women to make use of the programmes meant for them. WCADL organised various kinds of training programmes and awareness development programmes throughout the year.

Normally, in every training programme, there was active participation of about 50 to 60 women with interest and initiative from different villages and different social groups such as

Scheduled Castes (Madiga and Mala) and Scheduled Tribes (mostly the Lamabadas). Lambada women were numerically strong in the area among all the tribes and lived in the agricultural fields with agriculture as their main occupation and also attended to related activities. This tribe is also known as Sugalis. They were given training and orientation by the organisation in various themes such as status of women and their rights and responsibilities as equal partners in the family and society, the problems of child labour, importance of girl's education and their opportunities in changing times, awareness regarding general health and nutrition problems, special health problems of women and their treatment, awareness programmes in family planning and available techniques of family planning, specially for women such as tubectomy, importance of small family and various saving methods and insurance schemes for family welfare, etc. Further, other subjects like legal awareness, soil and water conservation, self-employment opportunities and their role in decision making of the family affair etc., were extensively discussed and the women were also encouraged to speak out their opinions on problems they confronted in the above matters.

To realise all these objectives, women were encouraged to organise money through 'Thrift Sangams' by contributing one rupee a day, i.e., monthly, thirty rupees within a group of 15 like-minded women in their close-knit groups. These 'Thrift Sangams' were initially encouraged and organised by paid social workers of the organisation but in the course of time they were organised by the women themselves. They managed 'Thrift Sangams' effectively by maintaining accounts and distributing the amount through their elected President and Secretary. The State Government has also been encouraging these thrift programmes of rural women by appointing a Mandal level liaison officer, normally a lady officer, who takes care of their problems, if any, and also who releases matching grants from the provisions of DRDA programmes of Rural Development to those 'self-help groups' of women by encouraging them to participate in such other development and awareness programmes of the government from time to time.

Field observation revealed that this is the only programme which has been successful among the various programmes and has presently become the core programme for the organisation of rural women for their own development, even though a lot of emphasis has been given to all the rural development activities in recent times.

In all these programmes of development, normally, the SC women were participating more than the ST women and other category of women for the following reasons. The main reason for SC women to participate more in the developmental activities was that they were nearer to the main village and they also lived as part of the village and like-wise were more responsive in adopting the programmes due to their accessibility to the organisers. Also, a few of them were literate and this was an added advantage for any development activity. Further, mostly they depended on either manual or agricultural labour or were paid servants for the farmers, etc. They lacked basic assets like land, capital, and livestock as means of production and hence they were more responsive and participated in all the development programmes to enhance their socio- economic credibility through the medium of the organisation which would otherwise be impossible for them to realise those set goals on their own, due to their weak position in society. In this respect they were unlike their counterparts like Schedule Tribes who lived away from the main stream of village life with distinct cultural identity and agriculture as their main occupation. Most of these Tribes possessed lands though not large in size. But these people including their women participate mostly in agricultural activities besides milching, poultry, sheep rearing, firewood gathering, and fruit gathering. Selling their products seasonally and vegetable vending were some of their vocations. They also worked as domestic servants. Thus, the tribal women played an important role in family management and production process. Therefore, training programmes like tailoring, etc., were less availed by ST women in comparison to SC women.

Women Education Programmes

WCADL organised programmes for adult education in about 1,005 adult literacy centres in about 600 villages of 18 Mandals in Mahabubnagar district. Among those centres, about 300 adult literacy centres were organised specially for women, by women teachers only during the nights. Further, there were 550 centres which were organised for men and women who were taking the advantage of this education programme without any problems. These centres were established depending on the local situation and cooperation where there were no functional problems.

The organisers firmly believed that in their approach to weaker community development, in educating first and next in understanding their problems and needs. Later they used to design programmes for development and to seek their target people's cooperation to participate in the programmes for benefit of the latter. This approach certainly yielded good results. Education is a confidence-building mechanism and most of the adult population including men and women who attended literacy programme centres attained some level of education mostly reading and writing to some extent due to the effort of the organisation. Some of them who were elder in age were able to sign, whereas in the past they used to put their thumb impression as and when they were to sign. It was surprising to observe during the field visits that many target people used to receive the research team respectfully, gather spontaneously and used to express their gratitude to the organisers, specially to Mr and Mrs Francis for working for the advancement of SC and STs. They affirmed that credit would go to the couple, if there was any change in their lifestyles.

Further, it was observed that the process of thinking and expression of the SCs and STs women transformed from a local level to a wider area and their interaction extended from their intra-caste groups to inter-caste groups. There was lot of qualitative change in the behaviour and orientation of these women towards their own individual selves and their society.

Income-Generating Economic Programmes for Women

The consistent and systematic efforts of the organisers with their unique voluntary method of working through adult education and awareness programmes, resulted in increasing social awareness by participation in various kinds of weekly, fortnightly, monthly, quarterly, half yearly, yearly and other meetings of the organisation and on the occasion of National and International importance. The level of consciousness among men and women increased. This has resulted in the capacity of women to bargain for better wages for labour, better organising the family, better personal relations with their own family and community members whereby they can depend on others in their day-to-day needs with better planning for future needs, etc. This has also resulted in more earnings of their men folk, controlled their bad practices and habits of alcoholism, smoking, etc. When most of the women in a community are aware of their rights, naturally it would reflect in their organisation of family, as such the women who are to become victims of their husband's bad habits and management individually, automatically became one and united through their developed consciousness which has helped in healthy social solidarity, primarily among women and later on among men and as such community as a whole. In the context of educating the children many families were sending their school-going age children to school, without discrimination of boys and girls. Now most of the women are aware of importance of family planning and most of them are practising family planning techniques through tubectomy operations. Further, unlike in the past, due to the effort of organisers, through the concept of Sangam, people used to take decisions in their demand for increased wages. In the process, the wages of their labour including man and women has improved and the level of bargaining capacity has gone up in comparison to the past. In almost all the districts of Telangana most of the agricultural labourers belong to scheduled caste and scheduled tribes and this is further more in Mahabubnagar district. In view of the increased consciousness due to the effort of the organisers, the lifestyles and chances of the SCs and STs have gone up in terms of food habits, dress pattern, rest and recreation, health care and hygiene, literacy and in various other aspects. The situation was not so in the past, when men and women had to work for the landed gentry on the latter's terms and conditions, and wages were not paid regularly. Generally, women were forced to do 'vettichakri' (free labour) at the houses of local landlords by sweeping their courtyards early in the morning, cleaning their cattle sheds, removing cow dung, etc. For this labour the landlords never used to pay any money except that now and then these women labourers were given leftover food stuff.

It was reported in the field by an SC women who was middle aged: "Sir, in our young age, Dalit women and their husbands never had the experience of sleeping together at home in the nights. We and our husbands used to work in our young age in the fields of landlords in the day time and in the dusk landlady would throw a few pieces of 'Jonna Rottelu' (maize cakes) at us. Whether they were sufficient or insufficient we had to adjust by filling our stomachs with water. If we asked extra they abused a lot in vulgar language. Further, landlords used to search for our husbands in the dark rooms of huts behind mud pots by lighting the match box (pulla geechy) when our husbands would want to escape from going to the fields in the nights for guarding the field from animals and thieves and to attend the work of 'Mota' i.e., drawing water from the well for the agriculture purposes. If anybody disobeyed, the landlords used to beat the Dalit labourers with the Tamarind sticks (Chintha barikelu) in front of all the villagers and the relatives of the victims and their wives and children." This inhuman and uncivilised system of 'Vetti' (free labour) practice now disappeared due to the voluntary effort of Mrs and Mr. Francis and subsequently all practices of Vettichakri are not practised now. It is totally stopped and the women of SCs and STs communities are taking care of their domestic work and using their time in other kinds of profitable occupations. Thus, it resulted in emancipation and liberty to choose their own occupation. Bonded labour, child labour and 'vetti labour' which are against constitutional rights and law almost vanished at least in the villages where WCADL had been working. Further, the organisation made special and risky efforts in order to liberate the SCs and STs from the bondage of slavery, suppression and untouchability.

Tailoring Training Programme for Women

This programme which has already been mentioned earlier was meant for the girls of SCs and STs and sometimes conscious women among other backward castes used to receive training at the two major tailoring training centres of the organisation. This programme was very much encouraged by the organisation because it is a good occupation for the young girls and enables them to earn reasonable livelihood, irrespective of their education and family background. Through tailoring, they can improve their income and attend their other kinds of work also. Normally, girls or women who practice tailoring feel that their status has enhanced in comparison with those of others. It is also an occupation that can be learnt within a period of 6 to 12 months while earning. Much investment is not required for this programme. In this sense the organisers have rendered a tremendous service to the rural SC and ST women. As per records of WCADL, it was observed that as on December 1996, 477 girls and women were trained in tailoring. It was also reported that about 300 sewing machines were supplied to those who had undergone the training and who were in need. These machines were supplied on subsidy, borne by WCADL and the remaining amount had to be paid back in easy repayable instalments. It is interesting to note that among those beneficiary women who availed themselves of the programme of owning sewing machines, almost all of them are SC women but no single ST woman has availed of this programme. This may be due to various reasons. The traditional dress pattern of STs, especially women, is cumbersome and complex; making or stitching such dress could not be taught by the trainers. The other reason was that they lived mostly in far-off places from their main village. Hence, it was not profitable for ST women. Further, these women were busy with some agricultural pursuit or the other or they preferred to work as agricultural or manual labourers which perhaps suited their spirit and temperament. Even if they learnt tailoring it would be difficult for ST women to pursue tailoring as an occupation since they lived in far-off places from the main village and other people would prefer to give tailoring work to those who were non-tribals and easily accessible. It was also reported that most of the trained girls and women belonged to SCs and BCs and they were earning their livelihood in their respective villages and leading a better life than that in the past.

Subsidiary and Income Generating Programme

WCADL has also organised some subsidiary income-generating programmes specially for women. These programmes included providing milch cattle on loan, training in leaf-plate making, mat making, and 'gongadi' (woollen blanket) making, sale of vegetables and fruits, etc. For the above income generating programmes of women, financial assistance on repayable basis was provided from 'village Sanghams' in easy and short-term instalments without any penalty. As such, 1,500 women were benefited from these programmes. This resulted in a lot of change in the women beneficiaries confidence in terms of earning and expenditure pattern.

Thrift and Credit Programme

Among all those income-generating programmes, thrift and credit programme was a very important programme. WCADL organised at least 165 such thrift and credit Sangams in various villages of their working area of Mahabubnagar district. About 24,785 women became members of this thrift Sangams. In every group there would be at least 15 to 20 members and they would contribute every month a minimum of Rs 30 each and more depending on the decision of the Sangam members. The amount so collected through the Sangam leaders like President and Secretary elected by the members, would deposit it in the nearest bank. In recent times, the government of Andhra Pradesh has also been encouraging the thrift Sangams by providing a matching grant through the Department of DRDA which could be deposited in the name of the Sangam account concerned and used for the members who are in need, at a nominal or reasonable rate of interest. Similarly, the money contributed by member women and the equal matching grant by the government and interest amount from the loans, all would be revolving regularly. Through this programme, women became money-earning and money-lending members of the family and society. Thus, the status and the role of rural women specially the women who participated in the WCADL programmes were enhanced. These Sangams helped to develop unity among women-folk in sharing the difficulties, helping each other in need, getting the disputes settled in respect of various members of families specially in the problems of young girls and wives and husbands. If this programme is split community-wise there were only 17 groups which belonged to STs among 165 total numbers of groups organised by WCADL. An examination of the opinion of the respondents in relation to the effort made by WCADL in organising Thrift Sangams reveals the following facts

Table 8.1

Role of WCADL in Thrift Sangam

Nature of role	*Number*	*Percentage*
Initiated	241	79.3
Supervision	12	3.9
Guidance	51	16.8
Total	304	100.0

The above table presents the data on the role of WCADL in the organisation of the women thrift Sanghams. Out of 304 respondents as many as 241 (79.3%) stated that WCADL initiated the organisation of thrift Sanghams (i.e., Podupu Sanghalu). Among the remaining only 12 (3.9%) and 51 (16.8%) respectively that WCADL only played the role of supervision and guidance in the organisation of thrift Sanghams of women.

Cultural Programmes for Women

The other important approach of WCADL was to initiate programmes of cultural activities consisting of songs, role plays,

Burra Katha, Oggu Katha and dancing, dialogues, plays, etc., which were very much attractive to the local weaker communities who were ready to take part in them. The WCADL through these programmes used to educate, unite, motivate the people for change. This was the most attractive means of communication and also the form of recreation. The WCADL used this technique more extensively for organising the women folk in the study area. The following table reveal the importance given for cultural programmes by WCADL for the development of women:

Table 8.2
Cultural Activities for Women

Cultural programme organised	*Number*	*Percentage*
Organised	142	46.2
Not organised	162	53.2
Total	304	100.0

The above table furnishes data on all respondents, not only the women from various villages where WCADL worked but also women from other villages also benefited through the cultural programmes organised by WCADL.

The data show that 142 persons out of 304 stated that cultural programmes were organised by WCADL to involve the women for their education, recreation, awareness and social development. The programmes organised were mostly singing the folk songs and folk dances etc.

Likewise, WCADL did yeomen service for the upliftment of weaker community women through the programmes of adult literacy and training programmes in general and training in civic issues like income generating economic programmes, tailoring programme for women, thrift and credit Sangams, health programmes, etc.

The following sections are devoted to an evaluation of the importance of women involvement in the development effort made by WCADL for the weaker community women. This has been done in terms of role of women in the process of development, gender equality in decision-making and designing the programmes, the roles given to women in the organisational process, the programmes designed for women such as thrift and credit schemes, their functioning, aid given by the government and the role of WCADL in organising the women to take part in all the matters of their concern and village development.

Role of Women in Development Process

It is a general practice that women in Indian society are not given importance in the process of decision-making. Hence, the development remains incomplete and incomprehensive. As such, in recent times the development planners have changed their views and argued that women should be given a leading role in the process of decision-making.

Table 8.3

Role of Women in Decision-making in WCADL

Equal importance	*Number*	*Percentage*
Yes	244	80.3
No	60	19.7
Total	304	100.0

The above table indicates the degree of importance given by WCADL to women in organisational matters. Interestingly, 244 (80.3%) out of 304 stated that they were given equal importance in the process of development whereas only 60 (19.7%) stated that women were not given equal importance.

Table 8.4

Reasons for No Equal Importance

Reasons	*Number*	*Percentage*
Lack of talent	24	40.0
Lack of self-initiative	20	33.3
Lack of cooperation	10	16.5
Any other	6	10.0
Total	60	100.0

Table 8.4 above indicates the various reasons for women not being given equal importance in development programmes.

Out of the 60 respondents who stated that women were not given equal importance in development programmes, 24 (40%) stated that women had no talent, and 20 (33.3%) stated that there was no self on the part of women and initiative 10 (16.5%) stated that there was no cooperation among women and 6 (10%) implied other reasons.

Table 8.5

Role of Women in Organisational Matters

Role given	*Number*	*Percentage*
Organisational	145	47.6
Social education	52	17.1
Others	47	15.4
OK	60	19.7
Total	304	100.0

The above table reveals the opinion of the respondents in regard to the role given to women by WCADL. It indicates that out of 304 who stated that women were given various roles in WCADL 52 (7.1%) stated that they were given social education roles. And, 47 (15.4%) stated that they were assigned various roles whereas 60 (19.7%) stated that they did not know.

Table 8.6

Mahalaxmi Podupu Sanghalu

Mahalaxmi Podupu	*Number*	*Percentage*
Yes	203	66.8
No	101	33.2
Total	304	100.0

Table 8.6 reveals the various women development programmes initiated by WCADL. From the above table it can be concluded that out of 304 respondents, a majority of them, i.e., 203 (66.8%) stated that Mahalaxmi Podupu Sangalu (thrift and credit

programme) were organised for women participation. Savings and credit facility in household needs was met by the organisations. Thus, it may be noted that WCADL encouraged women to conduct podupu sangalu themselves in a successful manner.

Table 8.7
Economic Programmes for Women

Economic programmes	*Number*	*Percentage*
Yes	129	42.4
No	175	57.6
Total	304	100.0

The above table shows the opinion of the beneficiary respondents in regard to WCADL effort of supporting the women in their economic activity such as mulching, vegetable vending, etc.

Surprisingly, the opinion of the respondents in relation to women's economic development activity was intriguing. Only 129 (42.4%) out of 304 respondents stated that various programmes of economic development were organised for women. Surprisingly, a majority of the respondents, i.e., 175 (57.6%) out of 304 responded negatively.

Table 8.8
Singing and Dancing Programmes

Singing and dancing	*Number*	*Percentage*
Yes	106	34.9
No	198	65.1
Total	304	100.0

The above table shows opinion of the respondents on WCADL in regard to its organising singing and folk dance programmes for the target women for their development.

It is interesting to note that only one-third of the respondents, i.e., 106 (34.9%) stated that singing and folk dance programmes were organised by the WCADL for the cultural development of women while the remaining majority, i.e., 198 (65.1%) gave a negative response.

Table 8.9

Economic or Thrift Sangam Programmes in village

Thrift Sangam in village	*Number*	*Percentage*
Yes	118	38.8
No	169	55.6
Can't pay	17	5.6
Total	304	100.0

Table 8.8 explains the beneficiary respondent's understanding of having a thrift Sangam in their village. Out of 304 respondents, surprisingly only 118 (38.8%) mentioned that there is a thrift Sangam in their village. But a large number i.e. 169 (55.6%) did not have any awareness of the thrift Sangam in their village in spite of the fact that almost every village had a women's thrift Sangam.

Table 8.10

Member of Thrift Sangam

Member of Thrift Sangam	*Number*	*Percentage*
Yes	57	18.8
No	61	20.1
NA	186	61.2
Total	304	100.0

The above table depicts the number of people among the respondents who were members of the thrift Sangam.

Surprisingly only 57 (18.8%) claimed that they were the members of the thrift Sangams. This may be due to the fact that the majority respondents are men and women organising the thrift Sangam.

Note

1. Usha Rani and P. Jay Ram Reddy, (1998: 36) "Women in Rural Development: A Brief Analysis", in Y.B. Abasayulu (ed.), *Women in Developing Society: Marching Towards 21st Century*, Delta Pulishing House, Delhi.

9

Tribal Development through Voluntary Effort: Change and Continuity in the Lambada Tribes

This part of the study deals with Tribal development through the voluntary effort of WCADL. Since its inception in 1976, WCADL has been taking up various programmes for the development of different communities, especially SCs and STs in the rural areas of Mahabubnagar and Ranga Reddy district of Andhra Pradesh. It is a well-known fact that any development organisation has to initiate developmental programmes corresponding to the felt needs of target people belonging to various sections. Since WCADL mainly aims at developing the weaker communities of rural society, naturally SC and ST communities are gaining importance as target communities for the upliftment effort of WCADL. It is also a well established fact that most of the weaker communities in rural areas particularly in the Telangana region of Andhra Pradesh belong mostly to Scheduled Caste communities, i.e., Madiga, Mala and an insignificant number of families who belong to those sub-castes such as Baindla, Byagri, Daccali, Sindhu, etc. As such, there are also numerous tribal groups in the Telangana region of Andhra Pradesh especially in Mahabubnagar district. The numerically dominant tribal population among the tribes is 'Lambada' or Sugali and other forest tribes. However, most of the tribes inhabit outside the main stream of the village life. The Lambada tribe, which is numerically and socio-economically strong in comparison with other forest tribes and other splinter groups, are also known as 'Banjara tribe' historically and they trace their origin to the Rajput community in Rajasthan. It seems factually and logically their claim of origin is unquestionable and also reflects the reality. Their physical and ethnic features reflect those of Rajputs in Rajasthan. Their physical features reflect intelligence, courage, tradition, hard work and cultural practices which are entirely different from those of other tribes and which are rich in wisdom and more social in the context of economic factors, family, marriage, religion and polity, etc. Their dominant occupation is agriculture and a substantial population depends on agricultural labour and other kinds of labour mostly related to physical work.

Owing to various natural reasons of declining rainfall in Mahabubnagar district and increasing population of Lambadas – and the related problems of fragmentation of landholdings and subsequent loss of employment at their living places led to their migrations from their place of origin which are popularly known as Tandas or hamlets of the main village for the administrative purposes. Otherwise those living places of Tandas are autonomous and the Lambadas lead a secluded life.

This part of the study mainly aims at understanding the general socio-economic features of the Lambada tribes in Mahabubnagar district and the WCADL effort in changing their socio-economic and cultural life through various programmes of development. Here, an analysis is attempted to understand the approach of WCADL and its initiation of types and nature of programmes and participation of tribal population, utilisation of programmes and consequent changes in their social, economic and cultural life. It also discusses the constraints in the process of change and continuity of their customs and tradition.

It is obvious that any study, which aims to understand the tribal communities mostly, needs to use various methods of data collection such as observation, caste studies, group discussions besides the historical method. Further, to reflect the present general conditions of working and living of those tribes under study the survey method was also used. As such this part of the discussion reveals the role of WCADL in changing socio-economic conditions of tribal people specially the Lambadas who are the main partners in the development process of weaker communities. Further, it mainly examines WCADL's effort in the context of changing social and cultural life of the Lambadas in Mahabubnagar, since other tribes are numerically and otherwise insignificant and suspectible to development approach. Though a few other people than the Lambadas derived the benefits of the development programmes of WCADL the analysis and discussion centres around the Lambada tribes, since most of the beneficiaries belong to the Lambada tribe.

Socio-economic Profile of Lambadas

Kalya Pavana (2002),[1] in her study "Socio-economic Development of Lambadas", a case study of Nalgonda district of Andhra Pradesh, described the distinct socio-economic and cultural features of this tribal community and their change and continuity due to various programmes of the government to uplift them since 1956-1983. The author while referring to Thruston (1909) stated that this tribe is found in all the three regions of Andhra Pradesh with different names and the word Lambada is synonymously used with Sugali, Banjara and she is of the opinion that Brinjali, Bonjari, Baipari, Sugali or Sukali are one and the same and the Lambadas of the Andhra and Telangana regions of Andhra Pradesh are similar in their way of dressing, customs and traditions. The author categorises the Lambadas into two: one, which is conservative, and the other which welcomes change. The conservative Lambadas say, "What is the use of or the fun in cutting and killing a colourful tradition which gives more happiness and provides more fun to the people and going on for a new practice which is a second hand imitation, dry and void of life". "The persons who want change say that sometimes they are ridiculed for their customs if not in their presence but in their absence. Hence they need a change from the old customs which means deviation from the generally accepted social norms and customs of their people and castes residing in their area". The author further observed that "Lambadas in

Telangana are favouring change whereas their counterparts in Andhra and other regions adhere strictly to their old traditions".

Kalaya Pavana, in her study (op. cit.),[2] highlights the general economic conditions of Lambadas. She says that "the Lambadas are settling in the area leaving their nomadic ways and it is difficult for them to earn a good living. They are also known to be criminals. It is difficult for them to be accepted by the other communities. Their income was less and it has forced them to be the poorest of the poor in the social circle. It is easy for the men to be accepted, as there was not of much difference in their dressing. But it is women who have been a neglected lot. And this places the Lambadas in the below poverty line sections of the society".

Though the above features are generally seen in this tribe, there are certain changes taking place in all walks of their life. The change is slow but steady. The change of lifestyles goes with various factors, such as sex, age, education, occupation, place of living, size of landholdings, etc. Whatever may be the economic status of Lambadas, even today their social status in relation to other castes and other religious communities is one and the same. Mostly they are mistreated, whenever they interact with other sections of population in the affairs of their day-to-day life. They are not treated equally even by the low caste Hindus and people belonging to low economic status in other communities. But these Lambadas learnt to live or put up with these social conditions, which are mostly suppressive and exploited for centuries. It is more often reported in the press that Lambdas women are raped and molested. They are beautiful looking women with fair complexion. Even today, most of the women prefer to wear their colourful traditional dress. But the younger generations are now used to dressing like other women. Because of their poor condition constant exploitation, men and women look strong, confident and courageous. They enjoy a lot of freedom in their natural abodes with full natural wealth. There is no segregation and social stratification among them. They enjoy the same status among themselves. Even the economic affluence of a few does not create any kind of discrimination among themselves. Normally, all the members of the tribe including children are exposed to all styles of their life without any inhibition. They believe in community life and do involve all people in all the community activities. Women and children participate more in their seasonal colourful feasts and festivals. They celebrate festivals grandly in different seasons and stages of agricultural activities. Though, their lifestyle and cultural practices look distinct, by religion they are Hindus. Their religious practices, faith in relation to gods and goddesses are mostly similar to Hinduism except for a few unique features. Their dominant occupation is agriculture and agriculture labour. Their habitations are out of the main village and mostly far away from the main village. They are mostly secluded places originally and normally unconnected to main roads. This is a deliberate settlement pattern of Lambadas. May be it was planned originally to keep them away from exploitation by others and keep up their own traditions and customs intact. But later, on due to the effort of various governments and voluntary organisations, there developed 'kaccha' roads or link roads laid to connect them. Yet they lack even today, basic facilities like protected water, schooling, health facilities, 'pucca' houses, sanitation, etc. Most of their agricultural fields are barren and dry lands. Mostly they depend on rains and wells for irrigation. If there are no rains and no water in their wells and even for a family with average size of landholding it is difficult to sustain. Their other subsidiary occupation is sheep and goat rearing. Every family also maintains a family poultry. They further depend on forest goods like firewood and seasonal fruits. Every family knows how to make use of their backyard for raising vegetables. All the members of the family old, young and children involve themselves in their agricultural practices. Very old and small kids below five years are at home to look after their siblings under five years. Mostly, men before 6 A.M. and women after 9 leave their houses for field work and come back in the evening. Their women work very hard in comparison to man. The men look after the field and financial matters of outside the house. But the women manage the entire household work besides their routine fieldwork. It is a very common and striking feature of this hard working tribe that due to fragmentation of land, irregular rains and continuous droughts and due to loss of livelihood, they had to migrate in search of work and livelihood to far-off places all over the country. Since most of them are illiterate and untrained they look for physical work, i.e., agricultural or manual labour. The kind of jobs is normally without regular timings. Labourers should work from morning to late in the evenings at farms, agricultural fields without any weekly off and any other additional benefit. It is very pathetic to observe that small kids of school-going age are mortgaged to the village landlords from year to year. In some cases the boys work for many years for want of liquidation of their parental debts. Some people work as bonded labourers even today. Child labour and bonded labour are very common among this tribe. Attached labour, i.e., yearly contract labour either to the landlord or to the labour contractor who hire the labourer, on a yearly basis for construction work is very common among this tribe. Those who enter into agreement with the landlord have to live in the Kottams (cattle sheds) of landlords along with cattle without any protection from mosquitoes and in unhygienic conditions. These labourers and boys are not allowed to go to their parent's houses even when they fall sick and during festivals. Many times, it is reported that people with serious ailments and non-treatment of fever and diseases died and no compensation was given by the landlords. They were not even provided with minimum clothes to protect themselves from cold and rain, etc. The foods given normally consist of leftovers and measured, not sufficient to quench the hunger and taste of the labourer. The conditions of the people those who work as manual labourers for construction contractors are further pitiable. They have to work in far-off places, i.e., 100 to 1000 kms away, as hired labourers for a year and live at the work place without basic conditions of living such as proper food, clothes and shelter. Further, they have to work in all seasons and even when they fall ill. Women, those who work in such conditions, are more often exploited by their contractors and the local people. Politically, this tribe is also playing an important role at village, Mandal, district and the regional levels. They constitute a substantial population among the tribes and play an important role in the democratic polity. Though they are a hardworking class indeed, normally they prefer to vote to the Congress Party due to the political dominance of the Congress Party since independence. Though, there is a change in the power structure and the Congress Party lost power in the state except once out of four General Elections, their loyalty is mostly shown to the Congress Party. However, the younger generation are showing interest in TDP (Telugu Desam Party) and other regional parties substantially but not totally. Irrespective of age, education, occupation most of this tribal people prefer to vote for the Congress Party. Old people mostly adore the ideal image of Indira Gandhi, Rajiv Gandhi and now they see their leader in Sonia Gandhi. The meetings of the Congress Party and 'dharnas' or any other political activities of the leftist parties are mostly attended by these Lambadas. They participate mostly in all public meetings in hot summer as well as in cold winter. Their dances are organised in political meetings of public importance. To mention the importance of tribal population in national life, Pandit Jawaharlal Nehru the first and foremost Prime Minister of India, once stated that India has a lot of natural resources manpower and rich traditions. The tribal people of India are rich in their culture, they sing, they dance, they love beauty and possess lot of natural endowments. But, the modern civilisation is destroying them. This is like the loss of nerve to the nation's body.

Even, after 56 years of India's Independence, in Telangana districts of Andhra Pradesh, Lambadas are playing a crucial role ranging from village labourers to industrial labourers, from rickshaw pullers to lorry drivers; their women from forest to farm maid servants, their children and old people are working day and night for the comfort of cunning and exploiting people of various castes and classes in the rural and urban society. Their socio-economic and political plight even today, depicts ceaseless suffering and labour. Yet, they bear their suffering silently. All the development programmes initiated after independence, planned or unplanned could not change their oppressed and suppressed conditions of life. They only know physical labour and work day and night. There has not been any movement so far for their upliftment ideologically or otherwise by themselves or by others.

People prefer to derive pleasure and benefit from their physical beauty and their labour but never allow them to live in their traditional way or in the so-called civilised way. Hence, a number of voluntary organisation, are gaining importance in recent times in the development of this unfortunate section of humanity all over the world. There are a number of national and international organisations who are really concerned about the problems of human suffering including ILO, UNO, World Bank, state and national governments, showing a planned concern for these unfortunate and innocent people who have been constantly victimised, suppressed and subjected to inhuman suffering. Yet, the society in general or the enlightened people who execute the task of this onerous responsibility of development are playing a mischievous role and are creating a stumbling block in the liberation and development of these Lambada people.

However, a few philanthropic and fair-minded social workers like Mrs Lucy Francis and Mr Francis worked their best in principle and ideology within the given constrains of the socio-cultural milieu and under the conditions imposed by the sponsoring agencies like the state and central government. They have worked relentlessly for about 25 years. They are working even in their old age and have not stopped their tireless mission of serving the poor and needy even though unlike in the past there is lack of support.

The following presentation, examines the development and change brought about by WCADL's voluntary effort in mitigation of suffering of the tribal communities specially the Lambadas who include men, women, children, adults and the old and thus on the whole, the entire Lambada community. This study is a comprehensive study which has used all the methods of data collection including field survey to examine the opinion of the beneficiaries of the organisation and the public in general. As already mentioned in the Methodology, about 304 respondents belonging to various villages and tribal Tandas of Mahabubnagar district, where the WCADL initiated its programmes, were interviewed. Among those about 54 respondents (17.8%) out of 304 are from the tribal population. Most of them are Lambadas. For the convenience of analysing of voluntary effort in tribal community development a few families were chosen as case studies for the detailed analysis. The following discussion throws light on the effort of WCADL in developing the tribal population in terms of the various programmes initiated, their impact on the people in terms of continuity and change in the life of the beneficiaries and their community as a whole.

Tribal Development

Pochammagedda Tanda: A Case Study

The inhabitants of this village, Pochammagedda Tanda are tribals known as Lambadas. The village where they stay is called a Tanda. They live far away from the main village. Their inclination to stay away from the main village originates from their desire to maintain their cultural identity and to avoid the problems of inter-mixing. This is not because of any factors like untouchables as in the case of the Scheduled Castes (Harijans) but because their culture and identity are different from those of the other castes and communities of India. They have their own special kind of dress for their women folk; their women perform a typical dance accompanied by rhythmic beating of drums by their men. The vigour of clapping and jumping during the dance by women, depends upon the frequency of the drum beating by men. Their tribal settlements are in the midst of their own agricultural fields. They are not scared of settling down in a far and remote area, even in a forest – like wild environment. In contrast, the other castes and communities live together in a village. For example, the Scheduled Castes live at one corner of the village.

It is reported about Lambadas that, in olden days, when transport and communication facilities were not so much developed as in the present day, these tribals used to travel on horse back to far away remote villages to sell salt, chillies, food grains etc. During such journeys they used to be away from their home for months together. And it is almost a century or more only since they have adopted the life of settling down in a village and have taken up agriculture as their occupation. Even now in the remote rural areas, some of these people still retain their old habits like dacoity etc. But, by and large, most of the members of this community have abandoned such violent habits, abandoned their nomadic life and have taken up agriculture. But even now during the lean agricultural season, sometimes both men and women and at times men alone, migrate to nearby cities like Hyderabad and to distance cities like Mumbai from Mahabubnagar district and from the other districts of Andhra Pradesh.

The members of this community, both men and women are sturdy and strong and are hard working. In several cases it has been observed that women of this community are no longer wearing their traditional dress and have taken to other dresses like the women of other castes and communities. The reasons may be that to stitch their traditional dress is a labourious task, it is not easy to wash and clean like other dresses, and not so convenient for physical work in the fields. The Lambada girls who go to school, women who have the chance to go to offices frequently to meet the officers do not wear their traditional dress when they are way from home. It has also been observed that young and adult girls who are absorbed in the formal schooling and educational systems are not so much interested in learning and practicing their traditional dance which is very much specific to their culture. Because of the cultural transformation which is taking place in the Lambada community, as years pass by, their culture may become extinct and they may be absorbed in the main cultural stream of the country. Though the Lambadas have their own gods and special practices of worship, they have started making pilgrimage to Hindu temples and worshipping Hindu gods and goddesses.

Uncertainty of Crop Yields in Dry Land or Rainfed Farming

Pochammagedda Tanda is a village with the characteristics of Lambada culture which is in the process of transformation. There are about eighty families in this Tanda. In each family there are members from three to ten. This village has an area of about 600 acres of land which is mostly dry; there only eight agricultural bore wells which together have the capacity of irrigating about 30 acres of land in summer season and about 60 acres during the monsoon. Therefore, the major portion of the land in this village is subjected to dry farming or rain fed farming. Monsoon rains are unpredictable, both in quantity and timing. Therefore, agriculture in dry land farming is a gamble with the monsoon. At times the monsoon rains are much less. It is too much as it happened this year. Because of excess rain most of the cotton farmers have suffered heavy losses. Sometimes the monsoon rains are so delayed that they fall when the sowing season is over. Some other times it is untimely for instance when the crops are ready for harvest. In such cases also the farmers suffer a lot. At times the monsoon rains come all at once in which case it will be impossible for the farmers to take up any agricultural work.

Crops in Dry Land Farming

Food grains such as jowar and ragi, pulses such as red grams, bengal grams and horse gram, oil seeds such as castor, ground nut, sun flower, other cash crops such as cotton and varieties of vegetables, chillies, etc., are grown in the dry land farming sector.

Irrigation Wells: Sources of Wet Cultivation in Dry Land Farming Sector

Irrigation wells in the dry farming sector render yeoman service to the farming communities like oasis in the desert. These irrigation wells help to supplement the shortage of water in the non-monsoon season and serve as the only source of water for crops in the monsoon summer months. But even these sources of water are not available in all the fields of the dry land area. Availability of such underground water sources are assessed by geologists and by traditional water diviners. In certain cases the traditional water diviners have proved to be more effective than the scientific geologist. For example, a geologist with all his scientific equipment gave a negative report about the availability of water in the fields around the Rajapur office of WCADL. But, a traditional diviner could locate in the same field a point where there was abundant supply of water.

It is reported that in the recent past, the underground water level has gone down to a great extent due to low rainfall and due to very poor soil and water conservation methods. During 1970 and 1980 an open well of about 10 metre depth and 4 metre width could supply water for about 5 acres of land. Gradually the water level has gone down to such an extent that it has become almost impossible to dig open irrigation wells. Now water is available only at depths varying from 40 to 50 metres and more. Now farmers are resorting to digging bore wells with the help of rig machines. Such bore wells are very deep as mentioned above with a diameter of six inches. The cost of digging open wells by manual labour and by machine with the above depth and width is more or less the same. But the difference is in the cost of motor and pump sets. A motor and pumpset for an open well costs about Rs 7,000 where as the cost of a motor and pumping set for a bore well is Rs 25,000.

The Catalytic Role of WCADL in Pochammagedda Tanda

In the year 1983, WCADL came into contact with this village. After repeated visits, contacts, formal and informal discussions with the people in the village by the staff of WCADL, a Sangam and a literacy centre were commenced in this village. With a small financial contribution from WCADL and with the contribution of a lot of labour by the villagers a small semi permanent community hall was constructed. This served as a shelter both for the literacy classes and for the weekly Sangam meetings. Literacy classes and Sangam meetings helped the adults to achieve a certain level of literacy and more insight into and awareness about their own development, and to take care of themselves against exploitation of the vested interest groups.

Among the adults who attended the literacy classes, a man by name Babia and a woman by name Vali appeared for the 7th class public examination conducted by the government and passed. Babia himself later on became an adult literacy instructor in the same village. Vali worked for some time as a 'women development worker' with WCADL. During the course of a discussion held in an agricultural field of this village, Babia narrated his first encounter with WCADL in one of the Sangam meetings in the village. (The discussion in the field was on 12 January, 1999). As reported by the Director of WCADL, the gist of the discussion is as follows:

In the initial stages of the Sangam meetings in which one or other of the staff of WCADL also would be present, the practice was that each participant had to stand up and speak something. Such practice was used to help them to overcome their stage fear in facing an audience, to have enough courage to speak in any office or in any similar situation. The meetings in this village were conducted in the small community hall which had only one door. The staff member stood at the door to make sure that no one went out to avoid his or her turn to speak. Babia was very much nervous to stand up and to speak. Under the pretext of passing urine he wanted to get out before his turn came. But he dared not do so for the fear of the staff member standing at the door. As he had no other chance to escape, he picked up courage to stand up and utter a few words which he said he himself did not understand. But such an experience laid the foundation for his courage to stand up and face any audience consisting of any number of people. He says that now he is not at all afraid to speak out in the presence of any officer.

During the same discussion on 12 January 1999 one of the participants said: "Sir, with the arrival of WCADL in our village we have now more problems than in the past". Then Francis asked Babia, "Is it true? What is this? Babia said, "It is true". "How is it true?" asked Francis. Babia said that before WCADL organised a Sangam and commenced literacy classes in the village, there were only a very few people who claimed to be enlightened and clever. These few were the leaders and the majority appeared to be unwise and therefore remained subordinate to the wise minority. The wise minority exploited the unwise majority. The latter could not resist the exploitative situation, and therefore remained silent victims of exploitation. Now, the situation has changed. The then silent majority have become vociferous and started questioning the traditional wisdom of the exploiters. Naturally, this has led to some kind of friction in the village. Then Francis told them this was what development meant. The silent majority are awakened and conscientious and therefore can take care of their own development. This is very much in accordance with the theory of development propounded by Karl Marx. According to him, in the process of development, there ought to be a situation which he calls 'thesis', i.e., the situation of an established system not suitable for the development of the poor. Therefore, the poor will revolt against the established system and this is called 'antithesis'. This will result in some sort of compromise which is called 'synthesis'. But even in the process of 'synthesis' there is bound to have some friction and hence the process of development. Thesis, antithesis – synthesis will go on until the exploited masses gain an upper hand and shape their own destiny.

During another discussion in the same village it was reported that on 2 February, 1999, one of the participants said that a certain politician promised to do certain favours to the youth. Then Mr Francis told that they need not fully believe all the promises made by politicians and government officers. But, all the same, they should try to make use of such promises as much as possible by taking whatever benefits they can take from them.

Then, Ramji, one of the participants said, "What, Sir (Francis) told is correct. The intention of such political leaders is not to improve the lot of the poor but to remain in power. For this they use many tactics". To substantiate his view he narrated the following incident.

Ramji was employed at a local government office to repair the hand pump sets of bore wells used for drinking water. He was employed as a temporary worker which meant that he would get his wages on the daily basis for 24 days in a month (excepting Sundays). For this he has to submit his tour dairy and other bills, etc. Once during a meeting in the local government office, the local politician, a Member of the Andhra Pradesh Legislative Assembly (MLA) questioned him about the slow progress in repairing the bore well pumps in different villages. Then Ramji told him that there were not enough tool kits for all the workers to do the work. At this, the politician asked him, "Why did you not tell me about this? There are so many tool kits lying down in my house, come and collect". Accordingly, the following day Ramji sent some of his assistants to collect the tool kits from the politician's house. When they went and asked him for the tool kits the politician was angry with them and questioned, "How can I have tool kits in my house?" Then Ramji's assistants reminded him about the promise which he made the other day. Then the politician retorted, "We people make many promises in public like this. Don't think that all these promises are to be kept up". So Ramji's assistants had to return with out any tool kits. When Ramji narrated this incident, some of the participants said, "Yes, politicians and officials are not to be believed in all what they say. They make promises. But they do not keep them up. They make promises and go away. They really do not mean the development of the poor. But WCADL is not like that. WCADL is happy when the poor people make improvements in their lives. WCADL moves with the people and understands the feelings of the people".

Ramji narrated another experience of his. Once, in order to get his monthly wages, he submitted all the bills and other required documents. At last when it came to the accounts officer, who is a lady, there was a delay of the payment under some excuse or other. Ramji repeatedly pleaded with her to pay his money. But at last one day she told him if he could get for her five litres of kerosene for her use in her house, she would try to pay him his money. Ramji was quite annoyed about it and said to her, "I too have a wife and children to take care of. You people sit in the office and draw better salary; I go about in the villages and do my work. If I give you bribe how can I feed the members of my family? Yes, I will bring five litres of kerosene, pour it on you while you are sitting on this chair and strike a match stick and throw it at you". Having said these words he went away. The next day the officer called him and paid his money. After narrating this incident Ramji said, it was only to threaten the officer that he told her so and that he did not mean any harm to her. In this way he said that each one had to use some tactics to survive in this world. On the whole it was a fruitful discussion on that day.

Apart from the conscientising education, WCADL also has helped the people of Pochammagedda Tanda with small financial help for desilting of their old wells, or for pump sets, plough bulls, fertilisers, etc. Later on, they themselves managed to make very substantial improvement in their economic life and also in educating their children by sending them to the formal schools, to professional institutes for getting trained in certain skills, etc. Some examples are given below:

Kethavath Bikia

Bika had six sons, no daughters and ten acres of land. In the past he received about Rs 3,000 from WCADL for making a bore well in his open dug well. More than this he was a regular participant in the literacy classes and Sangam meetings. By way of literacy, he himself might not have achieved much. But he had learned the art of living and the value of education. So much so he sent all his sons to school. His first son educated up to 10th class, learned driving and is working in Hyderabad drawing about Rs 2,000 per month. This son is not married yet. His second son also studied upto 10th class and is helping his father in agricultural work. As agriculture needs more people, the second son is married. The third son has also studied up to 10th class and is now working in a factory drawing about Rs 1,400. The fourth son after completing 10th class is undergoing training in typing. The fifth one is studying 10th class and the sixth son is in 6th class. In his ten acres of land Bikia made a bore well and fixed a pump set to it, which together cost him about Rs 30,000. For this he has not taken any loan from anyone. His sons who are employed bare part of the cost. Rest of the cost he met from his own savings from agriculture. In the past he took a loan of Rs 8,000 from a bank which is being repaid in instalments.

Kethavath Shakru

Shakru has four daughters and two sons. The first three daughters are married. The fourth daughter studied up to 10th class, and later underwent training in electricity mechanism. However, at present she is unemployed. The first son is a graduate. It might be possible for him to get a job as a teacher. But his policy is not to work under anyone. He wants to be a free man like the birds in the sky. He is married and has two children. To a question, how he would feed his wife and children if he did not do any work, his reply was that he would do some business or take up some self-employment. At present, he and other members of his family namely his wife and children survive on the income of his father who is not very happy with him. The second son of Shakru alone was working in the agriculture farm. While the first son used to simply wander about in the village.

Shakru was also a regular participant in the literacy classes and Sangam meetings. He took a loan of about Rs 6,000 from WCADL for various items like making a bore well in his open well, for plough bulls, chemical fertilisers, etc. In the course of time he got used to taking bank loan, government subsidy, etc. He took a loan of Rs 30,000 from a bank for a bore well, a pump set, etc. Out of this loan of Rs 30,000. Rs 10,000 was given directly to him. The rest Rs 20,000 was paid by the bank in Shakru's name to a business man who sold motors and pump sets. It was the responsibility of the business man to get the motor and the pump sets fixed to the bore well. But unfortunately while the motor and the pump sets were being fixed by the mechanic they fell in the deep bore well and it was not possible to pull them out as the bore well was more than 40 feet in depth and the width was only 6 inches. Shakru tried his best to pull the motor out but he could not succeed. As it was the responsibility of the business man to fix the motor Shakru approached him. The latter did not extend any help. Desperately Shakru filed a case against the business man in the consumer court. Meanwhile, the business man who had the business in a town close to Shakru's village closed his shop and went away to Hyderabad located 120 kilometres away. The business man's address could not be traced for a long time. At last, recently Shakru managed to get the address. He submitted the same to the court and is now waiting for administration of justice to him.

As Shakru is a man not to loose his courage in adverse circumstances in life, managed to make another bore well and fixed it with a pump set and now he has been growing rice in four acres of land. He has a total of ten acres of land. He says that the encouragements and enlightenment which he received from WCADL helped him to carry on with life cheerfully even in adverse circumstances.

Kethavath Anthyanaik

Anthyanaik was also a regular participant in all the programmes of WCADL in his village. He has four sons. His first son is married and has three sons and one daughter. After educating him up to 5th class Athyanaik put him incharge of their agricultural work. The second son studied up to 10th class, underwent training in an Industrial Training Institute (ITI) as a fitter. As he could not secure a job he was also engaged in agricultural operations. The third son got educated up to Intermediate, underwent training in typewriting and at present his employed in the Electricity Department. He is drawing about Rs 4000 per month. The fourth son after passing 10th class is undergoing training in an ITI to become a fitter. Now the question to be asked is: when already one son with ITI training is unemployed, what is the use of another son to undergo training in the same trade. The answer is that the training institutes do not select the candidates for training according to the aptitude and wishes of the candidate. They select them for imparting training according to the availability of vacancies. Imparting training in such a way would not always be of much use to the trainees.

Anthya Naik has nine acres of land which of course will be shared by his four sons. He took a loan of Rs 16,000 from WCADL for various items like desilting of his irrigation well, purchase of an electric motor and pump sets, purchase of plough bulls, etc. He has paid back the loan. Later he managed to get a loan of about Rs 60,000 from a commercial bank for various items like a bore well and pump sets, purchase of plough bulls, laying of pipe lines to take water to the other end of the field, etc. He has also cleared all these loans. He also took crop loans for agricultural operations. Now he has an outstanding loan of Rs 10,000 to the bank which he repays as per the repayment schedule. He says that even if there is enough money to invest in agriculture, even if there is water source, agriculture is not safe because of natural calamities like hailstorm can destroy the crops ready for harvest. Recently, he suffered such a loss and therefore, became a defaulter in the bank.

Kethavath Thakianayak

Thakianayak together with his four brothers have about 60 acres of land. They have together two bore wells and pump sets which irrigate about ten acres of land. Thakianayak has seven sons. The first son, Babia, has no formal schooling but is engaged in agricultural work. But he regularly attended the literacy classes and appeared for the 7th class public examination conducted by the government and passed. Later he himself became the adult literacy teacher in the village. The second son of Thaika is an attender in a government school. The third son is also engaged in agriculture. The fourth one Ramji is a hand pump bore well mechanic about whom mention has already been made earlier in this report. The fifth son studied up to 10th class and is also doing agricultural work. The sixth son who also studied up to 10th class underwent training in Industrial Training Institute as a fitter. Now he is engaged in agriculture as he could not secure a job. The seventh son studied up to 5th class and is now taking care of the sheep and goats of the family. The entire family members of Thakia are associated with WCADL. They have also taken loans from WCADL for various items of agriculture and have cleared all the loans.

Kethavath Lacianayak

This family was also very much associated with all the activities of WCADL. Lacia's wife attended the literacy classes, appeared for the 7th class examinations and passed and later on for some time worked as a women worker in WCADL. But she stopped as she has enough work in her own fields. Lachia, besides doing agriculture also has milch cattle. He himself takes and sells the milk in a nearby town. This family also has taken loans for agricultural operations and has repaid the whole amount. They also have a bore well and pump set. They have constructed a decent house. Their children are sent to an English medium school in the nearby town, and monthly fees of about Rs 30 per child are paid. The have two sons and one daughter. They have a bank saving of about Rs 9,000. This is the only family in the village which owns a television set. The neighbours rush to their house in the evening to watch TV programmes. Once, during the day time, some children went to watch the cricket match on the TV. But they were not allowed to watch the programme as it was day time and as no one among the house owners could stay back home for they had to work in the fields. In the evening on that day these children retaliated by switching off the power supply for the entire village.

Kethavathvaali (Lalcha)

A woman aged 30 who works in her field stated that she studied up to 7th class and she was taught by Mr. Devaiah, the cluster organiser of WCADL. They have five acres of land and cultivate another two acres of land which belongs to others. She is the one of the executive members of WCADL. She has been associated with WCADL since 1992. The reason for her association was that she was influenced by the talk of the organisers. WCADL organisers used to conduct meetings in which all the community people in the Tanda used to sit together without any difference or discrimination.

Earlier, a labour contractor used to engage a couple (i.e., wife and husband) on an yearly contract basis by paying an advance of Rs, 2000-3000. WCADL helped them to liberate themselves from bonded labour. Now they are working in their own fields, living on their own earnings, doing work of their own occupation. For them there is no need at present to go to far-off places in search of work.

Out of 6 Mandals, 36 villages and hamlets studied for the evaluation of the voluntary effort of WCADL, eight Tandas are tribal settlements. They are Kothoor Thanda, Mallapur Thanda, Kodicherla Thanda, Rangapur Thanda, Nadigama Thanda, Gandhipalem Thanda, Pochamma Gadda Thanda and Pullagiri Thanda (Darga thanda).

Kothoor Thanda

Kothoor Thanda is located just in front of the WCADL's main office at Kothoor. The Lambada tribe seems to have benefited significantly from the WCADL. It is because of several reasons such as proximity to the highway and Mandal field officers of WCADL. This Tanda is just in one of the two Field Office of WCADL. The observation shows that people of this Tanda acknowledge that they get a lot of benefit from WCADL. Prior to the effort of WCADL it is reported by these Lambada tribes that "Vari Annam Ante Bangaram" that is rice food is like gold to them. Owing to WCADL's support, they were able to dig wells, drill bores, raise paddy and eat rice food and in paying back loans to WCADL. One of the tribes stated that in the past they had no clothes, not even a mat to sleep on and now they got all these because of WCADL. WCADL supported them in digging wells, drilling bores in the old wells to purchase oil engines and electric engines and supplied fertilisers, etc. WCADL supported all these landholders in all agriculture needs and investments. As a result, almost all of them have now permanent tiled houses and a community hall. Almost all of them including women learnt to sign and their children are sent to school. As a result of the various social educational programmes, many of them including women are now aware of their rights and duties. Their lifestyles have been drastically changed, food habits have changed. They are raising various kinds of common crops such as cotton, horti-culture, vegetables, etc. However, they still appear to remain as victims of their vices such as alcoholism, superstition, lack of land, health problems, etc.

However, they need to be guided constantly and supported financially in their agricultural needs. They are seeking financial assistance regularly from WCADL and paying back the loans after sale of crops and again seek financial assistance for their needs through the Sangams. It is also reported that, whether there are proper crops or not, they are paying back the loans regularly by undergoing many troubles in order to keep their credit worthiness in the looks of WCADL. They have also reported that nowadays nobody is working as annual servants, i.e., attached labour (jeethagadu) under landlords and also stopped manual labour (Cooli work) for others.

Mallapur Tanda

One tribal women by name Smt. K. Kamalamma (Mallapur Thanda) a widow associated with the WCADL for the last 10 years stated that the organisers helped them in various ways and educated them in civic, health and hygiene matters. They are paying back the loans taken from WCADL regularly as per their word because of their confidence in themselves. If one does not pay, the other members of the Sangam together borrow money from some other source or the other and pay it to WCADL and take the loan again. Now WCADL keep the borrower's passbook of the land as security. She further reported that in the past she was unable to speak even proper Telugu. Because of the night school she and several other members are able to speak Telugu and they learnt in the night school the importance of cleanliness, health awareness, etc. They used to have weekly meetings in the night time. The staff used to teach them Atapatalu (games and songs) and Matalu (vocabulary). Through these programmes there is a tremendous development of unity and cooperation in this community people who have learnt to help each other in their various daily needs and problems, unlike in the past. There is also a lot of change in their dealings with other people outside their community in various matters. The present social relations are on the basis of mutual respect dignity and interest, unlike in the past which were exploitative to the advantage of the people of other community. Their dignity and self-respect has been recognised by others unlike in the past. WCADL has regularly been giving assistance in their agriculture pursuits such as drilling bore wells, buying bullocks, milk buffaloes, sheep, fertilisers, etc., They have also encouraged the women folk to organise Maha Lakshmi Podupu Sangalu (saving societies) by regular contribution of a minimum amount by every member of the Sangam which usually consists of 15-20 members. The money collected will be deposited in the bank under the guidance of the organisers of WCADL and subsequently they seek the matching grants from the State government through the Mahila Liaison Officer of the Mandal headquarters. The liaison officer, incharge of Podupu Sanghalu, is responsible to help in the matters of organisation and to provide the matching grant to the Mahila Sanghalu. This has become a women's movement in collective action for solving the problems of families, community and to involve the people in civic activities as effective members of a democratic society, unlike in the past. They are also settling a number of problems related to women including the family problems of wife and husband.

In conclusion it may be said that there is a tremendous change in the living conditions of this Tanda. Yet many of them are feeling insecure about their future. Due to the regular failure of rains and subsequent water shortage for irrigation purposes which is a serious problem in the entire Mahabubnagar district, the normal life of all the people who depend on agriculture is very badly affected. Irrigation bores are regularly drying up. In sufficient land, i.e., unviable land size also makes them depend on other sources of income which results in migration, shattering their regular life. Most of them are aware of the importance of family planning and are practicing it. The better-off families are sending their children to the nearby schools. In the case of poorer families sending their children to schools depends on the interest of the child. More often, parents pressurise a boy or a girl to attend agricultural work. Girls are normally not encouraged to go to school. People are helpless in serious health problems. They compromise with their fate and leave the matter as it is.

Rangapur Tanda

The Rangapur Tanda is one of the Tanda where WCADL has been working for a very long time. This Tanda is away from the main road but it is nearer to and on the way to Mandal headquarters. There are about 100 families in this Tanda depending on agriculture and agriculture labour as the main occupation. Interestingly this Tanda is the main attraction for the foreign visitors who used to sponsor the development programmes under the title 'Rangapur Committee'. These tribes still reflect all the features of typical Lambadas of the Telangana region. Their social and economic life is much the same, besides their routine agricultural pursuits through the financial assistance provided by WCADL for bore wells, fertilisers and pesticides, etc. They also work outside their own family, work in nearby villages and towns. Most of their children are also going to schools but many of them are stopping their education before completion of school education. Younger women are changing their traditional dress pattern. Old people are still wearing their traditional dress. There is no compulsion in wearing the traditional dress. But people feel that they are carrying their colourful tradition and it is lively. Interestingly, in every Tanda somebody suffers from some mysterious health problems. These people also believe that due to the effort of WCADL and their main organisers Lucy and Francis, they are able to lead an honourable life. They are of the opinion that they are in need of constant financial and other ways of support. They are now leading a free life without working from childhood under the clutches of landlords unlike in the past.

Kodicherla Tanda

Kodicherla Tanda of Kothur Mandal is an interior place. It is far away from the Mandal headquarters. Goli, a Lambada woman, whose husband was killed, reported that WCADL taught them to lead a life intelligently. They provided them with financial aid to purchase buffaloes, sheep, to dig wells and established night schools, etc. They have also provided them with financial and material aid in agricultural pursuits. They provided timely supply of fertilisers, etc. She stated that they believe in the Sangam and it is the only organisation which works for their upliftment. WCADL has also provided big lights in the night which would attract and kill 'Bonthapurugu' an insect which eats the crop in the fields. This is an innovative social work. It shows the commitment of the organisers. She also reported that WCADL worked day and night for the socio-economic and political upliftment of the tribal and helpless people. It has educated them in various ways including good health and hygienic practices. It is reported that at present WCADL has stopped almost all the activities except a little bit of financial aid through the revolving fund to help the people in their agricultural needs. The study teams feel that there is a constant need of help for the poor people until they become self-reliant, which of course is a gigantic problem for WCADL.

Rediya Nayaik who also belongs to Kodicherla Tanda stated that WCADL has served their community a lot. They provided them with a night school and taught them civic life and educated them in health and hygiene matters. He confidently said that he can sign now. WCADL has provided them with electric motors, bore wells, social education, financial support in agricultural needs, supplied fertilisers, provided a light in the field at night to attract and kill Bonthapurugu (a crop-eating insect) which eats all the crops in the field. All the financial assistance was provided at the rate of one per cent interest and payable back after the crop season. Again the farmers will be given loans from the revolving fund. To collect the loan, the responsibility is given to Sangam members. But, unfortunately there is no guarantee of crop due to various reasons. But they have to pay back the loans after the crop season. Otherwise, they would not get the loan again. This is the limitation of WCADL. If WCADL provides us financial assistance to start some other business it would help them not to depend totally on agricultural pursuits which are not an occupation with guaranteed income. Crops are not guaranteed because of the shortage of rains, ground water, shortage of electricity, etc. Rediya Nayaik's dream is to lead a life without purchasing rice for their family needs. That is, he wants to grow the necessary quantity of rice in his own field. But it is reported that people are now able to consume better food in comparison to the past. Their social conditions are also better than in the past. He is also of the opinion that he needs more children who would earn more and that would help the family. Hence, he would not like the idea of family planning. He has also stated that prior to the commencement of WCADL, their living condition was very bad and most of them used to live in huts. Now, most of the tribals are living in tiled houses. As such WCADL has brought a tremendous socio-economic change, but the study team is of the opinion that there is a necessity of continuing the socio-economic programmes. But WCADL has withdrawn most of the activities and restricted the activities only to a few villagers. The reasons for doing this are best known to WCADL itself.

Kodavath Tanda or Pullagiri Tanda

This is an interior Tanda away from the main road and the village of Thimmajipet Mandal. Gogia, a tribal, stated that this tribe was known as criminal in the district. They used to indulge in various criminal activities in the past which attracted the attention of the District Collector. When Mr. Subramanyam was District Collector, he took a number of rehabilitative measures and programmes to involve them in different development programmes initiated by the government and the special effort made by WCADL. However, this menace has been drastically reduced. Gogiya studied up to Inter and he is a member of WCADL. He reported that WCADL helped them in their different needs of agricultural pursuits on time without any interest, merely by collecting their beneficiaries pass books as security. Those who follow punctuality in repayment without becoming defaulters would be further given aid and help. However, the responsibility lies on the Sangam members. He further stated that there is a lot of socio-economic change. They were taught how to raise commercial crops and were supplied with fertilisers and pesticides on time. They were also taught saving habits and to maintain good health, etc. They are now confident to question the officials on matters of their concern without fear. WCADL educated them on all matters required in life through role plays, dances, night school, through social education, etc. He has also stated that there is a need for constant support of financial aid and other self-employment pursuits at local level. He has also stated that night schools should be continued, social education has to be given to change the unhealthy tribal practices. He stated that even today majority tribes prepare 'Gudumba' liquor made at their home and used it in their day-to-day life very lavishly. But this kind of preparation of Gudumba is officially prohibited by the government and there are a number of cases booked against these tribes in this connection. There are a number of police raids and raids by the Excise Department conducted in order to control the unlawfull activities of this tribe. Yet, these people continue the activities in disguise.

To conclude, he stated that there is a lot of socio-economic changes in all walks of life of the Lambada tribes due to the tireless efforts made by WCADL and its main organisers Lucy and Francis. Yet there is a need to continue all the activities of financial support and social education. Otherwise, the effort made by WCADL and the dedicated services of the main organisers so far seems unenduring and may not lead to sustainable development.

Notes

1. Kalya Pavana (2002) in her M.Phil study "Socio-economic Development of Lambadas", A case study of Nalgonda district of Andhra Pradesh (unpublished).
2. Ibid.
3. Notes from WCADL Reports/Records.

10

Summary and Findings

This part of the study presents the major findings and conclusions. The study was primarily concerned to understand the various conceptual and theoretical issues involved in the context of voluntary effort and the rural development with an emphasis on weaker communities' development, a voluntary organisation namely Weaker Communities Action for Development and Liberation (WCADL) has been chosen as a case for the purpose of the study to understand the empirical reality.

This organisation has was established in 1976 by Malayali Christian couple who have been sincerely devoted to the cause of upliftment of downtrodden and weaker sections started the social work to begin with the three villages in the backward Mahabubnagar district of the Telangana region in Andhra Pradesh. This organisation gradually spread its activities to the hundreds of other backward villages in Mahabubnagar district and neighbouring Ranga Reddy district. WCADL is very well known as pioneering social work organisation in Mahabubnagar district and its actives were at the peak stage during the period of 1976-1996. This is the time the activities of WCADL were in peak stage and thousands of people belonging to weaker communities specially SCs and STs, including women were actively participating, and it was a period of boon for the weaker sections in terms of somebody or some organisation speaking for the rights of age-old depressed and suppressed people. The areas chosen for social work are also known for its notoriety in terms of feudal socio-economic and political suppression and authority. Anyone who has some knowledge or familiarity of this area certainly understands and appreciates the courage of the devoted couple towards the poor and weaker sections. It is surprising and amazing to know about the method of working of the couple in the villages where landlords, Deshmukh and the upper caste mostly belong to Velma and Reddy communities who rule the roost. In spite of 60 years of Indian's independence and its planned and unplanned effort of developing the poor and unfortunate, besides the committed and sincere effort of the various social work organisations sponsored by the national and international organisations, the working and living conditions of the people of Mahabubnagar district even today is not that good. It is considered to be one of the most backward district of Andhra Pradesh in terms of literacy, employment opportunities, agricultural and industrial development. Further, the social life of the rural people specially the SC and STs is still dominated by ignorance, superstitions, child marriages, child labour, bonded labour, untouchability, ill health and without basic conditions of human living. Even today, most of villages and specially Harijans and Adivasis (Chenchus) lack the basic requirements of life, i.e., food, clothes and shelter. Many are suffering with numerous health problems and nobody is there to guide and support them in their day-to-day problems. Added to it there is a lot of ignorance and its related problems which are crippling the rural society. Further, it is a permanent drought-prone district as a result, most of the people who belong to weaker sections specially SC, STs and backward castes have been migrating for livelihood to neighbouring districts and to another neighbour states like Maharashtra, Karnataka, etc.

In view of the manifold human suffering in the district, philanthropic and social work organisations have come up in the district during the three decades. Yet, the human suffering of this unfortunate people who belong to weaker communities specially SCs, STs have not got reduced as it should have been. Several NGOs have entered in the district, they are getting lot of funds in the name of this unfortunate people, who prefer to be silent and at the most, if we provoke them to talk, they talk only positively in favour of the voluntary organisations. Very rarely a few people dare to express their displeasure or doubts regarding the real activities of this organisation. But they do not have any proof or records of swindling of the money.

In contrast to the observations about the NGOs in general, the main organisers of WCADL Mrs and Mr Francis to my understanding and to any standards of the research procedure, led the life as real social workers. They lived with the people day and night. They chose to work for the development of weakest of the weak, i.e., SCs and STs and very poor among the BCs.

They are fairly exposed to the various philosophical approaches and systems of thought including Jesus Christ, Karl Marx, Dr. Ambedkar, Paulo Freire and many other prominent thinkers and the reformers of India and the world. Both of them started their social work without any background of higher education but they are highly wisdomatic in the process of their three decades of social work and acquaintance with various categories of people including academics improved their qualification. This shows their urge for knowledge, besides their social work in the true spirit of learning. Both of them completed post graduation in social sciences through correspondence course. They have also acquired the required skills of writing accounts, typing, etc. They acquired all skills required to run the voluntary organisation without depending on others. Further, it is their commitment that, they should not have their own children if they want to serve the people sincerely and this was implemented in their life.

It is interesting to note that their approach is simple in lifestyle, strict in discipline, hardworking in nature and accessible to all. The couple worked together in the field, mingled with the people without any reservations and they were committed to the service, honest to the core, unambitious in expansion of the programmes, and realistic in planning.

The speciality of this organisation is simple in nature, i.e., working with the people, involving them in planning and programmes, as active partners of development process to develop themselves through the concept of collective action, i.e., "all with all". The assistance is given through the Sangams. It is repayable by the individual beneficiary to the organisation. But in the case of failure of the repayment of an individual, the Sangam of the village is accountable. The amount thus collected is treated as 'revolving fund' which will be used for further needs of this unfortunate economically and otherwise deprived sections of humanity.

Organisers are chosen from local people who belong mostly to weaker sections, who are not even literates before joining WCADI, - such people are trained to train others instead of choosing qualified social workers. Sangam meeting used to be held once in a week, cluster meeting are held every fortnight; in addition monthly, quarterly, half-yearly meetings are held to review the progress and an yearly general body meeting is held, besides special meetings on the days of national and international importance. Women were given equal importance in all the programmes such as decision-making in various issues concerned with the organisation, individual, family and community and as partners in the development process. Even in getting funds from local government, national government and international organisations they had their own approach of personal touch and acquaintance rather formal and contractual relations. It is observed that a number of times, if any member or members from international sponsoring organisation come to visit the field area, the organisers used to accommodate them in their house rather than meet them at star hotels and waste the aid given in unnecessary matters. The visitors appreciated this very much and felt at home to receive Indian hospitality.

Lucy and Francis worked together day and night limiting their activities only to few mandals and villages of Mahabubnagar and Ranga Reddy district, without aiming at popularity and spreading the activities for the sake of name, fame and money. It is very interesting to note that they wrote a number of articles and published in prestigious social science and academic journals such as *Rural Development* journal published by NIRD Hyderabad and *Social Action* journal from Delhi, besides publishing number of articles in academic and non–academic Journals and News.

The other important feature of WCADL and its leaders Lucy and Francis is that they were publishing a monthly Telugu magazine by name *Mana Marpukosam* (for our social change). This was an excellent magazine with a lot of information about the local issues and the local people. The articles and poetry were contributed on various social problems by the local people and the participants in the development process. This was one of the effective tools used by WCADL to educate and conscientise the people, not only by the Sangam members but also the elite groups to strike off their arrogance and work for a social change to bring about the Indian society to an egalitarian one. This journal *Mana Marpukosam* has reached the nook and the corner of the Andhra Pradesh.

Lucy Francis though she is a Malayali but learnt Telugu language and she can fluently speak and write on various issues in Telugu. She used to edit the magazine. She used to give talks on the All India Radio on various socio-economic issues and thus educated people in general and the people of Mahbubnagar in particular. She has also trained and encouraged rural women to speak on All India Radio on various issues of rural society. She also trained the cultural programmes troops of WCADL to broadcast quite a lot of educative and conscientise generating programmes in All India Radio Station of Hyderabad. Lucy Francis is thus inculcating social awareness and effecting social change by making use of the mass media such as publications of articles in journals of national and international repute, by editing and publishing a journal of its own and by making use of All India Radio. Thereby, laying the foundation for building up of an egalitarian Indian society was done by the efforts of WCADL. Lucy Francis was chosen and appointed as one of the advisors in the rural development programme planning members of the All India Radio, Hyderabad. For many years working in this capacity she has done a yemon service to the country. The magazine published by Lucy Francis has become a source of reading material for those who were trying to read and write through the adult education programmes. The success stories of the various programmes were also published in the magazine which was an another unique feature and approach of WCADL organisation and its main organisers. They have also made every effort to educate and unite the unfortunate and deprived sections to develop socially, economically and to transform them culturally.

The other unique approach of this organisation was to meet the people through the programmes of adult education, to discuss the various issues of development and change in the adult education centres and subsequently organised the people through the approach of the 'Sangams'. Likewise, WCADL supported the people in their economic needs of livelihood pursuits with a condition of repayment including the share of expenditure on development programmes except on the adult education. Thus, people were awakened, organised and actively involved in the programmes of development designed for the development of the weaker communities. It is to the credit of WCADL in general and to the credit of Mr and Mrs Francis in particular that some of rural unlettered or semi-lettered men and women were chosen by the All India Radio Station, Hyderabad to sit in the studio in the company of specialists chosen from the universities and other fields of specialisation and have discussion with them, argue with them, to ascertain, convince the experts and specialists, the views and the knowledge of the rural people on issues and topics such as water moisture and soil conservation in the agricultural fields. The role of cultural programmes in the process of social education, family programmes, etc.

In connection with the anti-liquor campaign launched by Krishna Kant the then Governor of Andhra Pradesh, WCADL organised a mass meeting on 29 September, 1993 in which thousands of WCADL sangam members and the large portion of the public, politicians, bureaucrats, personnel of security and mass media participated. The Governor and his wife Suman Krishna Kant were the chief guest for the function, while the main speakers on the occasions were the illiterate and semi-illiterate women. The chief guest and the audience at large were amazed and wonder stuck at the way, these women bravely, fearlessly and without any stage fear delivered their speeches and brought forth the issues on which they spoke. Governor Krishna Kant who later rose to be the Vice President of India and one of the Presidential Candidates of India, wanted to try and know whether or not the speech(es) delivered by the women were tutored, He posed several extempore questions to the women speakers. He conversed with almost all the participants in the public and was stunned and taken back by the intelligent and up to the point extempore replies given by the women speakers. After the conclusions of the Public meeting the Governor couple and some of the officials and bureaucrats complimented Mrs Lucy for training the women in this way.

The main purpose of the study is to understand the voluntary effort in weaker community development in contemporary times and its impact on the target people, conditions imposed by the sponsorers of the programmes, the response of social workers towards the sponsoring agency, problems in launching the programmes, opinion of the target people in regard to voluntary efforts and the main organisers, the opinion of the other organisers, and the evaluation reports of the sponsors, continuity and change in the lives of the people and the various activities of WCADL and problems and the prospects of the organisation.

This study consists of ten chapters. The first chapter deals with the conceptual and the theoretical issues of voluntary efforts against its historical evaluation especially in India in terms of types and approaches in the field of development and its related problems, etc. The second chapter deals with a brief historical evolution of WCADL from its origin to present stage. It also discusses the social background of the founder members of WCADL, their ideological convictions and influences on their personality and the main aim and objects of WCADL. It also deals with the unique approach in the upliftment of the weaker communities, etc. The third chapter deals with the organiser's presentation of methodology or research procedure which consists of nature of data, methods of data collection, tools and techniques of data collection, identification of universe, sampling procedure and analysis, etc. This part also deals with the limitation of the study. The fourth chapter deals with the socio-economic conditions of Mahabubnagar district and social profile of the beneficiaries respondents such as age, caste, occupation, liability, income, type of family, etc. The fifth chapter deals with the establishment of beneficiary's relation with WCADL. The sixth chapter deals with programmes of economic development such as nature and types of programmes and their impact on the people. Seventh chapter deals with the socio-economic and political development of the weaker communities and the programmes initiated and their impact on the weaker communities. The eighth chapter deals with the women and development and the programmes implemented specially for the development of rural women and their impact on the women, family and community etc. The ninth chapter deals with the development of tribes specially the Lambadas in terms of their development in the context of continuity and change. The last chapter deals with the findings and conclusions.

However, it is observed that the organisers had to face a number of problems to establish contacts with the target groups in a feudal dominated society and especially with the weaker community people such as SCs and STs. It was very difficult for the organiser to reach the target people and seek their cooperation. It is as usual the dominant features of the suppressed people, is not to trust anybody except their caste and community leaders in all the problems of their day-to-day life. But they are more often cheated by such leaders but they still depend on them only, instead of establishing their relations with the officials, elected leaders and people concerned with the development.

There was a lot of mispropaganda against the main organisers and they had to take risk of their life to establish contacts with the target people through the leaders of weaker communities and educated people who were interested in the development. However, when we asked the beneficiaries with regard to their reasons to establish contacts with WCADL, many of them stated that "All joined so I have joined". We were organised to join, to bring change and development through the programmes organised by the WCADL. Initially, every day in all Sangam meetings they had to sing a song that in a Mana Malupu (one or the other songs specially prepared to inspire them for their own change) which used to be inspiring and its main content is collective action in the development of weaker communities by initiative and active participation of the weaker community people through unity and for the dignity of those unfortunate people who have been suppressed since centuries.

The problems of the target people in availing the programmes were numerous besides their ignorance and illiteracy. First of all, they were not in a positive mood to understand the concept of voluntary effort of NGOs who mainly aim to develop those unfortunate people by seeking their cooperation in helping them to help themselves with least cost and effort. Further, any development of community or a section of community essentially involves mainly by the utilisation of skills, talents, the natural and other resources for the development of themselves and technical guidance and support is naturally expected to be given by the voluntary organisation.

A common feature of underdeveloped individual and communities is that they do not possess assets such as land, technical skill and any kind of assets. It is surprising to note that many people who belong to the weaker sections do not even posses proper shelter to live in and they do not possess a buffalo or bullocks to cultivate on lease the land of others. Land mostly belongs to the upper castes in rural India and most of the upper castes landed gentry even in the rural Telangana leave the land deliberately uncultivated, not because of the lack of investment and yield they get, but due to lack of social responsibility towards their fellow villagers who normally suffer for want of land labour, occupation and income. As a result they had to go far-off places to earn their livelihood in the nearby towns and cities of the same state and other states. The perennial problem of Mahabubnagar is droughts and subsequent migration of labourers in thousands and lakhs who are known as 'Palamoor labour'. They work in agriculture fields, farm houses, and constructions as manual labour, day and night for meagre wages at living places without basic requirements, proper food and clothing shelter and water and ill health conditions.

The problem of any NGO is that they cannot get sponsorers to support the innocent and deprived people in purchasing the assets required by them and provide capital investment. It is an unfortunate feature in rural India and also in rural Telangana that even after 60 years of Indian Independence, banks do not come forward to provide loans individually to a few thousands of the people who do not posses assets and marketable skills, rather they violate all procedures and come forward to sanction loans in lakhs of rupees to those who are already developed and possess lot of property. Banks are more often cheated by those loanies who are influential and who know the loopholes of the banking system. As such there are a number of banking scandals in India to the tune of crores of rupees. It is also surprising to note that even in the field of NGOs and voluntary efforts there is a lot of corruption in the process of getting programmes sponsored specially through the government departments and in their process of implementation. This fact has been established by a number of prominent scholars who studied the field activities of some of the voluntary organisations. It is reported that out of Rs 100 sanctioned for the project only about Rs 15-20 is really going to target beneficiaries and it is slightly more than this in the case of voluntary effort. From this, one can infer the outcome of some of the voluntary efforts of the NGO field in India.

The other problems in the development of weaker communities are unity of the target people and collective action and approach of the development organisation rather than the individual family approach. It is a major hurdle for the achievement of the desired results because of the levels of understanding of the people, their individual requirements, family size, possession of assets and assistance required. Further, the needs of all the people in the same community are also not similar to those of each other. The collective approach of the voluntary organisation more often, reflects the needs and aspiration of those under-developed people. Further, whatever may be the philosophy and commitment of the organisers when it comes to a real execution of the programme the approach is mostly authoritarian and the social workers invariably depend on the opinion of leaders who are also mostly subjective and biased in their approach even in relation to their kith and kin. In their development approach NGOs in spite of their rich experience of many years in India, they did not change their method of working for the poor and innocent.

However, I feel as an objective observer, that equal amount of importance is to be given to the collective family and individual approach in the development process. It was noticed that in the villages where the financial assistance was given to people through Sangams and the repayment was also made through Sangams during the harvest season, it is reported by the villagers that more often they had to pay back whether they got proper crops or not. It is obvious that in the failure of crops due to various reasons some people, if not all, may not be in a position to pay back the assistance taken from WCADL after the crop season. As a result, certainly some become defaulters and consequently the Sangam members pressurise the defaulters to pay back at any cost. Otherwise, the other members who paid back also will not get further assistance which is a condition of WCADL. It is noticed in the field study that those who could not pay back the loans had to sell their assets such as land, bullocks etc., due to the constant pressure of the Sangam members to clear the loan. It is a situation when all the borrowers do not pay back it is impossible for any organisation including the government to regularly render financial help to the members of weaker communities in their pursuit of occupation, specially agriculture.

However, there are a number of income generating and employment oriented economic programmes which were initiated. These include open irrigation wells, deepening of existing open wells, drilling of bore wells, purchase of oil engines and electric motor and pump sets, surface bore wells, and submersible motors and pump sets for irrigation purposes, land reclamation, house repairs, purchase of seeds, fertilisers, vegetable vending, fruit vending, hire purchase of tractors, purchase of fruit trees, milch animals, plough bullocks, bullock carts, cycle repair shops, slipper making, woollen blanket-making, sewing machines, consumer loans, wood cutting machines, sheep rearing, bank loan clearance, grocery shops, fair price shops, tea shops, barber-shop, crane services, band set, musical instruments, etc.

The number of families who benefited under the above programmes of income generation and employment, community-wise SC families are about 2,684 and ST families are about 289 and BC families are about 455 and OBC families are about 33. The total number of families who benefited through the income generation and employment programmes is about 3,457 and amount spent for the above programmes during 1976 to 1993 was Rs 35,86,406. Further, it is to be noted that the amount spent on income generation and employment generation programmes is being reinvested either on the same beneficiaries or on new beneficiaries on revolving pattern and as stated by the organiser.

Further, as stated by the organisers and as the organisation records, the government subsidies received directly by the beneficiaries by the intervention of WCADL during 1976-1979 for 111 milch animal and sheep rearing beneficiaries in 6 villages was Rs 65,652. Further, in 1991 the subsidy received for castor seed for 197 farmers in different villages was Rs 3,767; seeds production subsidy (castor seed) for 57 tribal families in Kodicharla Tanda village was Rs 30,403. Subsidy for castor seed production was received from 'Andhra Pradesh Seed Production Corporation' and 'Indian Commercial Seed Production'.

Central government's aid subsidies multiple asset creation programmes through DRDA, Mahabubnagar in 1992 – Mallapur Tanda of Kothur Mandal and Reddibai Tanda of Balanagar Mandal for 68 tribal beneficiaries was Rs 2,25,000. Release and rehabilitation of 224 bonded labourers in 25 villages Rs 9,37,970. Bank loan arranged from all sources directly to the beneficiaries Rs 44,95,260.

The amount spent on community organisation, adult education, meetings, training programmes, etc., was Rs 52,51,825. Amount received from the Central Government for adult education programme Rs 25,000 in 1979 Rs 97,170 in 1983 and Rs 30,000 in 1984. The above amount received at different times was Rs 1,52,170 approximately received directly by the WCADL. The amount received from the donor agency for these purposes was Rs 52,51,825 and for health care programmes Rs 6,00,100.

As narrated by the founders of WCADL the main objectives of education and conscientising and awareness-generating education programmes of WCADL were to make the poor self-sufficient and self-reliant. Due to the financial crunch it is not possible for an organisation of the status of WCADL to rescue all the Sangam members at all times in all their needs, because human needs and wants are unlimited, although it is quite easy for any outsider to point out that the communities with whom WCADL has worked "have not become self-reliant and self-sufficient" etc. Even the Central and State governments with unlimited resources and large administrative machinery at their disposal could not raise even 50 per cent of its population above the poverty line. Hence, one can imagine the position of a voluntary organisation dealing with a pittance of money. Therefore, WCADL through their adult education and community organisation programmes has instructed their participants to benefit as best as possible from the development programmes of the government. To assess this, WCADL conducted a survey in 151 villages covering about 2,512 beneficiaries. The result was that they benefited by an amount worth Rs 2,05,35,985 from the programmes of the government. The development philosophy of WCADL is not to promote the dependency of the participant-beneficiaries on WCADL but on the contrary to ween them away from WCADL and to educate them to look for other avenues to meet their needs.

Women have played a very major role by way of active participation in all the programmes mentioned above. The data reveal that out of Rs 35,86,406 spent on income-generating economic programmes, about Rs 1,00,000 was spent exclusively for the benefit of women on items such as supply of milch animals, woolen blanket-making, mat-making, leafplate-making, vegetable, fruit vending, etc.

The philosophy of WCADL is that nothing would be given free of cost except the services of the organisation in the form of guidance, social education, health education, civic and adult education etc., for income-generating economic programmes, financial assistance, including supply of fertilisers, pesticides, and instruments, bullocks, milch cattle, etc., had to be paid back to

WCADL during the harvest season, the total amount or at least part of it in the case of failure of crops, etc., to get further assistance for the subsequent crop. However, the assistance was provided for the day-to-day needs of the target people on the recommendation of Sangam members and on the recommendation of the cluster organisers on the condition of repayment with 1 per cent of cost expenditure depending on the background of the beneficiary and on the basis of programme of assistance, form of assistance, such as long-term or short-term, etc. For agricultural assistance it is reported by the respondents that their pass books are deposited with WCADL as a guarantee and to assess the interest of the beneficiary.

In the event of violation of rules and the procedure, basically the assistance would not be provided if it was already provided and if the beneficiary had become a defaulter, he would not be entertained in other and the same programme for assistance along with others. However, it is noticed that in the course of long years of voluntary effort by WCADL, quite a number of families have become defaulters due to various reasons and the programmes of WCADL reduced to a few and to a limited area because of various reasons as already explained. This is because the beneficiaries are educated to deal directly and benefit from the development programmes of the government, priorities for financial assistance by an aid-giving agency are changing as the attitudes and aspirations of the people in the villages are also changing in accordance with the changing political scenario both at the State and the Centre. The data reveal that due to the unique approach of the main organisers and Mrs Lucy Francis's special interest in the field of upliftment of weaker communities unlike in other organisations who appoint paid workers, to organise the unfortunate women. This organisation, i.e., WCADL could give tremendous importance to all categories of women specially the weaker community women, which is due to the special interest and ability of Mrs. Lucy Francis, whose more positive approach and patience in handling the women brought them under the fold of WCADL activities. Mrs Lucy Francis used to sit with these weaker community women wherever and whenever they were available, at home, or on the field, morning or evening, out of the house, in the house, even in their kitchen to talk with them, inspire them, change them and so made them participate in the programmes. As such, the women had made use of a number of programmes along with their husbands which were specially meant for them.

The type of programmes for which assistance was given to women were, mat-making, basket-making, stitching, milk vending, vegetable vending, etc. It is also observed during the study that the more number of years the Sangam members participated in the activities of WCADL, the better off, they are, in comparison with those who associated with WCADL for a fewer number of years. But it is difficult to conclude whether or not they have reached the take-off stage. Still many of them are indebted to WCADL. Such state of affairs is neither due to the failure of the development workers nor due to the mistake of the beneficiary participants, but due to the defect in the age-old Indian feudal system and the failure of both the Central and State Governments in the strict implementation of land reforms and the failure in equitable distribution of assets which are being monopolised by the elites in the country. The main drawback or hurdle in development of weaker communities is that they can do only physical work related to agriculture. But they do not possess the required land and they do depend for work on others who have land. It is also a common feature in the villages of rural Telangana that those people who own small landholding do not cultivate due to the non-availability of investment capital and not getting profitable returns. If at all large land owners cultivate the land, they do it for the sake of name and fame and for the purpose of keeping the land under their control but not with the intention of creation of employment and helping others.

The quantum of indebtedness of the weaker communities to WCADL, government, and other organisations varies depending on their ability of borrowing and their financial and the social position. However, most of the weaker sections are indebted to one or the other agency and they strive always to repay their debts.

The quantum of assistance depended on the purpose of the loan and the family as a unit of collective responsibility. Normally the assistance was given for agricultural activities and self-employment purposes. Sometimes the giving of assistance may not correlate with the timely need of the respondents. It is repeated by the people, that sometimes to get timely assistance was a problem.

In the context of self-reliance, many respondents without any hesitation stated that they needed constant support of financial assistance in their occupational pursuits, especially in agriculture. This is possible only through the voluntary organisation (i.e., WCADL) and its committed effort. Banks do not show that much concern and commitment to these people and their policies and priorities also do not reflect the felt needs of the poor and the conditions of the banks. They do not reflect the living and material conditions of the poorer sections. Further, the reasons for not being self-reliant are lack of viable landholding, lack of regular employment, regular failure of rains and frequent droughts, indebtedness, ill-health, ignorance and over population.

However, due to the voluntary effort of WCADL in the villages and areas where the organisation worked since two and a half decades, the lifestyles and socio-economic health conditions of the weaker communities have improved substantially. There is a lot of improvement in their social and political consciousness and condition of living. Unlike in the past, the living conditions of the weaker communities have improved in terms of cleanliness, good habits, food consumption, health practices, self-confidence in facing problems, collective approach to common problems, awareness of their legitimate social rights, etc. Many of the beneficiaries due to the effort of WCADL and through night schools and adult education centres learnt slowly to read and sign unlike in the past. It is observed that even the old people including women and men were signing instead of affixing their thumb impressions. It is also noticed that there is an improved unconscious psychic unity and confidence among most of the weaker communities unlike in the past. In the past, people were living in the social conditions of disunity, lack of interest, fear, and a feeling of deprivation. It is also further observed that there is a feeling of self-respect and exhibition of social etiquette. It is a very interesting phenomenon that there is a tremendous social change in the field villages of

WCADL. Also there is no rigid caste system as it used to be in the past. There is a lot of intermingling of the people at lower level of the various caste groups. The practice of untouchability is gradually getting reduced. There is no practice of two glass system in public places and village tea stalls in the areas of WCADL like in other villages. There is no bar on one taking one's own position in the context of public gatherings and public meetings. It is further noticed that there is a lot of cohesiveness in matters of community interests particularly in relation to the SCs. They are asserting their position in all matters of the village unlike in the past. Many of them are not following or continuing socially disapproved bad or unsocial and unhealthy habits such as smoking, drinking, beating wife and children, practice of bonded and child labour, neglecting old people, practicing of witchcraft and sorcery (Chethabadi, Bhanamathi) White magic (Bootha Vaidyams) which are now openly rejected. But still some believe in those practices in some health problems in a hide and seek manner. Many of the respondents openly rejected the white magic (Mantralu and Tantralu and Tayattulu) in solving their health problems. But still some find psychological satisfaction in resorting to magical practices in getting their problems solved because they are cheap in practice and low in expenditure, and can be done in a day or within few days of practice of rituals, unlike the other system of medicine which requires regular monitoring by the doctor, costly medicines and long treatment.

Many of the weaker community people are aware of the importance of family planning and most of them are practising it unlike in the past. In Sangam meetings there are apprehensions in the context of male sterilisation method of vasectomy, that it may affect the male capacity of handling hard jobs and there are cases which failed in the context of tubectomy and in some cases the health of the women is affected, but more women came forward to get tubectomy operations than men. Some of the young people among the women are also using pills for gap in childbirth. The family planning practices are more among women than men in SCs and STs. It is practiced more by SCs than STs.

It is also a significant contribution of WCADL in developing the socio-economic and political consciousness of the weaker communities. Though the organisers did not enter into political controversies, and did not proclaim any ideological affiliation they were always working for the poor and the deprived through a spirit of service to mankind and used to derive inspiration from such great thinkers who propounded such theories and ideologies. Many weaker community people in the area are familiar with regard to various legal aspects such as minimum wages, right to work, anti-untouchability, child labour, bonded labour, Anti-dowry Acts, etc. It was amazing to see in many villages that the disputes concerning the various castes such as BCs and other upper castes were also settled by the elders of the SC community. All the people concerned with the problem, in the process of settlement were choosing the elders from SC communities while settling disputes without the feeling of discrimination and instead with equal respect and esteem. WCADL has also trained some people among the SCs and STs to handle the problems of these communities in matters related to court cases, police stations and revenue departments, etc. It is interesting to note that nowhere is it mentioned and observed that people are exploited by the elders of the village in the matters of settling disputes as in the past. Irrespective of the socio-economic background, people of all castes were enjoying freedom in the presence of top echelon of the village, i.e., upper castes or landlords who were either withdrawn from village affairs or left the village to settle in Hyderabad.

In the context of political awareness and participation most of the weaker communities' people are aware of their village president, his political party, etc. But some of them do not know about their MLAs and MPs political party background, ideology etc. This lack of interest and awareness of the people is not due to the lack of effort of WCADL. But it is not supposed to be the agenda of any voluntary organisation. It would create rift among the people if voluntary organisations start taking interest in favour of political parties. However, people including women know the marriage age of girls and boys, unlike in the past.

Women and Development

The role of women in rural development has been recognised by WCADL since 1976. As such there are a number of policies and programmes initiated by WCADL to involve women as equal partners in the process of development. Likewise, WCADL has also initiated a number of special programmes for women besides making the women to participate in general programmes. The achievements in the area of women development is remarkable and marvellous. This is due to the effort of Mrs Lucy Francis as an equal partner in establishing and visualising the organisation of WCADL and working for its success day and night along with Mr. Francis in addition to discharging her household responsibilities. WCADL could survive so long without being deviated either morally or socially because of the presence and participation of Lucy Francis in all the programmes since the inception of the organisation. She had to spend her precious lifetime, i.e., about 25 years in the nook and corner of the Mahabubnagar district to motivate, activate, encourage people to participate and to achieve the aims and objectives of women development. Lucy Francis is more popular in the study area as she has became a role model by working along with her husband Francis without slightest difference with him who has been making tireless effort collectively for the upliftment of the weaker communities. She used to organise the people, do the bookkeeping, get involved in the planning and participate in all the programmes of the target people and also actively participated in the activities of the people such as singing, dancing, making speeches, guiding and guarding the organisation. She also used to handle the health care programme. Further, she used to participate in all the activities and programmes of WCADL such as meetings, evaluation, monitoring, etc. Further, she used to compensate the absence of Francis when he is away from headquarters. She has been the source of inspiration and spontaneous guidance in any matter. She was an ideal and model personality which reflects the ethos of Indian family and culture which I think is a further attraction for the foreign sponsorers who used to be very friendly and affectionate in their behaviour and relations with WCADL. Francis and Lucy never compromised on ideals and meticulously and sincerely worked in strengthening the organisation by involving locally available simple, sincere and talented people and giving them responsibility to manage the affairs of WCADL, instead of depending on professionally qualified persons and making it an alien organisation. It can be observed even today that this couple go to any part of the district and to the field area with confidence and courage and they are received with extreme happiness, joy and pleasure by the people who treat them as a model couple devoted to the cause of poor sufferers. Many women under the leadership of Lucy Francis were liberated from the age old clutches of social customs, cultural practices which were unhealthy. Further, she helped them in organising 'Mahila Sanghalu' and 'Maha Laxmi Podupu Sanghalu', 'tailoring centres', giving training in basket-making, leaf-plate making, saving money, building consciousness of health and hygiene besides involving women in colourful local cultural programmes, feasts, etc., besides making them speak on the days of public importance of national and international levels such as 15 August, 26 January, 2 October, May Day, International Women's Day, etc.

On the whole the role of Lucy Francis in the service of downtrodden and success of WCADL is immense and inspiring in various ways compared to the other organisation that are in the field of social work. This is also one of the major reasons for me to initiate the study of this voluntary organisation where wife and husband devoted their life for the cause of reformation and rehabilitation of the suffering mankind i.e., SCs and STs of Mahabubnagar and Ranga Reddy districts of A.P.

Tribal Development

Development of tribal communities is also a challenging field of voluntary effort. As already stated, among all the tribes, Lambada tribes who live mostly in plain areas are away from the village settlements. They maintain distance in the settlement from the main villages. The habitation place popularly is known as 'Tanda'. This distance of settlement from the main village is to keep their tradition and culture intact without being disturbed by other people. The Lambada community is also known for its social rigidity and mostly depends on agriculture and agricultural labour and on forest goods and activities such as fruits, firewood, sheep rearing and animal hunting, etc. Their lifestyles, cultural and religious practices are similar to those of Hindus and they celebrate all Hindu festivals. They claim their origins from Rajasthan and they trace their lineage to the Rajputs of Rajasthan. The people of this community including men and women who are good-looking with the physical features which reflect the Aryan race. They exhibit courage and bravery in their day-to-day life and challenges but they are submissive to the people of locally dominant castes and classes irrespective of caste status. They feel themselves as a superior race but they are ill treated by others. The men of Lambada tribe normally behave like 'Pedda Manishi' called Nayak, which means a leader. His social behaviour reflects the individuality, independence, courage and confidence and he also abides by his word. This is a very hard working community where women and men, young and old involve in the mode of production and possess one single status within their own tribe. Though there is no special dress pattern for men, women wear their traditional unique colourful dress which is cumbersome and full of mirrors and embroidery work. The blouse they wear only covers their breast but the back is kept open. They also wear a lot of brass and sliver ornaments. Their hands are seen with various designs of tattooing, etc. A woman is supposed to live with her husband's family only, without much dependence on her parent's family throughout her life. Women rarely visit their parental family. Women do more work than men. Women, besides their household work, child rearing, attending to old people, have to equally participate in the agricultural and occupational pursuits. A woman in this community is a major economic contributor to the family. Her social position is subordinate to man and there are a number of social taboos on her behaviour and social interaction, like in other communities. Lambada women are more often the victims of other community men because of their natural and physical beauty. In unseasonal leisure time, they collect firewood and forest fruits to earn a little by selling them in nearby villages and towns through which they try to meet the basic needs of the family. Most of them are illiterate including men. Nowadays boys and a few girls are allowed to go to school in nearby villages and towns depending on their economic position. Further, because of changes in the agricultural practices and mode of production, such as usage of electric motor operated wells, bore wells, extensive use of fertilisers and pesticides, use of high-yielding variety seeds and consequent changes in their socio-economic and cultural life, the status of the Lambadas in the general society has slightly improved. The status of women within the Lambadas families and communities has gone up.

Owing to the constant effort of WCADL under the leadership of Lucy and Francis, the socio-economic and cultural conditions of the Lambada tribes have been changed significantly in comparison to other Lambadas. There is a lot of change in the economic life of this tribal community due to the financial assistance of WCADL for agricultural and other related pursuits including construction of houses and purchase of milch cattle, bullocks, land, etc. Many Lambada women were trained in WCADL organisation in various economic activities such as stitching, vegetable vending, leaf plate-making, etc. Now due to the effort of adult education many men and women have learnt how to sign. Their food habits, health practices, dress design, social behaviour and customs have been drastically changed. Yet, they still prefer to continue their age-old style of living. But there is tremendous change in the lifestyle and socio-economic conditions and status of the people in the context of general society and in their own context. They have also stopped their criminal activities and unscientific practices due to various economic and social programmes of WCADL and the efforts of the government.

Thus, it may be concluded that there is a remarkable change in the lifestyles and status of the Lambada tribe. But more change is visible in young men and women rather than the old people. Yet this tribal community has been facing numerous problems such as unemployment, poverty, discrimination, etc.

Limitations of Voluntary Effort

It is a very crucial and important factor in the field of social work to trace the needy and poor, because the poor and the needy do not come forward to avail themselves of the programmes automatically meant for them in a greedy and selfish manner. Hence, identification of real target people is a crucial factor in the voluntary effort. Further, all the needy and target people do not posses any kind of assets except their physical form. The limitation of voluntary effort is to help and guide the people to help themselves. It also seeks the cooperation of the people to help themselves. Unfortunately, most of the poor and deprived in India live in a socio-economic cultural environment with characteristic features not conducive for the development effort. People do not believe in cooperative work and helping each other. Mostly, they are suspicious and doubtful about strangers and unknown people. They do not mingle with all the people of their own community. They carry a mindset that they are living in such conditions due to their 'Karma' (or fate). What others think about their conditions does not occur to them. Even drawing the minimum contribution from their side to start the programme is very difficult in the beginning. Rural people on the whole do not feel free to communicate and express themselves in the presence of strangers and even poor people in cities. This kind of attitude still prevails in the behavioural pattern of the rural people.

Upliftment Levels

Upliftment levels of the people of weaker communities vary from community to community, group to group and family to family within in the same community. The limitation of voluntary effort is that it cannot view or look at individuals and groups, and plans for the entire community. It only designs programmes where people are involved with common interests. It is difficult to make people work for their common interest. Their uncommon interests is more important due to individuality. As a result, except for the adult education and awakening programmes all other economic programmes such as community irrigation wells, community organisation, etc., could not succeed. It is reported by the people that the programmes of sustainable development such as community irrigation, community irrigation wells, oil engines, electric engines, cultivation of waste land, bore wells individually and collectively become dried up within the span of two to three years due to shortage of rains and lack of groundwater and excessive use of groundwater. The increasing competition, leave alone among the better off communities, even among the weaker communities, has become a hurdle in sustainable development due to duplication of programmes.

Role of Government and Banks

A positive role of the government and banks in the development process of weaker communities is highly required for the development of weaker committees. The government machinery and local leadership should come forward objectively to identify the deserving, needy and the poor. Surprisingly, contrary to the spirit and the objectives of the programmes, beneficiaries or target people are selected normally on the basis of their caste and party. To shirk off their responsibility, they blame the local leadership in execution of the programmes of development. The administrative machinery, more often works in the last minute and to fulfil the agenda, they execute the job not according to the norms of the programme but according to the subjective choice of the leader. It is reported that in spite of voice raised against the unlawful and biased decision of the leaders and bureaucratic duplication of programmes, allocating various schemes of development or benefits only to a few people is more common. The people who are deprived are helpless and their voices are uncared for and unaddressed to. The bureaucracy is insensitive and it is mostly in the hands of landed gentry and upper castes in rural India. It is a common feature that the bureaucracy and the rural leadership mostly take decisions which are always in favour of those who are already benefited.

Role of Banks

Normally, nationalised banks do not prefer to come forward to help those people who do not have assets such as land, house, or an occupation of commercial value. In their programme of action, expectedly weaker community people, those who live below the poverty line should find a place. It may be surprising to note that in reality even after 60 years of India's Independence this is not the case. Even for WCADL to utilise the facility of banks in favour of the poorest of the poor is a difficult task. Even in government sponsored programmes, payment of matching grants or margin money of 10 per cent to 20 per cent depending on the programme which is a condition to be fulfilled by the target people in availing the programme, is a very difficult task. Voluntary organisations are forced to manipulate the records to show the payment of margin money or matching grant to avail the development programmes for the benefit of the weaker sections.

The farmers cooperative credit societies are also not able to fulfil the objective needs of the farmer; leave alone the people who lack land and assets. Weaker community people generally do not figure in the farmer's cooperative society and cooperative banks. In spite of assertion and emphasis of the government on cooperative effort in rural development, the banks could not fulfil the social obligations in reaching the needy, marginal and small farmers, leave alone the landless agricultural labourers and the those people who are out of the farm work of agricultural pursuits such as nomadic tribes, settled tribes, SCs, STs and other dependent castes and communities.

However, it is a fact that the cooperative banks and nationalised banks have become subservient institutions of those who can manage them, who are usually rich and powerful rather than the poor and assetless people. In the above circumstances, whatever may be the commitment of the voluntary organisation in the service of the poor, certainly fails in their desired objective and obligations in reaching the poor on their own due to the encouragement and financial support of the banks and governments. The programmes of development consists of numerous conditions besides being collective in approach in the case of poor rather the individualistic approach.

Role of General Public

The role of general public other than the target people in the volunteer effort for the development of weaker communities also plays an important role. It is observed that any programme initiated for the benefit of the poor is unutilised or misutilised. It is because of lack of the commitment of those who are in the labour affairs on the one hand, and the support of the general public, on the other. It is commonly experienced and reported by the individuals and the voluntary organisations which work for the upliftment of poor and weaker sections that they face stiff resistance of the rich and the powerful people. Normally in rural society an opinion leader mostly belongs to landed gentry or upper caste or those classes which oppose the policies and programmes for the benefit of the poor and the weaker communities in spirit. They try to do everything to stifle the programme and dilute it covertly as well as overtly which is a major hurdle for the development effort. People who belong to weaker communities knowingly watch helplessly and sometimes they agree perforce what the opinion leaders are doing. It is surprising to watch the drama of an opinion leader's overaction of serving the poor and the suppressed people's covert feelings of deprivation. In this context WCADL has also faced numerous problems and threatening letters and messages. The courage exhibited by Lucy and Francis is really appreciable in such circumstances in the initial stages of the organisation. General public normally spread rumours against the good intentions of the organisation and the organisers. This was so because, if the poorest of the poor are uplifted they do not find the persons to serve them in servitude in an unquestioning manner.

Paid Workers of WCADL

The role of the paid workers of the organisation is also all the more important. It is difficult for the main organisers to meet the demands of the volunteer effort in terms of seeking funds from national and international agencies, meeting the officials in time of need and attending the administrative work, organising the poor, executing the programme, monitoring the programmes, planning for the future programme accounting, assessing the impact, response of the people, hurdles, etc.

Hence, there is a need to appoint some paid workers depending on the requirements of the programme under execution. The kind of appointing the paid workers depends on the needs of WCADL, in terms of long- and short-term employees. Office and transport require recurring and long-term staff and field staff is appointed depending on the project duration. It also requires to seek assistance as and when required from the specialised people such as agricultural officers, irrigation engineers, animal husbandry, forest management, industry and education departments, etc. WCADL in the long history of 27 years of weaker community services, appointed many people in this context. A few of them are still working with WCADL. Many of them shifted to various other organisations of their choice. An interesting fact about WCADL is that it choses people from among the local area. The criterion to appoint them is not qualification and external appearance. It is purely on the basis of skill and sincerity. This is the unique approach of the WCADL. Some of the people who are appointed as paid workers in WCADL were illiterate; while some of them were literate. Such people were given opportunities to work with WCADL to organise the people at village level, at the cluster level and the management level. The people who had no history and background were given opportunity to work as paid workers at various levels by paying them monthly salaries fixed in the present budget which more or less coincided with the local rates. This approach has really inspired the poorer sections who had no exposure of this kind of works. After appointment, they were educated, trained and given responsibilities by the organisation. They managed all the affairs of WCADL from the village level to the level of the head office. Hundreds of people benefited from this organisation in different projects and in different periods during the long history of WCADL. It was amazing to note through field observation that even the people who left the organisation long ago and working elsewhere have been showing respect to the organisation and the main organisers Mrs Lucy Francis and Mr Francis. They expressed their gratitude to the organisers for the opportunity given to them to work in WCADL which changed their whole life. They were amazed to have the experience of working under the leadership of Lucy and Francis who are devoted and dedicated disciplined social workers. They were acknowledging that they learned everything in life from WCADL, personal to public behaviour. They were benefited in all aspects of life due to the effort of WCADL. Now they are able to lead a honourable life in the society because of the devoted couple. They were appreciating the meticulous planning, strict discipline, punctuality in working, courage in facing the public which were most attractive qualities of the couple. However, they also, as usual, expressed feeling of low payment for their work. In comparison to the official work they were getting lower payment. But they were happy because it was compensated by getting benefit of the schemes. Working with the organisation their social prestige had also gone up. This kind of organisational approach of giving opportunities to the people who were not exposed to public management, increased the morale of the uncared and the poor and inspired many others.

Role of the Beneficiaries

Any development effort normally succeeds not because of the planners and the programmers but because of the interest and participation of the beneficiaries and their effective and active role in utilisation of the programmes. In this context the beneficiaries of WCADL exhibited unusual spirit and cooperation in the process of development effort. The beneficiaries consist of SCs, STs and BCs. A large number of beneficiaries are SCs. Next the people benefited by the organisation are the STs specially the Lambadas. An insignificant number of people who have benefited belong to BCs. The unique feature of WCADL is involving the women in the process of development and also giving equal importance to them. Women have been playing very crucial roles in the organisation like ordinary members to active organisers. They have grown from silent house-bound women to active organisers to a level of public speaking. This was possible due to the special attraction of Mrs Lucy Francis. She was encouraging the women as equal partners in the family and in the development process. There are a number of special programmes organised for the benefit of women from adult literacy to awakening programmes to be active partners in the economic development. The WCADL organisation succeeded in mobilising them, motivating them, activating the people, involving them in programmes of development and subsequently changing the people to construct a healthy and a dignified human society. Likewise, WCADL has fulfilled all the conditions to be called a model voluntary organisation which sincerely worked for the cause of the weaker communities; at times the governments are increasingly depending on the role of NGOs to implement the development programmes.

Evaluation Reports

In the context of the academic evaluation of WCADL's effort in fulfilling its aims and objectives, the public opinion in general and that of the people of weaker communities in particular are highly appreciative. Interestingly, those who have not benefited and those who are unconnected to the organisation have also slowly withdrawn from the role of stumbling blocks to the functioning of WCADL activities as and when required. It means even the general public approved the activities and achievements of WCADL in the service of poorer sections and weaker communities. The opinion of the weaker communities also needs objective scrutiny to understand the real work done by the organisation and the commitment of its leaders. Though the individual families have benefited differently depending on their real conditions of living and subsequent ability of making use of the programmes, it is marvellous to see their satisfaction, gratitude and respect they show instantaneously without any reservation to the main organisers, i.e., Mrs Lucy Francis and Mr Francis. Beneficiaries treat the couple like their parents and respect them whole-heartedly. It is because of their day and night struggle in the interior villages by meeting the people, motivating them, involving them in the programmes, organising them for collective approach in the development, uniting them, breaking their social shackles and finally making them feel free like birds. It was not an easy task. It needs basic human elements, then conviction and urge to serve the people, then transform commitment to appreciative action, resolving and facing the crisis and challenges and succeeding in the ultimate goals of liberating the people from their deprived socio-economic cultural conditions. This is the ultimate aim of any development organisation and civilised human beings. By applying this yardstick to the success of this couple in the service of weaker communities, poorer sections, what they achieved cannot be compared with that of other organisations which is much less because of their approach of dedication and working both day and night with a matching spirit to realise the goals they set for themselves. The title of the organisation itself indicates the internal spirit of its authors.

However, the main sponsoring organisation 'Bread for the World' the donor agency and its evaluation team consisting of two foreigners and two Indians made certain observations to strengthen the organisation in terms of its future continuity and expansion of activities to more areas and to extend the benefit of WCADL to a larger number of people. Their observations are not unanimous and collective but opinions of those members who represented the donor agency are taken note of here. The nature of observation is not to find fault with the spirit or service done by the main organisers but to restructuring the organisation to suit the organisational needs and attracting funds rather depending on a single source and restricting the activities. Further, in the context of continuity of leadership they felt that there is a need to create alternative leadership in view of the authors of the organisation are getting old and may not be in a position in future to carry forward the numerous responsibilities of serving the poor. In the context of the structure of the organisation it is observed that it is "outlined to satisfy the statutory requirements" and the meetings of Sangam members are not regularly held. It is further observed that there is a need to appoint people who are qualified for various jobs from outside. But it is difficult to implement it because they need to be paid heavily and there is no guarantee of their working sincerely which any organisation cannot risk for the sake of experiment that too in the field of social work. The finances of WCADL are also limited for a particular purpose and it is very difficult to manage such highly qualified specialised people in a field where poor are involved. The success of WCADL is mostly due to the utilisation of local skills among the local people and putting them in lead position which should be the spirit of any voluntary organisation and in this context WCADL leadership succeeded in completely running the organisation through carefully trained and talented local people which has inspired the target people because the managers are not strangers but their own people, and they too can do such management jobs. This was the message given to the people. In the context of utilisation of the services, government departments in serving the target people was not found adequate. While the governments intend helping the poor by enlisting the services of the NGOs, yet these NGOs are not given the freedom to enable them to execute their programmes for their target groups effectively. There are a number of conditions to be fulfilled which is not possible by the organisers. It is time consuming and ultimately the result will be marginal.

Further, a comment is made on the interest charged on the credit schemes for the investment purpose. It is a fact that depending on the scheme and the size of the credit 1 per cent of interest is charged to meet the administrative expenditure of the scheme. It is also not sufficient but only levied to make the people to be careful in properly utilising the scheme and pay back dues and not to be careless in paying back the investment amount. If interest is not charged slowly it may lead to depletion of the funds and ultimately nothing may remain. In these circumstances of limited resources and unlimited need of funds, with the beneficiaries paying 1 per cent interest on investment it may be possible to keep the corpus intact for it to continue the economic activities to help the helpless in times of need and more so, in the absence of getting funds. Finally the suggestions of appointing the 'accompanier' which means nominating an outsider by the sponsoring organisations to be in the management, planning, monitoring, controlling, and maintaining close contact with the international organisation may not be acceptable to any organisation which has self-respect and which may leave the matters of continuity to circumstances rather to plan to loose its original spirit and sacrifices without notice. Hence, there is a need to free the voluntary organisation from the conditions and spirit of local needs rather and to look at externals or matters outside the real situation.

However, to conclude, WCADL and its authors and leadership have been successful in serving thousands of needy people who were mute and silent sufferers but are now actively raising their voice, living collectively, going ahead with confidence, courage and hope. Thus, the organisation has succeeded in its commitment to weaker communities service and to put in their action for development and liberation of these communities.

Conclusion

Whatever may be the opinion of the sponsoring organisation in regard to the development effort of WCADL and it leaders, as long time partners in the process of upliftment and development of the deprived and suppressed sections of Mahabubnagar district of Telangana region of A.P., by any yard stick, this organisation and organisers could withstand the pressure and dominant tactics of the landed gentry who are always against the poorer sections on one side and also uncharitable and unscientific evaluation and consequent withdrawal of the support of international organisation, certainly affected the helpless but these factors could not succeeded to scuttle the pride and spirit of the couple who decided to serve the cause of the needy and the poor. Even though, they could not become national figures in the field of social work by spreading the numerous activities with professional zeal and gaiety, they could succeed in serving the suppressed sections in their all-round development in a limited area with limited funding, but unlimited horizons of success. Though they could not lead a luxurious life with numerous attendants but as a healthy and happy couple even at the age of nearly seventy, do every work including driving, by waking up at 4 in the morning and going to bed not before 11 in the night. Though they did not appear to be highly ambitious or posses contemporary dubious style of modern intellectualism, they still represent the philosophy of simple living and high thinking and what is preached is to be practiced and what is practice in only to be preached. Further they live away from the clutches of family bondage. They shifted their place of living from Hyderabad to a nearby field area only to be in touch with those people for whose sake their lives are dedicated.

However, it may be concluded that the sincerity of the devoted and dedicated social work of the Christian couple did not succeed in realising their ideal expansion and extension of their social work. They could succeed in enkindling the light of development in the lives of the deprived and suppressed communities who were engulfed in darkness and the couple showed the individuality and Indianness in social work to the donors of international agencies in serving the needy, the poor and the deprived. Let us be optimistic that this torch of light lit by the couple will be taken over by progressive skill workers of India. It is with this hope that it may be concluded that this study will pave the way for such leadership in social work in order to build a democratic equitable and just society in India.

Bibliography

Bandopadhyay, D. 1997. "Voluntary Organizations", *Main Stream,* Vol. XXX, No. 16, 29 March.

Basu, Sisir. 1994. entitled, "Rural Poor: Failure of Growth Models", *Deccan Chronicle.*

Baviskar, B.S. 2001. "NGOs and Civil Society", *Sociological Bulletin*, 8 October, Vol. 50, No. (1).

Bernard, Amanda, et al. 1998 *Civil Society and International Development*, Paris: Council of Europe and OECD.

Betteille, Andre. 2001. "Civil Society and the Good Society", *Sociological Bulletin*, Vol. 50, No (2), September.

Beveridge, W.H. Lord. 1948. *Voluntary Action,* George Alien and Unwin.

Bhatiya, Arun. 2002. "Stealing from the Poor", *The Hindu*, 24 November.

Brahmnand Reddy, K. 1976. "Role of Voluntary Organizations in Tribal Development", New Delhi: Ministry of Home Affairs, (occasional papers on Tribal Development – 2)

Charyulu, U.V.N. 1981. "Voluntary Organisations and Rural Development", *Rural Development in India: Some Aspects*, (ed.) NIRD, Hyderabad.

Das, Debendra Kumar. 2000. *Dynamics of Rural Development: Role of Voluntary Organization in Financing Rural Development*, Deep & Deep Publication, New Delhi.

Dave, P.C. 1966. "Voluntary Organisations and Welfare of Backward Class", *Vanyajati*, 14:4, October.

Debal, K. Singha Roy. 2001. *Social Development and the Empowerment of Marginalised Groups* (voluntary organization for social development and empowering the marginalised in Bihar) Sage Publications, New Delhi.

Desai, A.R. 1969. *Rural Sociology in India,* Popular Prakashan, Mumbai.

Desai, Vasant. 1988. *Rural Development: Experiments in Rural Development,* Vol IV, Himalaya Publishing House, New Delhi.

Dhanagare, D.N. 1998. "NGOs and Foreign Funding", *Man and Development,* 20 (2).

Farrington, J. and A. Babbington with K. Wells and D. Lewis. (1993). *Reluctant Partners? NGO's, the State and Sustainable Development,* London: Routledge.

Farrington, John and S. Bigges. 1990. *NGOs Agricultural Technologies and the Rural Poor Food Policy,* London, Routledge.

Fisher, William F. 1997. "Doing Good? The Politics and Antipolitics of NGO Practices", *Annual Review of Anthropology,* 26: 439-64.

Francis, C. 1976-1985. "Development Communication in WCADL", *Weaker Community's Action for Development and Liberation: Origin and Expansion,* p. 28.

Francis, C. 1976-1985. "Organisational Structural and Activities of WCADL", *Weaker Community's Action for Development and Liberation, Origin and Expansion,* p. 24.

Francis, C. 1976-1990. "An Experience in Working with Rural Poor", WCADL Report, p. 277.

Francis, C. 1996. "Poverty Eradication through Employment Generation in WCADL", in *Indian Poverty Eradication Foundation Bulletin,* Vol. 1, No. 1, July-September.

Gangrade, K.D and Sooryamoorthy, R. *NGOs: Retrospect and Prospect.*

Gangrade, K.D. 1987. "Development of Voluntary Action", *Encyclopaedia of Social Work in India,* Vol. (1), Ministry of Social Work, Government of India, New Delhi.

Ghali, Boutros. 1945-1995. "The United Nations and the Advancement of Women", Published by the United Nations, Department of Public Information, *Blue Book Series,* Vol. VI, New York.

Gupta, A. "Voluntary Agencies and Rural Development" (nd), 220. Research Project sponsored by ICSSR, New Delhi.

Jain, R.B. (ed.) 1995. "NGOs in Development Perspective", Vivek Prakashan, New Delhi, *Sociological Bulletin,* Vol. 50(2).

Jain, S.C. 1985. *Rural Development Publications and Strategies* (Role of Voluntary Agencies for Rural Development), Rawat Publications, Jaipur.

Kabra, Kamal Nayan. 1985. "Confused or Camouflaged", *Yojna* Issue on Testing Voluntary Agencies, June 16-30, pp. 9-11.

Kalimullah, Nazmul Ahsan. 1989. "The Political Environment of Non-Government Organisations in India," A study of three states in

Chaudhuri, Ranjit (ed.) *Conflict Development and NGOs,* Calcutta: Best Books.

Kaliya, Pavana. "Socio-economic Development of Lambadas." A case study of Nalgonda district (unpublished).

Kapoor, A.K., Dharm Vir Singh. 1997. *Rural Development Through NGOs,* Rawat Publications, Jaipur.

Kapoor, Rakesh. 1996. "Voluntary Action Survival, Politics and Transformation," *Social Action,* Vol. 46, January-March.

Khandwalla, Pradip N. 1988. *Social Development: A New Role for the Organisational Sciences.*

Khanna, B.S. 1991. *Rural Development in South Asia, Local Rural Organisation,* I&II, Deep & Deep Publication, New Delhi.

Lalitha, N.V. and Kohli, Madhu. 1982. *Status of Voluntary Efforts in Social Welfare,* National Institute of Public Cooperation and Child Development, New Delhi, 1982.

Lawani, B.T. 1999. *NGOs in Development,* Rawat Publications, Jaipur.

Maheswari, S.K. 1995. *Rural Development in India: A Public Policy Approach* (Voluntary Organisation and Rural Development), Sage Publications, New Delhi, 1995.

Masoni, Viltorio. 1985. "Non-Governmental Organisations' Role in Development", *Voluntary Action,* 277 (9-10), March-April.

Mathru, B.L. 1996. *Rural Development and Co-operation,* RBSA Publishers, Jaipur.

Mehta, P.C. 1994. *Voluntary Organisation and Tribal Development.*

Mishra, Satish. 2002. *Empowering People Organisation and Rural Development: Role of Inter Governmental Organisations,* Kanishka Publications, New Delhi.

Misra, Sunil. 2002. *Voluntary Action in Health and Population,* Sage Publication, New Delhi.

Mukherjee, K.K. 1980. "Voluntary Organisations in Rural Development", *Manthan* 3(2).

Nityananda, 2000. *The Emerging Role of NGOs in Rural Development of India,* Vol. 30, Nos. 344, September-December.

Non-Governments Liaison Service (NGLS). 1999. "Economic and Social Development in the United Nations System: A Guide to Non-government Organization", New York: UNO.

Nune, Sheel C. 1996. "Centripetal vs. Centrifugal Forces and the Role of NGOs", *Social Action,* Vol. 46, January-March.

Pal, Madhusudhan. 2000. "Rural Development and Easy Money", in *Frontier,* 28 April – 4 May.

Pandey, S.R. 1991. *Community Action for Social Justice: Grassroots Organisations in India*, Sage Publication, New Delhi.

Pandey, S.R. 1979. "Voluntary Experiments in Rural Development", *Voluntary Action*, 21(9) September.

Patel, Mohini. 1998. "Voluntry Organisation in India: Motivation and Roles", in M.L Dantwala et al. (ed.), *Social Change Through Voluntary Action*, Sage Publications, New Delhi.

Raj Kumar. 2002. "Capacity Building of Panchayats for Rural Development: Some Emerging Areas for NGOs".

Ramachandran, Vimla. 1998. "Voluntry Organisation: Professional Agencies or Sub-Contractor", in M.L. Dantwala et al. (ed.), *Social Change Through Voluntry Action*, Sage Publication, New Delhi.

Ramuany, M. 1992. "Role of Social Voluntary Organisations in the Effective Implementation of the Tribal Development Programmes of Eighth Five Year Plan", *Vanyajati*, Vol. 40 No., January.

Ranga Rao, K. 1998. In an edited book *Women in Developing Society: Marching Towards 21st Century* by J.B. Abbasayulu.

Riley, John M. 2002. *State Holders in Rural Development,* (Critical Collaboration in State NGO-Partnership) Sage Publication, New Delhi.

Sankaran, R. and Rodrigue. 1983 , *I. V.O: A Handbook to the Management of Voluntary Organisation*, Chennai.

Satyanarayana, G. 1992. *Changing Agrarian Structure and Labour Relations,* Rawat Publications, Jaipur.

Satyanarayana, G. 1998. "Voluntary Organisations and Emancipation of Dalit Women", In Y.B. Abasayulu (ed.), *Women in Developing Society, Marching Towards 21st Century*, Delta Publishing House, New Delhi.

Shalini, Rajneesh. 2002. *Rural Development Through Democratic Decentralisation: Role of Voluntary Agencies,* Deep and Deep Publications, New Delhi.

Sharma, B.D. 1984. *Planning for Tribal Development*, Prachi Prakashan, New Delhi.

Sharma, K.L. 1996. "The Indian State and the NGOs: Some Reflections", *Social Action*, Vol. 46.

Singh, D.N. 1985. Introduction: "A Prologue to Rural Development Strategies in India".

Singh, Katar. 1999. *Rural Development: Principles, Policies and Management*, Sage Publications, New Delhi.

Singh, Madhuri and Singh, K.N. 1985. "Voluntary Agencies: Their role in Rural Development in India". In K.N. Singh and D.N. Singh (eds.) *Rural Developments in India*, R.L. Singh Foundation, Varanasi.

Srikanth, H. 1996. "State, NGOs and Urban Community Development", *Social Action*, Vol. 46, January-March.

Srivastava, S.P. 1999. "Nature of Voluntary Action in India Today: A Critique", *Social Action,* Vol. 49, January-March.

Sundaram, I.S. 1986. *Voluntary Agencies and Rural Development*, B.R. Publishing Corporation, New Delhi.

Sundram, Satya. 2002. *Rural Development,* Himalaya Publishing House, Mumbai.

Tandon, Rajesh. 1996. "Changing Context and Challenges for Voluntary Action in India Today", *Social Action*, Vol 46.

Tandon, Rajesh. 2004. "Policy on Voluntary Sector", *The Hindu*, January-March.

Thurstone, E. *Castes and Tribes of Southern India, Madras,* 1909, Vol. 1, Asian Educational Services, New Delhi.

Todaro, Michael P. 1977. *Economic Development in the Third World*, London: Longman.

Tucker, Veena. 1999. "Role of NGO's in Participatory Communication", *Social Action*, Vol. 49, January, March

United Nations Assertion: "The Advancement of Women" in the *Blue Book Series,* Vol VI.

Usha Rani and P. Jay Ram Reddy. 1998: 36. "Women in Rural Development: A Brief Analysis", In Y.B. Abasayulu (ed.), *Women in Developing Society, Marching Towards 21st Century*, Delta Publishing House, New Delhi.

Varma, Ram K. 1996. *Policy Application to Rural Development*, Voluntary Action Publication by Printwell, Jaipur.

Webster, Neli. 1999. *NGO's and Local Government: The Democratisation of Local Development,* in Rajasekhar D. (ed.).

Articles

Bhat, Ganesh S. 1999. "Rural Entrepreneurship and NGOs", *Kurukshetra*, November.

Bhatt, Anil. 1995. "Voluntary Action in India, Roles, Trends and Challenges", *Economic and Political Weekly*, Vol. XXX, No (16).

Charyulu, U.Y.N. 1990. "Voluntary Organisations and Rural Development", *Kurukshetra*, Vol. XXVIII, No (15), May.

Daye, P.C. 1966. "Voluntary Organisations and Welfare of Backward Class", *Vanyajati*, October.

Day, S.K. 1985. "Voluntary Action or Collusion", *Kurkshetra* (Annual Number) 34(1), October.

Deoganokar, S.G. Warora. 1989. "Role of Voluntary Agencies and Tribal Institutions in Social and Ecological Development in Tribal Areas", Vol. 37(4), *Vanjajati*, October.

Dhangare, D.N. 1988. "Action Groups and Social Transformation in India", *Lokayan* Bulletin 6 (5): 37-59.

Ghosh, D.K. 1990. "Voluntary Agencies and Rural Uplift", *Yojana* No. 34(18), October.

Gibbs, Christopher, Claudia Fumo and Thomas Kuby. 1999. "Non-Governmental Organisations in World Bank-supported Projects", A Review, Washington DC, The World Bank.

Hariecharidram. C. 1982. "Futuristic Role of Voluntary Organisations", *Khadi Gramudyog* 28(7).

Hegde, Odeyer D. 1982. "Role of Voluntary Organisation's in Tribal Development", *Kurukshetra*, 30(13).

Jain, Deveki. 1976. "Role of Voluntary Agencies", *Voluntary Action* 18(3-4).

John, Mencher, 1999. "NGOs are they a Force for Change", *Economic and Political Weekly*, 34(30).

Kidar Nath, 1975. "Tribal Uplift: Voluntary Agencies needs to be Encouraged", *Economic Times.*

Kishore, Saint. C. 1974. "Catalyst Role of Voluntary Agencies: A Conceptual Frame Work", *Peoples Action* 8(11).

Klugman, Barbara. 2000:1-2. "The role of NGOs as Agents for Change", *Development Dialogue*- A Journal of International Development Cooperation published by the Dag Hammarskjold Foundation, Uppsala.

Krishna Murti, V. 1982. "Voluntary Agencies and Rural Development", *Kurukshetra*, Vol. 30(16).

Kothari, Rajni. 1995. "Under Globalisation: Will the Nation-States Hold?", *Economic and Political Weekly*, 30 (16): 1593-1609.

Lakshmaiah, T. 1999. "Tribal Development: Role of Voluntary Organisations", *Kurukshetra.*

Leach Melissa. 1988. "Becoming a People's Sector Indian Voluntary Agencies at Cross Roads: Community Development" journal.

Lucy, T.V. 1993. "Social Reforms to Voluntarism in India", *Legal News and Views*, December.

Paul Chowdhry, D. 1970. "Voluntary Action in Rural Areas", *Kurukshetra*, Vol. 18(2).

Rajaskharam, M.V. 1985. "Voluntary Organisations and Rural Development", *Kurukshetra*, 34(1).

Rao, V.Y. 2000. "TRYSEM Through NGO's", *Kurukshetra.*

Roy, Bunkar. "Let Voluntary Agencies Plan Their Own Scheme", *Kurukshetra* (Annual Number) 34(2).

Roy, Ajit. 1995. "Civil Society and Nation-State in the Content of Globalisation", *Economic and Political Weekly*, 30: 2005-10.

Sahu, Gopala Krishna. 2002. "Voluntry Organisation for Rural Development", *Kurukshetra.*

Sudha, K. and Bhargava, B.S. 2000. "Panchayats and NGO's in Social Change", *Kurukshetra*, Vol. 48, No. 10.

Varghese, B. George. 1977. "Voluntary Action: A New Mission for the New Missionaries", *Voluntary Action*, June-October 19(1) 958-86.

Reports

Francis and Lucy Francis. "A Profile of WCADL", pp. 9-10.

Francis, C. 1976-1985. "Interpersonal Communication Meetings", Weaker Community's Action for Development & Liberation, Origin & Expansion, p.28.

Francis, C. 1976-1985. "Organisational Structure and Activities of WCADL", Weaker Community's Action for Development & Liberation, Origin & Expansion p. 24.

Francis, C. 1976-1990. "An Experience in Working with Rural Poor", WCADL report p.277.

Francis, C. 1996. "Poverty Eradication through Employment Generation in WCADL" in *Indian Poverty Eradication Foundation Bulletin*, Vol.No 1, pp.14-15

Francis, C., 1976-1990 in their report "An Experience in Working with Rural Poor", WCADL Report.

Ibid., 1976-1990.

Kalya, Pavana. 2002. in her M.Phil study "Socio-economic Development of Lambadas", A case study of Nalgonda district of Andhra Pradesh.

Rao, Y.V. and C. Francis. 1993. in their article "Action Oriented Adult Literacy and Education in WCADL", pp. 625-651.

Usha Rani and P. Jay Ram Reddy. 1998. in their article on "Women in Rural Development," p.36.

WCADL Origin and Expansion, a Report 1976-1985, "A Brief History of WCADL". (typed notes) pp. 3-5.

World Bank. 1975a. Report, "The Assault on World Poverty: Problems of Rural Development Education and Health", Baltimore, M.D. Johns Hopkins, University Press.

Index